Applewood Pointe of Eagan

THE EXPLOITS OF BEN ARNOLD

D1568506

The Western Frontier Library

BEN ARNOLD (CONNOR)
From an old daguerreotype taken in the
early 70's

THE EXPLOITS OF BEN ARNOLD

Indian Fighter, Gold Miner, Cowboy, Hunter, and Army Scout

Map, Illustrations, Bibliography, Index, and Notes

by

Lewis F. Crawford, A.M.
(in collaboration with Josephine McCarthy Waggoner)

Foreword
by
Paul L. Hedren

University of Oklahoma Press
Norman

ISBN 0-8061-3105-5

The Exploits of Ben Arnold is Volume 64 in The Western Frontier Library.

The paper in this book meets the guidelines for permanence and durability of the Committee on Production Guidelines for Book Longevity of the Council on Library Resources, Inc. ∞

Copyright © 1926 by Lewis F. Crawford. Foreword by Paul L. Hedren copyright © 1999 by the University of Oklahoma Press. All rights reserved.

This book originally was published under the title *Rekindling Camp Fires* in 1926. Published as *The Exploits of Ben Arnold* in 1999 by the University of Oklahoma Press, Norman, Publishing Division of the University. Manufactured in the U.S.A. First printing of the University of Oklahoma Press edition, 1999.

1 2 3 4 5 6 7 8 9 10

To the Pioneers of the Old West and
their Descendants, this Volume
is affectionately Dedicated
by the Author

᭙

Beyond the sad shadows into the light of day,
Over the mountain that hides the way,
Beyond the surging river wide and deep,
Awakens a weary traveler from his sleep;
The somber granite that will mark his grave
Would sooner crumble than his spirt brave.
Though blasted by tempests, beaten by storms,
Unafraid, he crosses to the waiting forms.
Only a scout missing, lost in the fray,
But the trail leads on to a beauteous day.
                    — JOSEPHINE McCARTHY WAGGONER

Written on the occasion of the death of Ben Arnold Connor

CONTENTS

1

ILLUSTRATIONS

FOREWORD

LEWIS F. CRAWFORD's book, *The Exploits of Ben Arnold* (originally titled *Rekindling Camp Fires*), is the lively autobiography of Ben Arnold, a member of that colorful class of northern plains roustabouts that included Luther "Yellowstone" Kelly, John Hunton, Charles Allen, Charles Larpenteur, and a short handful more. All were westerners engaged on the Black Hills-Yellowstone-Missouri frontier when it was still distinctly "Sioux Country." Whether scouting, freighting, ranching, or fur trading, they roved comfortably between pressing civilization and the largely untrammeled frontier, advancing various business interests, engaging socially, marrying (often Indian women), and always retaining a visionist's eye to preserving their legacies. Our understanding of the social fabric of the American West is generously enriched by their lives and foresight.

Ohioan Ben Arnold (Connor) came west in 1863 in the enlisted ranks of the 2nd Battalion of the 11th Ohio Volunteer Cavalry, a unit expressly organized for duty on the Indian frontier. This was his third wartime enlistment, and he did so under the alias of Monroe, his given name being Benjamin M. Conner but his reputation already sullied by a previous desertion. Adopting the surname Arnold when needed, the fleetfoot bailed from the 11th Ohio as well, it having taken him up the Oregon Trail to the Platte Bridge Station, located today at Casper, Wyoming. Arnold ascribed his desertion to a feud with a fellow soldier and his fear of being murdered. He never looked back.

Arnold's wanderings carried him west to Fort Hall, Idaho, where he operated a ferry across the Snake River for a while; then to Virginia City and Helena, Montana, where he dabbled at placer mining; and later to Fort Benton, where he bull-whacked freight to the gold fields and once east to Fort Union, at the confluence of the Yellowstone and Missouri rivers. While wintering at Fort Union in 1865–66, Arnold and several mates trapped and poisoned wolves and coyotes but chiefly blended into the fort's unique social milieu.

From Fort Union's bourgeois, Fellows D. Pease, Arnold secured employment as an engagé to transport buffalo robes and other furs down the Missouri to market. Arnold was captivated by the river, and in coming years he found continuous pick-up labor at river forts and towns as a construction hand, wood hawk, and deck hand. This was menial employment at best, but in later telling Arnold gives us delightful insight into such plaintiff exertions as cutting and cording wood, loading steamboats and mackinaws, and social intercourse with neighboring Indians. Always we meet an arresting array of commoners just like him, and soon an Indian wife named Itatewin. We also sense his wanderlust on the loose-knit frontier.

In 1868 Arnold witnessed government commissioners presenting the now infamous Fort Laramie Treaty to the Hunkpapa Sioux at Fort Rice, in present-day North Dakota. There he gained the acquaintance of men like Father De Smet, Gall, and Running Antelope, the latter Sitting Bull's great friend. Arnold knew Sitting Bull, too, and Isaiah Dorman, the black roustabout who later perished at the Battle of the Little Big Horn. In the next several years Arnold roamed the Fort Sully-Grand River country driving beef to the local Indian agencies, farming, and carrying business and military dispatches under contract. Later forays took him to Wyoming and Nebraska, again chiefly trailing cattle to the Indian agencies in Dakota. And his wanderings drove him predictably to the Black Hills in the mid-1870s, where he nosed about the diggings and was credited with carrying the first formal mail south from Custer City to Nebraska in February 1876.

During the opening movements of the Great Sioux War, Arnold was frequently engaged as a dispatch rider from Fort Fetterman, Wyoming, north to Brigadier General Crook's field camps, traveling in the lustrous company of men like Frank Grouard, Louis Richard, and Baptiste Pourier. He happened to be in Crook's camp during Crazy Horse's furious attack at Rosebud Creek, Montana, and was later challenged by Crook to carry messages to Brigadier General Terry, encamped then on the Yellowstone River. Arnold would not go and instead carried a final mail bag to Fort Fetterman, thereafter bailing for Deadwood.

In the later 1870s and 1880s the "call of the frontier" kept Arnold largely in Nebraska and South Dakota, at times cutting hay, herding someone else's cattle, tending shop for others, and pulling and selling young cottonwood trees to incoming settlers so that they might "necessarily improve" their claims. In 1891 he relocated to Pierre so that his several children by a second marriage could be schooled. Even then "the call of the frontier was always strong," he said, but running a Missouri River ferry and helping settlers find homesteads were meager highlights for a man then in his fifties. And then his record withers. Ben Arnold died at Fort Pierre, South Dakota, on October 22, 1922, at age seventy-eight.

That Ben Arnold's story of wanderlust survives is a credit to the acknowledged editor, Lewis Crawford, and perhaps chiefly to Josephine Waggoner, an educated Hunkpapa Sioux mixed-blood and ironically the daughter of Arnold's deserted Indian wife, Itatewin, from her second marriage. Waggoner had befriended the aged Arnold and induced him to share his stories. With permission she began compiling notebooks on his life and adventures, eventually filling some fourteen before his death.

Interested in seeing Arnold's story published, Josephine was led to Crawford in 1924. A Harvard graduate with a master's degree in history, Crawford was then superintendent of the State Histor-

ical Society of North Dakota and a North Dakota
history enthusiast. He had previously published
Badlands and Broncho Trails and *The Medora-
Deadwood Stage Line* with Bismarck's Capitol
Book Company, and evidently gladly undertook
the final production of Waggoner's notebook tales
from Arnold. For his part, Crawford annotated the
text and did his best—so he writes in the closing
chapter—to corroborate Arnold's stories, but where
no confirmation was possible Arnold's statements
were accepted as substantially true. Some scholars
have refuted Arnold's remembrances here and there,
but in the main Crawford's assessment of authen-
ticity holds true.

When this book was being prepared for reprinting
by the University of Oklahoma Press, several of
Josephine Waggoner's grandchildren came forth
hoping that their grandmother's role in collecting
Arnold's story might be properly credited. Alas,
the opportunity to cross-examine the principals
involved in the initial publication of 1926 faded
decades ago. Waggoner died in 1943. A Hampton
Institute graduate in Virginia, she returned to the
Standing Rock Reservation, where she married a
soldier from Fort Yates in 1889, birthed nine children, and remained intrinsically connected to the
saga of her people. Lewis Crawford, meanwhile,
retired from North Dakota in 1934 to operate a
book store in Minneapolis with his son, Ken. He
died there in 1936. In turn, I knew Ken in the
1970s and early 1980s when he ran an antiquarian

book business in North Saint Paul, and we occasionally talked about his father and about this book,
but Ken, too, is now deceased.

Internal evidence, however, suggests that Waggoner's grandchildren are right about Josephine's
involvement. In his introduction and conclusion,
Crawford speaks of corroborating Arnold's story, and
to receiving aid from several informants, including
Josephine Waggoner. His bibliography lists collaborative writings, but none having to do directly with
Arnold's life. *Exploits*, however, is written in the first-
person voice. Crawford does not speak to having
been the recorder of Arnold's stories, or of having
had any relationship at all with the old frontiersman.
But he does acknowledge Waggoner, if only casually,
as having "furnished some data taken down just
before Ben Arnold's death."

Let the record show, therefore, that *The Exploits
of Ben Arnold* was truly a collaborative effort between
Arnold and Waggoner, and Waggoner and Crawford.
Crawford did annotate and otherwise prepare the
text for the 1926 edition by Capitol Book Company,
but any publisher today would credit him as having
been an editor, not the author. More important,
readers today should take heart that Ben Arnold's
history "with the bark on" is back in print. He was
an ordinary man engaged in ordinary business at an
extraordinary time in the American West, and his
story is well worth remembering.

PAUL L. HEDREN

INTRODUCTION

THE STORY of the West must be written largely from human experiences. Documents and reports are useful; but vital, moving history must come from the lives and actions of men. Even in the youngest states there are few of the pioneers left from whom we can get first hand evidence.

Without the soldier, the Indian, the miner, the cowboy, the "bad man," there would be no West. These men were neither saints nor demons. They were men, even as you and I; some good, some bad. Even the good men, removed as they were from the saving grace of their own reputations, were at their worst. Men had to take care of themselves; and in doing so gave themselves the benefit of the doubt. One who left his own chance to fate, fell by the wayside. Good men are not always good; bad men are at times not so bad. On the frontier, life consisted largely in extremes, and every individual embodied enough of both good and bad qualities to make him an enigma when judged by the standards of a settled community.

This volume is not the biography of a certain man; but rather the story of the times in which a certain man lived and did his humble part. It is history with the bark on; no attempt has been made to edit out even the harsh things that went to make up the pioneer civilization of which he was not an unworthy part. I have not glossed over his or others' faults. The desire has been to present truthfully a few sketches as he saw and remembered them. In the narrative the desire for truth is stronger than the desire to cover up evil. When known, names of individuals have been mentioned. Some were morally delinquent, yet even they had some redeeming traits. Their shortcomings are not paraded; they are mentioned, not for the purpose of bringing odium upon them or their descendants, but simply to keep the historical narrative straight. Facts are stated with intentional fidelity; and I trust with sympathy and an average ability to see both sides of a question and the point of view of other people and other times; yet naught is set down in malice. Time has softened our judgments and we are now entitled to the whole story.

In a volume where details are given, errors must of necessity creep in. I hope those who find errors will call the author's attention to them, that they may be corrected.

Any one who writes on matter of fact subjects must of necessity call upon many for information. Such aid have I received from the following: Ed Monroe of Springview, Nebraska; Horatio H. Larned of Lansing, Michigan; and Wm. V. Wade of Shields, North Dakota — all old living friends of the subject of this sketch; from Mrs. Lula M. Price of Lidgett, Canada; Mrs. Laura Casady of Lemmon, South Dakota, and Mrs. Blanche Hanson of Glenham, South Dakota, his daughters; and especially am I indebted to Mrs. Josephine McCarthy Waggoner, a daughter of his Indian wife, Itatewin, by a second marriage. Mrs. Waggoner's knowledge of the Sioux people and their language enabled me to interpret facts and incidents in the story. She also furnished some data taken down just before Ben Arnold's death.

To all the above grateful acknowledgements are given.

Lewis F. Crawford

CHAPTER I

MORGAN AND QUANTRILL

WHEN Morgan made his daring raid north of the Ohio River in July, 1863, I had just enlisted in Company E of the 11th Ohio Volunteer Cavalry, which was recruiting a second battalion, consisting of Companies E, F, G, and H, for service on the western Indian frontier. This battalion was recruited to relieve the first battalion of the same regiment which had been on the frontier for the year past, but under the necessity of heading Morgan off, our battalion was called into active service immediately. I had already served under two enlistments in the Civil War,[1] and had just been recovering from a more or less persistent malady which had caused my discharge from the service.

Up to this time the Ohio River had been considered the boundary line of the war. When Morgan[2] crossed it, therefore, the whole state was thrown into con-

[1] Benjamin M. Connor. First Enlistment: Enrolled July 15, 1861, at Nelsonville, Ohio, was mustered into service Aug. 13, 1861, at Camp Dennison, Ohio, as a private in Co. C, 39th Ohio Inf., to serve three years, was honorably discharged April 5, 1862, at New Madrid, Mo., on a surgeon's certificate of disability for chronic bronchitis, following the measles.

Second Enlistment: Aug. 14, 1862, at Cincinnati, Ohio, mustered into service Aug. 18, 1862, private Co. C, 39th O. V. Inf., and left Nov. 5, 1862, near Grand Junction, Tenn. — *War Records*, Washington.

[2] See Gen. Basil Duke's *Life of Morgan*. Also L. J. Weber, *Ohio Archaeological and Hist. Pub.*, v. 18, pp. 79-104.

sternation. Indianapolis, Cincinnati, Columbus, and even Cleveland, were considered in danger. Governor Tod called out 50,000 militia, and all available Union forces in the national organization were put in motion to effect Morgan's capture. He was harassed on every hand, day and night. Seven hundred of his men were captured when he attempted to cross the Ohio at Buffington's Island ford into West Virginia, while he with 1,200 others escaped and continued northward. Finally, on July 26, after leaving a trail of devastation over the southern end of Indiana and clear across the state of Ohio, he surrendered and was sent to the penitentiary at Columbus. But Morgan's spectacular career was not yet over. On November 27 he and six others escaped by cutting through the stone floors of their cells with knives from the prison table. Tunneling under the walls of the building, they scaled the walls surrounding the grounds by the use of ropes made from bedclothes. Outside they changed their prison garb, and Morgan took the train for Cincinnati. Alighting in the suburbs of Cincinnati, he went to the Ohio, crossed the ferry, and found shelter among friends in Kentucky. He then went through Tennessee to northern Georgia, and from there to Richmond, where he was given an ovation.

After Morgan's capture, our battalion was loaded into cars and headed for St. Joe, Missouri, then the western railroad terminus of the United States, under orders to proceed to Fort Laramie. Our train moved at a fair rate of speed, taking due caution against a possible wreck due to the act of some disloyal person in placing obstructions upon the track or loosening the rails. In every town we went through signs of the war were much in evidence. Enlistment offices and drill grounds were frequent, and we saw many soldiers on furlough, many of whom showed emaciation from wounds or disease. In fact, all we heard and almost all we saw pertained to the war in which the nation had then been engaged for over two years.

On our arrival at St. Joe, we were all set to work unloading horses, mules, wagons, tents, supplies, and ammunition. Ferries were in waiting to carry us down the Missouri to a point opposite Fort Leavenworth, and on August 13, after a short march, we landed at that historic fort.

Although we had some supplies, they were wholly inadequate for our needs, and there was no place close at hand where more could be obtained. In fact, the needs of the various armies were such that supplies could not be manufactured fast enough to meet the ever-increasing demands promptly. While awaiting the necessary equipment, both officers and men busied themselves in getting together such personal belongings as life on the frontier might demand, knowing that the suttlers' stores along the way could supply only a limited quantity and that at a high price. We were all young fellows, for the most part boys from eighteen to twenty-one. The West was new to us and we were anxious to get on the road to the wild and romantic regions about which so many stories had been told, especially since the 49'ers had wended their way to Sacramento to pan over its gold-flecked sands.

On the morning of the 21st of August, our camp was thrown into great commotion. General Thomas

Ewing,[3] whose headquarters were at Kansas City, had come over to Leavenworth a day or two before on duties connected with his office. While there he received a telegram informing him that a band of Confederate guerrillas under William C. Quantrill had sacked Lawrence, burned the town, and killed nearly all the male inhabitants they could lay their hands on. Under the stressed circumstances, General Ewing called upon our battalion officers to render him what assistance they could. Only a few of our men had had horses assigned to them, and none of them had received their arms and ammunition. By early afternoon, however, about three hundred of us were mounted and equipped, and we set out under a forced march to intercept, if possible, the return of Quantrill and his marauding band to their old haunts in Missouri, whence they had set out for Kansas but a few days before.

I have seen few hotter days than the one we spent in the saddle in our ride from Leavenworth to the Kaw, or Kansas, River. The men were new recruits for the most part, unused to horse-back riding and the exhausting effort of active campaigning. The rapid riding was hard on the men, but even more wearing on the horses. When we left Leavenworth, it was thought possible that Quantrill, emboldened by his success, would attempt to go on farther West and attack Topeka; it was our purpose to head him off. Later, messages were received that lead to a change in course. It was found that Quantrill was heading for Missouri, so our line of march was veered to the east straight for De Soto, where we expected to find boats for crossing the Kaw

[3] *Rebellion Records*, Series 1, vol. 22, p. 572.

River. But no boats were present, and we were obliged to construct rafts. Consequently our crossing was delayed about six hours, which was good for the horses, but of little benefit to the men. As soon as we had crossed the river, we took a southeast course. Great columns of smoke were rising beyond the grove of timber far to the west, where but a few days before the city of Lawrence had stood in peaceful security. The city was out of sight, but the volume of smoke convinced us that the reports of her destruction had not been exaggerated. We rode all night long, although at greatly reduced speed. Our horses were fagging under the strain, and only intense anger and desire for revenge supported the men, who still claimed to feel ready for any emergency.

Quantrill and his men on reaching Lawrence had changed their jaded horses for fresh ones, and were consequently able to make better speed than any of their pursuers. Scattered here and there along the line of march was loot from the Lawrence stores which the marauders had been obliged to abandon in order to escape their pursuers who were converging upon them from almost every direction. It is idle to speculate what might have happened if we could have obtained a fresh supply of horses. But Quantrill was ahead and swept the country clean; so, although his men were more worn than ours, his mounts were fresher. None of the pursuing bands was able to keep a sufficient body of men in contact either to bring him to battle or to hold him until the wornout horses, plodding from exhaustion, could come up and bring a force large enough to insure victory. Quantrill's rear guard was able to hold the few Union men who could make a contact with it until his main body was some distance in advance; then the rear guard would fall back rapidly to the main body and safety. Thus the pursuers were unable to push them fast enough to bring them to a halt. If the Union forces had been able to force a general engagement, they would have been able to hold and surround Quantrill's company in a short time, and would probably have exterminated them. Their safety lay in flight.

To give the reader some idea of the exhausting efforts we were making, I need only mention that our command lost, as reported by General Ewing, several men from sunstroke, one of whom, David S. Dick, was first lieutenant in my company.[4] We had been out of Leavenworth but twenty-four hours, and notwithstanding a loss of six hours at the river crossing, had covered about a hundred miles. We had had no time to rest or sleep, and what food we had was for the most part devoured as we rode along.

When it seemed evident that Quantrill would escape to his old haunts in Missouri, the members of the 11th Cavalry were released from further pursuit and ordered to return to Fort Leavenworth. This we did after a little rest and refreshment, although at a more leisurely gait than on the trip out.

On the western horizon a column of smoke still ascended over the ruins of Lawrence, while back in Missouri Quantrill's band rested safe and almost unpunished. Such is war.

[4] *Roster of Ohio Soldiers*, vol. xi, p. 799. *Rebellion Records,* Series 1, v. 41; Sereis 3, v. 3.

CHAPTER II

Off for Fort Kearney

THE TRAIL leading to the northwest from Fort Leavenworth was rutted and worn by the thousands of live stock and wheeled vehicles that had passed over it. It had been used by Brigham Young and his followers in 1846,[1] by the stream of gold-seekers rushing to California in 1849,[2] by General Albert Sidney Johnston with his army of three thousand men and a supply train seventy-five miles long in 1857,[3] and by fur hunters, express riders, and numerous emigrant trains before and since that time. The route followed the Little Blue to its head, a distance of about two hundred and seventy-five miles, thence over a sandy prairie divide for perhaps thirty miles to the Platte valley, and then up the valley about fifteen miles to Fort Kearney, designated as the first stopping place on our journey. Eastern Kansas at that time had a few settlers scattered along the fringes of timber bordering the streams. The dwellings in all cases were constructed of sod or logs, and those who occupied them were poor and lived in the main from the proceeds of

[1] Cody and Inman, *The Great Salt Lake Trail*. R. F. Burton, *The City of the Saints*.

[2] Crawford's *Report*, Sen. Ex. Doc., 37 Cong., 3 Sess., for general information on this route.

[3] Johnson's *Life of Albert Sidney Johnston*.

garden truck and hay sold to the people who passed along the trail. The farther west we went, the shorter and browner became the grass, the scarcer the timber, and the less frequent the settlers' shacks.

In our traveling we made and broke camp according to the system in use by the United States army. Each wagon train of about thirty wagons was under the direction of a wagon master, or boss, as he was usually called, and an assistant. The disposition of the wagons in camp was under their direction. In making camp, the wagons were parked about one hundred feet apart, standing parallel with each other. A rope cable was then stretched taut between the wagons from hind to hind wheel, high enough to keep the horses from getting their feet over it. The cavalry horses were then tied to this cable, head to head, feeding being done by nose bags. Each man's saddle was laid behind his horse. The rows of tents were pitched directly behind the line of horses. The officers' tents were placed so as to give them the advantage of the wind. The mule teamsters and civilian employees had tents of their own and did their own cooking. A mule team consisted of six head, and worked stretched out in twos. When being fed these were tied three on each side of the wagon tongue, facing each other, the feed being poured into a long feed box chained to the tongue. At night two soldiers stood guard over the line of horses, pacing up and down on a regular beat. The teamsters, on the other hand, often arranged their wagons in a circle, closing the spaces between wagons with a rope. In the corral thus formed the mules and loose stock were turned.

When traveling through a country not deemed dangerous, we turned the mules and horses out to graze, and at night watched over them by relays of night herders divided into watches. The last shift on duty then brought the horses in, in the morning. When mules were turned out to graze, a toggle was fastened to one of the forefeet by a strap with a chain about eighteen inches long attached to it. If the mule attempted to travel fast, he would set his hind foot upon the chain and stop himself. The toggle was intended to give the animals freedom in grazing, to render them easier to catch, and to prevent their running off. Especially when grain feed was scarce it was necessary to put the horses and mules under herd or else hobble them or put a toggle on a front foot. They could not get enough grass to sustain them in a circle reached by a picket rope, or within the rope enclosure.

After breakfast was over we broke camp by bugle call, every tent-pin being pulled and every guy rope loosened at the tap of a drum. Each wagon had its crew of men to do the loading, and each man in the crew was assigned certain work; thus the loading was done quickly and without confusion.

When the train was strung out on the road, eight or ten men were always detailed as rear guard to pick up lost articles, gather in the missing or foot-sore animals, give relief to broken wagons, or ward off an Indian attack. This was a duty which none of us relished, as the trail was disagreeably dusty in the rear. As in our case, an army outfitted and equipped for service many miles from its base of supplies required long trains of wagons to transport the necessary provisions and stores of war. Each army wagon in the train was drawn by six mules strung out in twos, and carried about a three-ton burden. As the wagon train got farther and farther from its base, the loads became lighter, but often not light enough to adjust the burden to the waning strength of the work stock, and the trail was littered with furniture and equipment abandoned by emigrants for this reason. Often the trail could be followed for miles by the line of dust which at times rose in stifling clouds.

Ordinarily we tried to camp on water, but the grass was always overfed at the watering places. Occasionally we had either to drive several miles off the main trails or else make a dry camp between watering places. In the latter case it was necessary to haul fuel and water for cooking purposes. Good water and good feed are never found together along a main highway of travel like the old Oregon Trail.

When we left Leavenworth, all our equipment was spic and span. The wagons were just from the factory, all shining in their new paint; the harnesses were black and well-oiled, and all straps were present and unbroken; tents were tight and free from holes, and the uniforms of the men were clean and becoming. But before we had reached Kearney, the wagons showed wear, harnesses were broken and tied with straps, tents were rent and frayed by the wind, and clothes were torn and travel-stained.

At every camping place wrecks of wagons, skeletons of oxen, horses, and mules, pieces of ox-yokes, broken crockery, fragments of camp stoves and dutch ovens, barrel hoops, crumpled and runover boots, and scattered scraps of clothing littered the ground. In most cases things were thrown aside because worn out, but in some, thrown overboard to adapt loads to the weakened condition of the work stock.

The constant stream of people going and coming had killed off and scared the buffaloes back from this traveled thoroughfare, but all along the trail was the bleaching bones of these animals, most of which had been ruthlessly slaughtered by former travelers for the mere glory of killing. Mingled with the buffalo bones were the remains of horses, oxen, and mules that had given up their lives in the service of man.

On this great highway unnumbered thousands had traveled during the past few years — Mormons seeking an isolated home free from the law's interference; 49'ers impelled by the lure of gold; soldiers in the line of duty; bull-whackers and freighters with their long trains of supplies; messengers and express riders; gamblers seeking an unrestricted field to ply their trade; malefactors escaping the law; emigrants seeking new homes for their families. The trail, or rather series of trails, was cut into deep ruts by the assault of many feet and the grinding wheels that slowly followed. The dust rose and stood in hovering clouds over the trail, marking its winding way within the range of vision. There was scarcely a time when a train either coming or going was not visible, close at hand or in the hazy distance.

Young and full of vitality as we were, and accustomed to death in all the forms war brings, yet it was with a touch of sadness that we looked upon the scattered graves that dotted the highway and encircled every camping place. Among all classes the death toll was heavy; hardship and exposure, Indian foray and bandit attack, quarrel and suicide, sickness without medical attention or proper nursing — all contributed not a little to the daily death lists. The graves — some unmarked and revealed only by a ridge of clay or a sunken place in the sod, others with crude inscriptions cut with a pocket knife or painted with axel grease on a barrel stave or a board from a packing box — told a simple story, touching even to the most hardened.

CHAPTER III

Fort Kearney and Doby Town

Old Fort Kearney was on the south bank of the Platte River, whose broad and shallow waters were dotted with numerous islands clothed in richest verdure. Although shallow, the river is by no means easy to cross, owing to the ever-shifting quicksand which lines its bottom. The volume of water it carries is subject to great fluctuation, now overflowing the adjacent valleys, now sinking into an insignificant stream. In dry seasons it even disappears in places into its sandy bed, leaving pools here and there inhabited by turtles, small fish, and tadpoles.

Fort Kearney was established as one of a chain of forts in which United States soldiers were stationed to protect the travelers, mainly against Indian depredations. Our four companies were under orders to proceed to Fort Laramie, from which point we were to be distributed westward along the Oregon Trail to guard the immigrant trains and patrol the telegraph line which had been strung to Sacramento. West of where our four companies were to be stationed were placed the California troops, whose duty it was to protect the line from where we left off to the coast.

The United States Army paymaster paid us at Fort Kearney the wages due at that time, and told us we should get no more until we arrived at Fort Laramie, a distance of over 350 miles.

As we were getting into a dangerous country, Jim Bridger, the well-known scout and guide, was engaged to escort us to Laramie. The route lay along the south bank of the South Platte for a distance of two hundred miles. Fort Kearney was surrounded by a ten mile square military reserve on which no merchants were permitted to establish supply stores except licensed post traders, and travelers had to camp outside the reserve in order to save the grass for the cavalry horses and work stock belonging to the fort. Consequently a little trading post had been established on either side of Fort Kearney to get the trade of those who passed hither and thither on the highway. Dog Town, a tough pioneer settlement, was located east of the fort about twelve miles, and Doby Town was located to the west a little over two miles, just outside the reserve, which did not extend as far westward as it did eastward. Here civilians could purchase equipment and find feed for their animals, while still near the protection of the fort.

After a short stay at Fort Kearney we moved over to Doby Town, settled down for a little rest and repairs, and proceeded to spend the money the paymaster had temporarily left with us. Owing to the scarcity of timber, the whole town was made of "dobies," or sun-dried brick. It was supported wholly by immigrant trade. It was afterwards called Kearney Town, but has long ago ceased to exist, and nothing now marks its location except a few sunken depressions which were the old cellars and excavations.

Doby Town was a frontier settlement — the outpost of civilization, if its brand of conduct could be called civilization. There were no streets, and people built their houses wherever preference or caprice dictated. The townspeople were mostly frontiersmen who settled there for the sole purpose of trading with, or preying upon, those who traveled on the Oregon Trail. The population consisted chiefly of men: about two dozen permanent inhabitants, mostly gamblers and saloon keepers, some loafers who had no employment but hung around town to rob the passing immigrants, and a few women of well-known reputation. When immigrants put their herds out to graze, these fellows would sneak them away at night and run them off a few miles around a bend in the river, reporting that the Indians had taken them. To the immigrants the story seemed highly probable, as a number of indigent Pawnees hung around Fort Kearney to get their scanty allowances; so when any of the white man's stock was missing, the Indians were blamed for taking it. The immigrants did not know the country and usually had only a worn-out saddle horse to ride, so was glad to hire the loafer to hunt his stock for him. In other words, it was cheaper to hire the grafter to bring in the stock than to waste time trying to find it himself. The vagrant had no use for the stock, as most of it was poor and foot-sore, but he drove it off in the belief that the owner would offer a reward for the return of the missing animals. In a conveniently short time after a suitable reward was offered, the vagrant would go out and bring in the stock, deliver it to the owner, and get from the latter in return a liberal reward in cash and a hearty gratitude. There was no law in Doby Town, or at least none that could be enforced.

To induce the travelers to gamble was easy, and to induce them to drink was easier still. The saloon men paid no license. A man could run a saloon at any good water hole where travelers stopped to water their horses and oxen. An upturned dry-goods box and a few quarts of whiskey would start one in business, and a brisk trade would follow, especially in the spring when immigration was at its height. At such times wagons were often strung out for miles and miles with but a few yards interval between them. There was none to hinder the whiskey seller, and when business ceased to be good at one place, he could move on, stock, bag, and baggage.

There was a motley throng at the Doby Town station, some preparing for the next lap on their journey towards the mountains that lay weary miles beyond, and almost as many looking towards homes in the States, which they were anxious to reach. Every eastern state contributed a few members to the crowd; many came from Ohio, Indiana, Illinois, Kentucky, Tennessee, and Arkansas, and still more from Missouri. Every sort of outfit was in use. Some drove horses, others mules or oxen, and a few milk cows, hitched to wagons, buggies, or carts. When on the road the covered wagons were so heavily laden that only the driver, usually a woman, with possibly a few small children, rode in them. The remaining members of the party rode horseback or trudged on foot, driving the loose cattle and horses. Instead of walking and riding in the trail, they usually went parallel to it, to avoid the dust and give opportunity for the stock to graze. The glaring sun and parching winds had sunburned everyone until they all looked like tough customers, as some of them were. The men all wore whiskers, which combined with the dust and travelstain to make them look much older than they were.

Every morning from the various camps around Doby Town issued forth the women and children, practically all barefooted, with baskets in which to pick up what was commonly called "buffalo chips" for use as fuel. These buffalo chips make good fire in dry weather, but in wet weather it is hard even to get a smoke out of them. Yet this was the main fuel on the western plains, and as the buffaloes disappeared, the bed grounds of the work-oxen and domestic cattle were salvaged. There was no coal in use anywhere, and in many places there was only wood enough for emergencies.

The immigrants for the most part slept in their covered wagons or under them. The soldiers used Sibley army tents, and the officers had wall tents, which gave them room in which to do their clerical and staff work.

While getting ready for our onward trip, we had much leisure to visit the various immigrant and freighter camps. Most of the immigrants seemed to be refugees from the border states — Missouri, Kentucky, Arkansas, Tennessee, Illinois, Indiana, and Ohio. Those from the northern states in sympathy with the South were escaping the draft which was then being applied to recruit the Union armies. These Northerners in sympathy with the South were called "butternuts." Some of them wore a butternut pin secretly and belonged to a disloyal organization known as the "Knights of the Golden Circle." Those with stronger disunion leanings, who not only gave sympathy but even went so far as to give secret assistance to the South, were called "Copperheads" because they struck without warning. Some enlisted in our battalion from the southern border states because, while not favoring secession, they did not want to fight against their own states. There were all sorts of coarse songs and rough gibes about the Missourians from Pike county, the Hoosiers from Posey county, and the Arkansawyers from Izard county. While people from these counties were not less cultured than those from other parts of their respective states, yet since they were the butt of all jokes, they bore the stigma of being the most backward and ignorant people on the trail.

Those who were traveling eastward were not so numerous but formed equally as picturesque a group as those outward bound. These formed a motley crew of disappointed miners from Denver, Colorado Springs, and Pike's Peak; freighters returning empty to the Missouri River for another load of supplies; and disappointed emigrants returning home, as they expressed it, to the "States." These latter were in bad shape, their animals jaded, outfits sadly dilapidated, food scanty and unpalatable, and clothing in rags. Then, too, there were mule skinners, many of whom were Mexicans, scouts dressed in buckskin suits and broadbrimmed hats, bushy-whiskered fur hunters waiting for the trapping season to open, and men of royal blood looking for adventure in the chase.

Doby Town had a sod grocery store where one could buy tobacco, gunpowder, flour, sugar, and coffee. Baking powder was an unknown article. Bread was made exclusively of sour dough and soda, the dough being kept from meal to meal. There were no canned vegetables, and the process of condensing milk was yet undiscovered. We took our coffee black. The only canned goods I had ever seen at that date were oysters and sardines. The only ready-to-eat goods to be found in the grocery store were ginger snaps, crackers, and sardines. Beer was not used, as it was too heavy to haul that long distance; every man who drank at all, and there were few who didn't, was compelled to drink the more concentrated liquor, whiskey.

To Doby Town in the spring season came many people from the states, ignorant of the perilous journey ahead. Here they were held and organized into companies, instructed how to arrange their wagons in camp, and how to corral most quickly and effectively in case of Indian attack. In the season of heavy traffic, Fort Kearney and Doby Town had guides and scouts open to hire, who knew the country well and made a profession of guiding and piloting wagon trains across the plains. These guides knew all the water holes and bad-creek crossings, the best camping places, and the most likely places of meeting hostile Indians; and were always more or less proficient in talking with the Indians, especially in the use of the universal sign language of the plains.

Spending most of my time visiting around the camps among the immigrants, I was able to pick up much valuable information. From them I learned that we would probably not be attacked by the dreaded Sioux, as October was now far advanced. This was welcome news to me, as I had listened in my childhood in the peaceful valleys of southeastern Ohio to the bloody deeds of the Indians in the earlier days and naturally did not relish being attacked by them. I also learned that the Indians did not, as a rule, go on the warpath in the winter time, but that they usually selected a place with an abundance of timber, grass, and water in which to go into winter quarters, unmolested by the white man.

I met a well-informed Mormon gentleman who told me that he and his party were enroute with teams to the Missouri River, to meet converts to their faith coming from England, Wales, Norway, and Sweden, and to conduct them across to Salt Lake City. The Mormon Church paid all expenses of these immigrants, even providing the steamship fares from Europe. I wondered where the money to do this came from, but I ceased to wonder when it was explained to me that a tenth of all the Mormons produced was paid as a tithing to the church. The Mormons even at that time covered a wide scope of country in Utah and adjoining territories, and raised everything from live-stock to cotton, corn, and wheat. Even in the small villages there was a tithing office and a tithing officer stationed to receive and dispose of whatever was paid in. The church set a price on all products, and allowed no one to sell above or below this set price — a great protection to the poor immigrant who passed through their territory. Converts sent from across the ocean by the Mormon elders, whom the church supported as missionaries, were first put on farms under wages from the Mormon church until they learned the business of farming well enough to fit them for taking up and handling farms of their own. Most of the Mormon band I met were from Cash Valley, Utah.

At Doby Town was also located the stage barn to take care of the work stock on the daily stage line running from Omaha. This line went to Fort Kearney, and extended westward through Plum Creek, Spread Eagle Ranch, and to Julesburg, where it divided, one branch going southwest to Denver, the main line continuing up Pole Creek toward Salt Lake City, and the third branch following the North Platte to Fort Laramie. While I was standing one day at the stage barn, the stage with a four-mule hitch swung into view, surmounted by the driver and the express messenger. The coach was equipped for ten passengers inside, and a boot for baggage was hung on the hind end gate with the outer end suspended by chains from the top of the coach. The roof of the stage was floored solid and surmounted by a railing, so that mail sacks, and if necessary passengers, could be carried on top in the open when weather permitted. From the east-bound miners whom the coach carried I learned that the Sioux, Cheyenne, and Arapahoes had been running off immigrant horses and cattle along the trail and setting prairie fires, in a vain effort to keep the many bands of immigrants and the numerous Mormon trains out of their country by making it impossible to get feed for their stock. The killing and scalping of soldiers and citizens when caught out alone was a not infrequent occurrence. Every sort of crime or misdemeanor committed by stage robbers or horse thieves was laid to the Indians, and it was quite generally believed that the growing feeling of hostility on the part of the Indians against the encroachments of the whites would cause much bloodshed sooner or later. As I have already said, the Indians do not make war in the winter time, and it was felt that there would be no disturbance during the latter part of 1863. Most of the Indian bands had either gone or were preparing to go to their winter camps in the wooded regions on the Powder, Tongue, and Little Missouri rivers with their supply of dried buffalo meat, to remain in winter camp until the following spring. It was well known that the Indians always select a winter camp with a view to the wood and water supply, so the trail along the barren Platte was assured of safety.

October was just at an end, and the Platte Valley from Doby Town westward was bleak and open, without protection for stock and with scant timber. There were some small ash trees and bullberry bushes along the draws, but not enough to amount to anything as fire-wood, since most of this brush would be covered with snow and inaccessible in the winter season. Even the stage was generally discontinued during the cold weather, as traveling was too toilsome and uncertain, especially in times of blizzard or deep snow. The mail was then carried by pack horse. Both hay and feed were scarce along the trail, and when they could be had, were held at a high price. For these reasons travel by whites along the Oregon Trail was greatly reduced during the winter, and for the same reasons there was safety from Indian attack.

CHAPTER IV

A Saloon Orgy

After we had rested about a week in Doby Town it was found that our men had made the necessary repairs to their equipment and clothing and that the cavalry mounts and work stock had taken on some flesh and had regained their former spirits. Consequently our commanding officer decided to break camp and renew our westward journey. The orders were given out late in the afternoon requiring us to move early the following morning. As this was to be our last night, of course all of us were bent on having a good enough time in the few hours of freedom still remaining to last us for some weeks of monotony on the march.

In a small place like Doby Town there was little of life or spirits outside of the saloon and the ramshackle dance hall. Being impartial in our patronage, we went from one to the other of these places seeking such thrills as the coarse monotony of their daily program offered. Most of the men drank, some gambled, and others were merely interested spectators passing away the time. I belonged to the latter class.

The saloons were all built of sod and similar in size and appointments. The one in which I spent most of the evening consisted of a long, narrow room with a bar made of rough boards extending the entire length of one side. Out in front of the bar stood a few square pine tables covered with woolen blankets, which were used for card tables. Some gambling was going on night and day, but at night while we were there the tables were always full. When I stepped into the saloon I took a place behind one table of players and watched the game, an unobserved onlooker. The clink of glasses and the noisy badinage around the table were conspicuous. The languages in use were Mexican, French, English, and one other, common to all nationalities: profanity. Occasionally some exultant winner would express his delight by firing his pistol through the roof or into the sod walls of the saloon and a little loose dirt would trickle down. The air was heavy with the blue smoke from the guns and the lighter tobacco smoke; and the fumes of both, mixed with the stench of the liquors slopped over the bar by unsteady drinkers, made a combination of foul smells unknown outside a whiskey dive.

Dealing out drinks behind the bar was a dark slender young man named Jack Morrow, whom I met and worked under several times in after years. Jack was a good man for the place: he had strength, nerve, and speed — qualities necessary, not at rare intervals but daily, and almost hourly. It was occasionally his duty to drag an unconscious drunk across the dust-covered dirt floor to a back room where he would lie in a heap for hours, only to awaken with pockets rifled.

I stood and watched the game in which some of my comrades were playing and idly listened to the drift of their conversation. With frequent drinks the conversation grew louder and less guarded and they said things which sober caution would have kept secret. I was brought sharply to attention by a few chance words I heard, and listened closely thereafter. I observed from their dialects that these men were Southerners, which gave more credence to the plans they were discussing. I listened as intently as I could without betraying my interest (though it is doubtful if any of them would have noticed it in their intoxicated condition), and gathered that their intention was to get as many soldiers as possible to join them in a mutiny when we reached Julesburg. After that they planned to rob the stage coaches along the line to Denver, then branch off south and east toward Kansas, rob and plunder the scattered towns along their course, and eventually join Quantrill's notorious guerrilla band. Two men, both named John Sullivan, and two others named Crawford and Grey [1] were to give the grip of the Knights of the Golden Circle to test out those who were favorable to the mutiny.

As all soldiers were required to answer to roll call before taps, we did not dare stay too late at the saloon but started back in time to avoid the punishment inflicted on those who were absent from roll call. On our way to camp I could still hear my companions planning. This was no drunken dream but an organized treasonable plot. I was among rebels dressed in Union uniform. These men had joined the Northern army to

[1] See Vol. ii, *Roster of Ohio Soldiers*, 11th O. V. Cav., 561, 799-800. These four men were members of Co. E.

escape being drafted to fight directly against the South, knowing that the 11th Ohio was enlisted for service in the Indian country. Here they could serve and still maintain, and with narrow limits express, their pro-southern sympathies. I rode along silently behind the bibulous crowd, taking in every word of the treasons a few of them planned so boldly, yet uncertain how I should act in the matter. I was only twenty years old at the time, and timid. My instincts were all right, but I was wholly lacking in the maturity and dicisive-ness of judgment demanded by the seriousness of the situation. A soldier's duty is to obey orders. I hated to be a tale-bearer or informer against my comrades, for after all they might be a little less vindictive when sober than their drunken boasts had led me to believe. But, on the other hand, if I kept still I felt that I would in a measure share their guilt in case their plans were executed. After taps that night I went to bed and dreamed wild dreams of treason and mutiny in which I was trying to save my command but could not open my mouth.

CHAPTER V

Mutiny Planned and Averted

In the early morning we broke camp as planned and set out for Plum Creek. This was a swing station for the stage line, *i.e.*, a station where the incoming teams from each direction turned and went back over the route they had come. While I had thought much and worried not a little over what I had heard at Doby Town, I had said nothing to anyone, hoping that the men would give up their plans when the influence of the whiskey wore off. By giving them the benefit of the doubt I could excuse, though not condone, their actions when under the influence of liquor. They were, as I have said, Southerners. It was but natural at a time when the country was in the midst of a civil war, when the land of their birth was over-run by the hated "Yankees" and they, the rightful owners of the soil, were forced into involuntary exile, that the ties which held them to the Union under ordinary conditions would be weakened. They were made desperate by circumstances even to the point of betraying the Union they had sworn to protect. Thus I made excuses for them. In addition, there was still a lingering doubt in my mind as to whether, when it came to a pinch, they would ever attempt to carry out the plans their resentment prompted. But on our arrival at Plum Creek late that afternoon I noticed that the same men were scattered in several small groups talking in an undertone, and my suspicions were renewed.

I went to bed down-hearted, but was kept awake by the bronchial cough that had caused my discharge from the army some months previously. Later, when all were supposed to be asleep, I overheard Sullivan whisper to his bunkmate Grey, "You give 'em the grip, and they'll come around." They whispered more, but I could not understand it. I am sure that I was the only person awake to overhear this conversation, and was probably the only one in the command who knew of the plotting. These men were much older than I and paid little attention to me. I was only a youth, slight of stature and still emaciated from illness, and no one took me very seriously. Be that as it may, I knew about the plot and whatever was to be done was up to me. This feeling of responsibility earned me little better rest than I had enjoyed the previous night.

The next morning we broke camp and set out for Spread Eagle, which was a home station on the stage line, a station where the drivers stayed overnight. Camp was made in the early afternoon a short distance from the station and our horses turned loose to graze. I was selected as one of the two day herders. Camp having been made thus early, I had plenty of time to observe the actions of the men whom I suspected, and to make up my mind what to do. The mutiny was to come off at Julesburg, and Julesburg would be reached within a few days. So far as I then knew or ever heard afterwards, no other person except those in the plot and myself had even an inkling of the conspiracy. I did not know just how many men they had won over to their side. I had never seen a mutiny, but I knew it meant a fight and more than likely the death of some of our officers and men.

So, with these thoughts in mind, I made my decision: I would speak to our company officer, Captain Marshall. When my companion and I had brought the horses in from grazing and given them their grain, our work was over for the evening. In the gathering dusk I sauntered over to Captain Marshall's tent, no doubt with the seriousness of my mission written on my face. I saluted and said, "Captain Marshall, I have something to tell you if you will step outside a moment."

The captain looked concerned. "What is it Monroe?" he asked.

I then told him carefully and accurately all I had heard in the saloon at Doby Town and what I had seen since, calling to his mind the fact that a number of the men were from Kentucky and other southern border states. On my finishing, the captain thanked me quietly, "I've been noticing an unrest among the men the past few days, and this seems to explain it." I went to my tent feeling much relieved in spirits but still apprehensive. It would have been far easier for me to have kept quiet. I knew I was incurring the danger of bodily harm, for the leaders in the plot were fearless and desperate characters. I knew the captain would not mention his informant yet felt I would be suspected; and my peace of mind and safety were in constant jeopardy.

The next morning before breaking camp a sergeant and a squad of dependable soldiers placed the four ring leaders of the Golden Circle gang, the two Sullivans, Grey, and Crawford, under arrest. Their arms, consisting of a seven-shot Spencer rifle and a Remington revolver, were taken from them and they were told to fall in on foot behind the wagon train, under mounted guard. There was some whispering among the men but no open insurrection, and everything went off quietly. These ring leaders were compelled to walk all the way to Laramie, a distance of three hundred miles. No greater punishment can be meted out to a cavalryman than to disarm him and make him walk. The mutiny was thus happily averted, or rather, postponed, as we shall see later.

CHAPTER VI

JULESBURG differed from Doby Town in size rather than in quality. Being at the juncture of three roads as I have already stated, it was larger and livelier, contained more saloons, more stock rustlers, more gamblers, and more outlaws than Doby Town; otherwise they were identical.

From Julesburg one branch of the stage line ran south to Denver. The first station on this branch was *Caché la Poudre*, a French settlement so called because the French traders there had to *caché* their powder, bringing in a little at a time to trade with the Indians, because they did not want the latter to know how much powder they had. From *Caché la Poudre* the road ran on down to Fort Collins, named after Col. G. H. Collins of the 11th Ohio.

The second branch ran up Pole Creek. Feed was scarce along this trail as it had been used heavily by the 49'ers and the Utah immigrants. Much stock was lost along this route from poisonous water, insufficient feed, and loco weed. The loco seems to come in when the grass is overfed. The stock, being deprived of grass, first eat the loco from necessity and afterwards from desire, as a habit forming drug is taken by a person addicted to it. Cattle when locoed walk nervously around looking for the "weed." They become poor, their hair loses its gloss, their eyes become sunken and stary, and in disposition they become nervous and unmanageable. They seldom die of loco in summer but become so poor that they succumb to the first storms in the fall. The effect most serious to the traveler is that it makes the animals crazy and unmanageable.

The third trail out of Julesburg is the one we took to Laramie, of which we shall learn more as we go along.

Julesburg received its name from a Frenchman named Jules Remi who had settled there. We heard many tales of his death at the hands of Joe A. Slade,[1] the notorious superintendent of the grand central division of the Overland Stage Company, which stretched over six hundred miles of territory with scanty population and less law. It seems that bad blood had existed between Remi and Slade for some time. On one occasion Remi, taking advantage of his enemy when he was unarmed, emptied his revolver into him, then picked up a shot gun and discharged it into his prostrate body. Contrary to all expectations, however, Slade survived this cowardly outrage, even though his body bore thirteen pistol bullets and buckshot. Later, it is reported, Remi returned to the country with the avowed purpose of finishing the job he had left unfinished previously. Slade, hearing of this, sent four of his stage employees to capture Remi. They tied him to the corral at a station known as Chanson's ranch not far from Fort Laramie, and Slade shot him to death

[1] See Langford and Toponce for full accounts of Slade.

with a revolver. He then sliced off both his ears with a bowie knife and carried them for some time as watch charms. Among the frontiersmen acquainted with the facts, Slade was justified in what would have been classed as brutal murder under other circumstances. The stage company approved of his action and continued him in its employ.

They that live by the sword usually die by the sword. A year later when I was working on a ferry on the Snake River at the site of old Fort Hall, the stage came in bearing Slade's body. His widow accompanied the body, which she was taking to Salt Lake for burial as she did not want him interred in Montana where he had been hung by a vigilance committee. It is known that Slade had above average ability, and it is believed that if he had not acquired a habit of drink he would have been a useful man. His temper was always touchy, and when under the influence of liquor he was in an ungovernable rage. He had, however, some excellent qualities. He was fearless, although despotic. If a man refused to obey him he usually enforced his commands with a drawn pistol. He lived in a country where there was no law, and as superintendent he was responsible for the safety of the stage. Neither Indian nor white freebooter knew any restraint except fear, and surrounded by these, Slade got results in his rough and immediate way. No one ran over him, because those who knew him held his name in wholesome fear. He committed many acts wrong in themselves, but in part, if not wholly, justified by the circumstances.

After he went to Virginia City his name became a terror. He was guilty of many inexcusable acts of violence. He drank more freely than before and when drunk was both destructive and vicious. One morning following a particularly violent night the writ of arrest which the sheriff was reading to Slade was snatched from his hands by one of Slade's confederates and torn to pieces. Then the vigilance committee got together, arrested Slade and told him he was to be hanged. When he saw they meant business, he broke down and on his knees begged for his life. When he found his pleas unvailing, he asked that his wife might be sent for, from their little ranch home twelve miles away. It was agreed that his life was to be spared until his wife could come in; but fear that her presence might cause bloodshed was stronger than the promise and he was hanged at once. When Mrs. Slade arrived on a foaming stallion, flourishing a revolver, his body lay in the hotel. She flayed everybody for making Slade die the death of a dog by the rope instead of by a bullet. Mrs. Slade was a beautiful woman, and bore all the marks of an energetic and forceful one, too. Here she was bringing the body of her husband a distance of four hundred fifty miles for burial as a protest against what she called an outrage. Whatever his failings, Slade seemed to have inspired a very genuine devotion in his wife. I never saw Mrs. Slade again, although I heard years later that she had married a pioneer banker in Denver by the name of Kiskadin.

But to return to our camp at Julesburg. There was

a variety of nationalities in our company and members from many different states of the Union. A large percentage of them had deserted from a former enlistment and reënlisted under an assumed name. A few had gone under so many different assumed names that they would often forget the current one. One man had to look in his hat at roll call to see what name he had assumed last.

My case was hardly so extreme, but was similar. I had been going under my first and middle name, Benjamin Monroe, leaving off my last name, Connor. My first enlistment was under my right name and I was honorably discharged for disabilities after serving about nine months. On the margin of my discharge was written, "not to be reënlisted." I had joined the 39th Ohio in 1861 [2] when I was seventeen, falsely stating my age as two years over the minimum required. The need for soldiers was so urgent that the enlistment officers winked at these white lies and enlisted practically all who offered themselves, even though they suspected them of being under age. After receiving my discharge in April, 1862, I went to my Ohio home for a period of some four months, where I was fed codliver oil and other flesh builders. I made a rapid improvement and had a desire to reënlist, as I felt strong enough again to do a soldier's part. So one day when I met a bunch of recruits who were going to the front, assigned to various regiments whose quotas had been depleted by casualties, I presented myself to the recruiting officer and he took my name.

[2] See note 1, ch. 1, p. 15.

Within broad limits the applicant had a choice of regiment and I asked to be sent to the 39th O. V. I., which at that time was stationed near Iuka, Mississippi. I was put into my old company but the condition of my previous discharge did not allow me to enlist. I was not even given a medical examination. Being in the enemy's country and having no power to furnish transportation to send me back, our regimental officers could only muster me in and put my name on the rolls.

We fought under Grant up and down the Mississippi until September. Then my old malady returned. Sleeping on the cold wet ground and getting wet almost daily brought on a cough even worse than it had been before. At night I had fever, and several times in a delirium I wandered out of my tent and away from my command. One morning in November I found myself down by the Mississippi River, and my company gone. I was too weak and sick to follow. As soon as I felt able I took passage on an up-river boat to the mouth of the Ohio and up that river until my money was gone. Then I walked or caught rides as opportunity offered until I reached Zanesville. I had just strength to reach the house of an aunt, Margaret Connor, and then collapsed. For several months I was confined to the house, much of the time in bed, but under careful nursing improved so much both in health and spirits that I desired to enlist again. Not until then did I learn that I was reported as a deserter. The army rolls so carry my name to this day, but I am sure that my remorse and loyalty have more than expunged the technical offense; and no one can be found who has more consistently loved his country and its institutions than I.

So, in 1863, I enlisted for the frontier service in the 11th Ohio Cavalry, using the name Monroe, which was the maiden name of my mother, a cousin of James Monroe.

CHAPTER VII

BUT TO return to Julesburg. We remained there only one night, then resumed our journey up Pole Creek, across the North Platte, and then over a rolling country up to Fort Laramie. The atmosphere was high and dry. We passed many places of historic interest which travelers never fail to mention. Among these was Court House Rock, so called from its fancied resemblance to a court house. Not far east of our line of march was Ash Hollow, where Gen. William S. Harney chastised the Brulé Sioux Indians under Little Thunder, as related later in this chapter. We crossed Pumpkin Creek and Rush Creek, from which points Laramie Peak, over a hundred miles distant, was visible. The next notable point in our northwestward march was Chimney Rock — a sandstone which stood straight and tower-like for a great height. In the clear air it seemed near, and some of the soldiers started out to climb it; but they gave up when they found it was still over ten miles away. When we reached the towering column we all fell to deciphering the names and dates cut on almost every portion of its surface that could be reached by even the most agile climbers.

About thirty miles west of Chimney Rock was Scott's Bluffs. Through a cliff in these bluffs was a pass just wide enough for two wagons to pass each other. Jim Bridger told us that a few years earlier a man by the name of Scott had saved his life from pursuing Indians by taking refuge in the eroding cliffs of this bluff. On this, my first visit to Scott's Bluffs, the wind was wailing dismally through the gap, a circumstance which I found on later visits to be not unusual, especially in the fall season. The opening in the bluffs was named Marshall's Pass for the captain of my company.

Many years later when Ed Monroe and I passed this point on the road with an overland cattle herd from Texas, we saw what looked like a young growth of leafless trees but which proved to be the antlers of a herd of elks. Their bodies were so nearly the color of the clay background that we could not have distinguished them except for their lighter horns which looked not unlike a patch of scrubby timber. They were huddled motionless on the west hillside, but on noticing us they started to run through the gap and down the western sloping entrance. I jumped off my horse and ran to the top of a nearby ridge, which was almost too steep for foothold; I had on moccassins, however, and was able to clamber up. I counted the elk as we catch-count cattle, by tens, and the total number arrived at by this method was 1,700 head. To my readers this will seem a fairy story, yet it is true. Elk, like some other animals, gather in great herds in the fall.

Our next stop after leaving Scott's Bluffs was on Horse Creek, and before reaching Cold Springs we camped at a spring called Goes-in-the-Hole. A French beaver trapper had wintered there a few years before in a dug-out, and the Indians named him "Goes-in-the-Hole." I do not know whether the spring is still so called or not.

From Goes-in-the-Hole we proceeded to Bordeaux's trading post, nine miles east of Laramie. This is a historic spot, made famous — or rather, infamous — by the foolhardy bravado of Lieutenant Grattan[1] a few years before our visit. I have heard the Indians tell about it many times. It was in 1854 that some Mormon immigrants left a cow that was too lame to travel further. A few days later the owner came back from his camp near Fort Laramie to look for the animal, hoping the rest would enable it to travel; but he found it had been killed, as was afterwards learned, by a Minneconjou Sioux Indian. The Indian had found the cow unable to travel, and needing a piece of rawhide, killed the animal and stripped off as much of the hide as he needed, thinking, of course, that it had been abandoned by its owner. This Indian did just what you would have done had you been in his place. It is doubtful if the immigrant had previously expected to get anything out of the animal, but being close to the fort, he made complaint. The Indians offered him ten dollars for damages but he demanded twenty-five, which they were unable or unwilling to give. Even so, there would never have been any trouble had not Lieutenant Grattan insisted on being permitted by the acting commander of the fort to get the Indian who had done the killing. Grattan was inexperienced, hot-

[1] *Annual Report* of the War Dept., 1854.

headed, and a sort of "blow-hard." Instead of going out alone and getting the Indian, he took thirty men with a sergeant and two howitzers, went to the Indian camps, planted the men and howitzers in the center of the camp, and entered into a parley.   The Brulés and Ogalallas who had camps there were wholly innocent in the matter of the killing of the cow. The chiefs of both these tribes urged Lieutenant Grattan to wait until the agent, who was then absent, returned, and expressed the belief that the matter could then be settled amicably; but the request was refused. The chiefs even went so far as to go around and collect eight head of horses and offered them in settlement, but this offer was also refused. Had Lieutenant Grattan been a man worthy of the position he held an adjustment would easily have been made. But he kept demanding the guilty Indian, who was not there and could not be delivered; then ordered his men to fire. A number of Indians, all innocent, were killed or wounded, and the Brulé chief, Bear-that-Scatters (Mato Wayuha) a strong friend of the whites, fell with three bullet wounds. Incensed at this outrage, the Indians returned the fire, mostly with bows and arrows, and killed Lieutenant Grattan and all his men.

Shortly after being shot Bear-that-Scatters died of his wounds. He was a chief of good reputation. He had punished his own people for taking property from the whites, and on several occasions had put men of his own tribe to death for injury to the whites; consequently his death aroused much resentment among his people.

But the end was not yet. Col. William S. Harney was sent up from Fort Leavenworth in the following year, 1855, to "chastise" the Indians. On his march up the Platte he learned that there was a band of Brulé Indians under Little Thunder camped on Blue River, a short distance north of the North Platte, and there he marched. On sighting Harney's infantry Little Thunder began to pull down his lodges and move away, but was persuaded to stop and talk with Harney. The latter demanded that the slayers of Grattan be delivered up to him, which of course Little Thunder was powerless to do, since his band had had no part in the matter. In the meantime Harney's cavalry had secreted themselves on the opposite side of the Indian band, and the massacre began. Harney in his official report [2] says that eighty-six Indians were killed, five wounded, and about seventy women and children captured. Many of the killed were women and children. Little Thunder's band was innocent of wrong-doing, neither prepared for war nor expecting it. This was known as the Battle of Ash Hollow, in spite of the fact that the fighting was all on one side.

Colonel Harney went on to Laramie, again demanding the "murderers" of Lieutenant Grattan. Several of the leading men from the nearby camp came in, singing their death chant, and offered themselves as hostages. They, with their wives, all innocent, were sent to Fort Leavenworth prison.

In 1856 Colonel Harney held a council with the Sioux at Fort Pierre. He was still looking for the man

[2] *Annual Report* of the War Dept., 1855.

who had killed the cow. The Sioux agreed to deliver him and to make reparation for property destroyed. They did so, making a settlement which they would have been willing to make at any time except for the misguided efforts of the soldiers to enforce settlement.

Up to this time travel across the plains had been considered safe. Indians there were, scattered all over the plains, but they were harmless to those who treated them in a friendly manner. But after the Grattan massacre and the Ash Hollow tragedy there was bad blood between the whites and the Indians, which culminated in 1864 in murdering and plundering over a stretch of more than three hundred miles on the Platte River, from a short distance west of where Beatrice, Nebraska, now stands to the American Ranch on the South Platte. Many villages and farm houses were reduced to ashes, not a few white men killed, and some women and children taken into captivity by the Indians.

I was told later of another incident comparable to the indiscriminate killings mentioned. Two women were held captive near Fort Laramie [3] whom Chief Thunder Bear (Mato Wakinyan) wished to have turned back to the whites. He camped near the garrison with the prisoners and gave them a chance to escape. The garrison immediately sent out some soldiers, who killed one and captured three of a party of Indians they met. Two of them had been guilty of helping to take the women and hold them in captivity,

[3] The statements herein given are on the authority of Sioux Indians presumably familiar with the facts.

but the other one was Thunder Bear who had been instrumental in letting them escape. The three Indian captives were brought into the fort. The women who had been released pleaded with the soldiers to spare Thunder Bear who was their friend. The soldiers, however, were deaf to all entreaties and hung all three of them. Their bodies were left hanging all summer, dangling and swinging in the wind and dried to a shining black.

The hanging of the innocent man particularly irritated the Indians, and Spotted Tail planned a revenge. He and some others of the chiefs went to the garrison and told the commanding officer that there was a war party over the ridge camping along the creek, and offered to guide soldiers to the top of the ridge and show them the locality of the camp. They, themselves, could not go over the ridge, for the rest of the Indians must not know who had told the soldiers. Spotted Tail and the other chiefs led the detachment into a trap, and every soldier was killed. This is supposed to have happened about two years after Ash Hollow. Thus the Indians secured a measure of revenge for the outrages they themselves had suffered.

These stories I heard from whites as we passed through the country or from the Indians whom I learned to know well in after years.

CHAPTER VIII

Soldiering on the Plains

OUR journey was nearing an end and there was some hilarity among us when we descended to Laramie Crossing, within a short distance of Fort Laramie, where we were to camp. The Laramie River at this point is a mountain stream, clear, cold, and sparkling, and alive with trout. The garrison hauled its water supply from this stream, using six-mule teams and large tank wagons for the purpose. Here our command was given a few days rest before being scattered to different posts along the "wire" road farther westward. There was little vegetation around the post, and hay, when used, had to be hauled a long distance.

At this time the territory of Nebraska extended clear to the Oregon line, which was itself indefinite; no surveys had been made and legal bounds when established could not be made to square with the topography. The country hereabouts later became a part of Dakota Territory, which it remained until 1868 when Wyoming Territory was organized to include it.

The post at Laramie at the time of our arrival was usually occupied by two or three companies of the 11th Ohio which had been sent out the year before, and a portion of which could be sent to eastern or western stations as need seemed to be urgent. Laramie was an old post and the best known place along the Oregon Trail at that time. All the earlier structures were made of logs, but the barracks and stables were made from lumber from the little saw mill which had been hauled out over the plains and was now running at the foot of Laramie Peak.

Shortly after our arrival I, with about thirty other soldiers detailed from various companies, was sent north some thirty-five miles to Rawhide Buttes with the cavalry horses, as the grass was much better there than at the fort. We established a camp on Rawhide Butte Creek where there had been an old fur-trading outpost. A press for baling buffalo and other hides was still standing there. A bale of buffalo hides was as large as a bale of hay, but heavier. The hides had to be carried or hauled long distances to market and it was necessary to press them into as compact a bale as possible. Fuel and timber for buildings were plentiful at our camp, the grazing the best we had seen in months, and water and natural shelter all that could be desired.

We had been on Rawhide Butte Creek but a short time when an Indian and his family came in and pitched their buffalo-skin tent near us. Indians had always been objects of curiosity to me, as I had not known any in my youth and also because I wished to learn as much of the language as possible. I visited this family often. The man knew a little English and I was able to pick up a good deal from him. I learned that the Indians were hostile only toward emigrants, not to traders. They were glad to exchange their furs for knives, axes, cooking utensils, beads, and the like, and traders were welcomed.

After remaining here a month I was ordered in to the post to become a member of a detachment of thirty which was to take a station about one hundred miles westward at North Platte Bridge, some ten miles beyond the place where Fort Fetterman later stood. A fresh horse from the herd we were holding was issued to me and I set out for Fort Laramie. On arriving I saw the two Sullivans, Grey, and Crawford, the ring leaders in the incipient mutiny, shackled in ball and chain, chopping wood and policing the post. They had been court-martialed, found guilty, and sentenced to three months hard labor with pay suspended.

On our way to our new assignment at Platte Bridge we crossed a number of streams which emptied into the Platte. At every crossing was a telegraph station and operator. They were now able to keep in contact with the fort, but sometimes during the winter season weeks would elapse during which not a message got through over the line on account of wires having been broken by snow and storms. All the creeks had to be named so that headquarters at Fort Laramie could locate the place from which messages came and could locate breaks in the line easily. Among those we crossed were Horse Shoe, Bitter, Cottonwood, La Bonté's, Wagon Hound, Bisnett, Deer, Bedtick, and La Parelle. We passed over two toll bridges, Richaud's and North Platte, the latter built by Joseph McKnight. Most of the streams had worn out precipitous gorges whose walls were sometimes six or seven hundred feet high, relieved only by an occasional stunted cedar or a shrub of buffalo berry. These mountain streams were all swift with frequent rapids and cataracts down which the torrent splashed and foamed.

On our arrival at North Platte Bridge we relieved the other detachment that had previously been guarding it. There we found a horseherder with his feet badly frozen. He had been lying bedfast long enough for the flesh to slough from his instep to his toes, the bones being bare and in full view. As soon as an ambulance could be obtained he was taken to Laramie to have his feet amputated, but I never heard whether he survived the hardships of the long tedious trip and the operation or not.

A short time after our arrival, Lieutenant Rice, who was in command of my detachment, detailed Bill Lock and me to go south about ten miles with the horse herd to better grazing land. While there was much snow in places, the wind had swept portions of the hills bare and the feed was left exposed. We constructed a dugout with an open fireplace and chimney of stone and sod. The cooking utensils consisted chiefly of a dutch oven, frying pan, camp kettle, and coffee pot. For provisions we had sugar, coffee, tobacco, flour, and salt, but no meat. I had asked when we were packing our outfit to leave Platte Bridge, "Lieutenant, aren't you going to give us a little meat?" He looked at me in a whimsical way and replied, "Might as well send coke to Pittsburgh as to send meat to your camp," and walked away.

And we didn't need any meat, unless possibly a little

bacon. Black-tail deer were plentiful, and we killed enough to keep ourselves well supplied with venison. Buffaloes and antelopes could also be had, but they were not so close to us or so easily taken as the black-tails. For variety we could have sage grouse and rabbits.

The horses picked up in flesh and soon became located, so that herding was an easy and monotonous task; yet we dared not relax our vigilance for fear they might stray before some storm or be driven off by Indians. We did not see an Indian, or a white man either, all the remainder of the winter at this camp.

The name of my companion, as I have said, was Bill Lock. He hailed from Newport, Kentucky, and belonged to my company. He was a capital fellow, unselfish and willing to do his full share of all camp duties. Without companionship the long months would have been tedious indeed. As it was, while we had no books or newspapers, we kept busy making mittens, caps, and other articles of clothing from the skins obtained from our hunting. Our feet were encased in cavalry boots. We had no overshoes, in fact I had never seen an overshoe at that time.

The short winter days and long, cold nights dragged wearily on. We lost track of the days, the weeks, even the months. I never knew when Christmas or New Year's passed by. We were completely shut off from the outside. In the summer when the wire was in good repair the North Platte Bridge station got some news by telegraph; but in the winter there was not even mail carried along the Platte, as we were off the main mail

line which passed up Pole Creek from Julesburg and
went many miles to the south of us. In the dead of
winter at our horse camp we were cut off from communication even with our fellows.

When the spring days started the sap of the cottonwoods to flowing we cut down the young trees so that
our horses might browse on the bark and small
branches, which they ate with rare relish. We were
glad to take advantage of the moderation in weather
to ride in once in a while to see the rest of our detachment at the bridge. Two traders, brothers by the name
of Bernard, had a store near the bridge from which
they supplied some necessities to the travelers at what
would now be considered fabulous prices. They also
owned the bridge and collected a toll of $10 for each
wagon that crossed it. As the water was swift and the
crossing difficult, few had the temerity to attempt to
ford the stream in order to avoid paying the bridge
toll. Staying at the Bernard brothers was a Shoshone
Indian woman, captured some time before by the Sioux,
who had been returned thus far on the road to her own
people, and was awaiting spring before going further.

In the latter part of March our detachment received
word that we would soon be transferred further west
along the telegraph line, and other troops would be
sent on to relieve us. Lock and I were called in with
the horses and everyone commented on their condition,
for they had had to pick their own living, often from
beneath the snow.

When our relief had been ordered up from Fort
Laramie, an uprising among the soldiers was again

attempted. The two Sullivans and Patrick Grey refused to obey an order and were thereupon shot by
Lieut. John Brown and others of my company.[1] They
were all killed instantly or died of wounds received in
their attempted mutiny. The execution of these three
trouble-makers had a wholesome effect on some of the
other men who were inclined to want to take the bit in
their teeth, and after this we had no more trouble.
When we pushed over the bridge to make room for the
troops who were relieving us, I saw Crawford for the
first time since he was released from arrest. I did not
then know, nor did I learn for a month, that he had
found out who had reported him in the first place.

Our first stop on the westward march was at Sweetwater Bridge on the north fork of the North Platte.
We were now practically out of the Sioux country —
really on neutral ground between the Shoshones, Utes,
and Bannocks to the west and the Sioux, Arapahoes,
and Cheyennes to the east. The Snakes, Bannocks,
and Utes were at that time on friendly terms with the
whites and no trouble was anticipated with them.
Here at Sweetwater Lieutenant Rice's command was
divided, part of it remaining and the detachment to
which I belonged going still farther westward to Three
Crossings on the Sweetwater. Our location was all
that could be desired. Spring had now arrived;
meadow larks had come and the days were becoming

[1] Patrick Grey and one John Sullivan were shot May 12 and instantly killed and the other John Sullivan died of his wounds on
May 17. Crawford, who had been mixed up previously with the
above three, was honorably discharged July 14, 1866. See *Roster of
Ohio Soldiers, 1861-66*, Vol. ii, pp. 561 and 799-800.

warm and balmy. Travel would soon set in on the Oregon Trail.

Two soldiers with a supply wagon were sent from one of the eastern posts to us at Three Crossings. The supplies did not arrive as expected and we were much concerned as to the reason for the delay. A courier coming over the road found an empty wagon standing in the road, with both team and provisions gone. This news was telegraphed back to North Platte Bridge and it was ascertained that the wagon of supplies should have reached us previously. Lieutenant Rice selected James D. Thomas, John Kerns, and myself to go back to the wagon and get on trail of the team and follow it as long as there was any hope of recovering it or of catching the thieves. The ground was soft and it was thought that the six mules would make a trail by which they could easily be followed. We went north toward the snow-crested Bighorn Mountains for twenty-five miles, but lost all trace of the team and were obliged to turn back to camp with our mission unaccomplished. The driver was never found.

CHAPTER IX

A Fight with a Grizzly

While still keeping a close lookout on the bare chance of seeing the mules we discovered a dark object in the distance, and on approaching we found it to be a grizzly bear — the largest, I think, I ever saw in all my travels. On noticing us the bear stood up on his hind feet and took a good look. Kerns said, "Ben, you're the best shot; you shoot first," and I fired, aiming as nearly as I could for the vital spot behind his foreleg. As soon as I fired the bear pressed a paw to its heart, dropped down on its forefeet, and started to run for a thick clump of high sage brush, following a broken buffalo trail. He secreted himself there and after a short time in which we saw and heard nothing of him, we concluded he was dead. We dismounted and began to throw stones into the gnarled and matted sage brush. When this brought no immediate results, we scattered out in order to comb the brush patch. Shortly a shot from Kerns followed by a shout, "I've got him," rang out. We ran to him and were just in time to see the bear lurch to its feet, lunge for him, and knock the gun out of his hands. We retreated as fast as the brush would permit and held a consultation. It would not do to go back to the post and report that one of our number had been disarmed by a bear, so we again made a cautious sweep into the brush patch, trying as best we could to protect Kerns, who carried only a six-shooter which I had loaned him. We had gone but a short distance when Kerns with a shriek threw both hands in front of him in an involuntary effort to protect himself from the sudden onslaught of the grizzly. The bear swept both of Kerns's arms into its mouth, the impact carrying him to the ground with the bear on top.

Kerns, as he was borne to the ground by the beast, cried out frantically, "Don't leave me, boys." But in the meantime we had not been idle. Thomas was firing into the bear's head with a six-shooter while I was shooting into his side. We were both firing as rapidly as possible and at such close quarters that the powder singed his hair at each shot.

In spite of the noise of our shooting we heard Kerns gasp, "Roll him off, he's mashing me." The bear now lay quiet across his body, and it was all we could do to lift the immense, limp form enough to pull Kerns out, choking and exhausted.

Later, on recovering from the excitement, we examined the grizzly and found he had been pierced by thirteen bullets, several of which passed through his heart. I know of no other animal which is not instantaneously killed by a shot in the heart, but a grizzly will often run some distance and put up a terrific fight with a bullet hole entirely through his heart. I believe, however, that a bullet through the brain kills a grizzly instantly, just as it does any other animal.

We tried to lift Kerns to his feet, but he was groggy

and faint from loss of blood, which flowed freely from his mangled arms and a large wound across his abdomen, the result of a side swipe of the bear's claws. From a nearby pool we bathed his wounds as best we could, using a portion of his shredded shirt as a wash cloth. Fortunately, no bones were broken and after the first feeling of exhaustion and faintness had passed he made bold to assert that he was not as badly hurt as we thought. Even so, however, he was too badly torn to be able to ride and it would be necessary to bring out a wagon from camp to haul him in. Thomas volunteered to ride to camp after help while I waited on Kerns and skinned the bear. I had a loaded rifle at hand for fear another bear would make his appearance, and kept a close watch.

As camp was some miles away, about three hours elapsed before Thomas returned with a wagon and help. By this time Kerns's wounds and clothes were matted with blood and he began to suffer much pain from his lacerations which were now becoming swollen and feverish.

When the wagon came the mules objected to being driven up close to the carcass of the bear which lay on its spread-out pelt; but after much mule talk and the spirited use of the mule skinner, the rig was brought alongside and the man and bear loaded up. It was getting dark by the time we reached the post, but the whole camp turned out to see us with mixed motives of curiosity and sympathy. While such expressions as "Ain't he a whopper," and "As big as an ox" were being passed, we took Kerns out as gently as possible and turned him over to the two women who were laundresses for our company. Kerns's wounds, while painful, proved to be superficial, and he was up and around in a short while, much to our surprise and satisfaction.

The bear was an old fellow and too tough for eating. We did not even attempt to preserve the skin for bedding, as to cure it properly required much work in scraping off surplus flesh and tanning the hide. All we kept as relics of our fierce encounter were the claws, which we distributed among a few of our friends.

CHAPTER X

COMING OF THE DANITES

FOR SOME days after the encounter with the grizzly nothing happened to break the camp routine until one day a runner sent to our post brought the news that a train of disaffected Mormons from Soda Springs, Idaho, was on its way to our station, with orders for us to give it safe conduct to the next station eastward. The nearest division of California troops was conducting the train to our post.

The members of this band were seceding. While they espoused the Mormon church, they opposed polygamy and were trying to make their way to Florence, Nebraska, where it seems there were a settlement and church holding views and doctrines similar to theirs. It would not have been necessary for us to give them an escort had it not been that they were being pursued by a body of minute men, or "destroying angels" as they called themselves, whose duty it was to prevent any who wavered in their faith from getting out alive to spread heresies contrary to the teaching of the true Mormon church. The Destroying Angels, or Danites, occupied a position similar to police in enforcing the orders of the church, and were privileged to take not only the property but the lives of those who opposed the church authorities.

This organization was said to consist of men between the ages of seventeen and forty-nine. They were organized into bands of from ten to fifty men with a captain over each band. "Signs" and "grips" were given so the members would know each other day or night, and all were bound by the most sacred oaths to keep secret their works of darkness. They robbed, pillaged, whipped or killed those who fell into their disfavor. Originally called Destroying Angels, they later took the name of Danites, or Sons of Dan. They formed a sort of death society against the Gentiles and those of their own followers who fell from the faith. It was said that the Danites sometimes assumed Indian disguises before attacking whites, to protect themselves from suspicion or reprisal. The apostate Mormons and Gentiles were always under the dread of the terrible Danite vengeance. In 1858 the Danite organization burned provisions and destroyed ammunition to the extent of 450,000 pounds, intended for General Albert Sidney Johnson's army — for which they received no punishment.

When the disaffected Mormons reached our post and we saw many pretty girls in the company, we lost no time in getting up a dance for the evening. We had been almost shut off from female society for many months, and we all thought these Mormon girls were the loveliest it had ever been our good fortune to look upon. We had a rollicking time, and were sorry they could not stay longer.

Some of the refugees were short of rations, and to such the commanding officer ordered supplies issued from our own rather limited stock. A detail of eight soldiers was selected to escort them to the next station, Sweetwater Bridge, and to my joy I was one of the number. The emigrants' horses were so worn that we could not make good time and were obliged to camp at Split Rock, half way to Sweetwater Bridge. The trail was sandy, and to relieve the jaded teams the women walked all the way. The soldiers each carried a child from six to twelve years of age behind the saddle on his horse, and the teamsters whom we met on the road made much fun of our "military" bearing. When we arrived at Sweetwater Bridge we turned the Mormons over to the next command who escorted them to the Platte River Bridge. They were thus passed from one station to another until they reached safety, out of danger from either the Danites or the Sioux.

We enjoyed visiting with the soldiers at Sweetwater Bridge, all members of our battalion. A particularly warm friend of mine, James Lynch, plucked my arm and said he had something to tell me. We walked a sufficient distance away to insure privacy and he began, "I've been hoping to see you. Crawford has found out some way that you're the one who reported him at Spread Eagle Ranch. Killing the two Sullivans and Grey has stirred up some bitter feeling again." I asked him what he thought of it. He said, "Crawford is cowardly enough to kill you unawares, and even if he doesn't try it, there are enough Knights of the Golden Circle left that we know of to make trouble for you."

I thanked Lynch for putting me on my guard, and

began to notice things that had meant nothing to me before. I could see that Crawford kept aloof while the rest of the boys were shaking hands with me genially. As I have said, many men in our command were from Kentucky, and a few had come from other southern states. In case the mutiny had come to a head, bloodshed would have been unavoidable, and more disastrous still, a disorganization of the company, so in reporting the mutineers to Captain Marshall I had done what I thought my duty. Now it looked like I was to pay for it. Not all the southerners were disloyal, by any means. Lock, who stayed with me at the horse camp, and one of our sergeants by the name of Blades, were from Kentucky, yet we had no better soldiers or more loyal men in the company than they. Blades and I hunted black tailed deer together a number of times.

What Lynch had told me had made me uneasy and restless as I lay in my bunk that night. Now my persistent cough was a real danger, as it revealed my whereabouts in the darkness as well as in day light. I felt that Crawford would either kill me or I would be compelled to kill him. Even if I killed him in self-defense, some of his friends would probably lie in wait for me. I came of a proud and honorable family, and I hated to shed another's blood, even in self-defense. I had two brothers in the Union army, and my father had been discharged on account of age and disabilities. One brother was making a name for himself for his daring as a spy and a scout. Our family line ran back in America to pre-revolutionary days. My grandfather, Edward Connor, came across the water from Ireland when a mere lad. He joined the side of the colonists and fought in the Revolutionary War, after which he married Nancy Jane Cunningham in the justly famed Shenandoah Valley. He served in the War of 1812 and opposed the British when they burned the capitol at Washington. As I lay and thought of these ancestors of mine, and what our family name meant to us, I decided that whatever happened I must avoid bloodshed. If I had seen anything of disgrace in what I contemplated doing, I would never have done it.

The high mountain air had put me in the best of health, with the exception of the cough, which was persistent. We were out in the wilderness. There was no other post to which I could hope to be transferred. I realize now that the officers, out of gratitude for my past services, might have granted any reasonable request I would make, but I was ashamed to go to the commanding officer and tell him I was afraid to stay in his company. I was no coward, but saw no need of courting trouble. One man missing from the company would not amount to much, and I wanted to avoid being the principal in a feud that might endanger the lives of several. It was for this reason that I resolved to leave the army, or, to speak bluntly, desert. But I must say here that desertion had not the significance then that it has now. Men continually dropped out of the army, whenever it suited their fancy, and being punished for deserting was considered no more of a disgrace than being arrested for speeding is now.

When our mission to Sweetwater Bridge was ended, we returned to our camp. In making my plans for escape I had decided that I would have to take some government property — a gun and a saddle — as these were both necessary to mere existence on the plains. I had a small Indian pony of my own, which I had bought from some immigrants. We had received no government pay for some months, and I had more in wages due me than the combined value of the gun and saddle, so I could take them without any qualms. Besides these, I had only $10 in cash.

The pony was gentle — would stand for gun-firing from his back, and would carry dead game without shying or pitching — all invaluable qualities when one is alone in the wilderness.

So one day I started out hunting, as I had often done before, leaving the post with a horse, a gun, and a saddle, but this time never to return.

CHAPTER XI

A WANDERER

ON LEAVING the post, I traveled westward until I reached a telegraph station called Rocky Ridge where I stayed over night with the operator. I told him I was out hunting, which was not unusual for me. Even my failure to return to the post doubtless created no surprise among my comrades, as I had remained out many times before when hunting. There was no danger from Indians in the part of the country I had now reached, and I rode along in perfect security.

My route lay up Sweetwater and by Independence Rock. This huge block of granite covers almost thirty acres at its base and stands over one hundred and fifty feet high. It looks as if it had been dropped on the level plain. The trail passes to the north of this natural curiosity and the Sweetwater flows at its southern base. This famous landmark was named by some emigrants who had camped at its base on July 4th of some previous year. They not only named the rock, but cut the name Independence into the stone. Near this huge stone has always been a famous camping place, and it bears the names of thousands of travelers who have passed by on the Oregon Trail.

From Independence Rock the trail climbs upward through Devil's Gate by almost imperceptible degrees to South Pass, which has the appearance of a level plain rather than a pass. In fact, it is about twenty miles wide, more than twice as long, and over seven thousand feet above sea level. The next places of interest on the trail were Cold Springs — where ice could be found three feet beneath the sod all summer — and Pacific Springs, so named because its waters reach the Pacific Ocean. From this point several trails lead out, one going southwest by Fort Bridger (established by our old friend Jim Bridger) and Black's Fork to different points in Utah, and the other, which was the main traveled thoroughfare, leading northwest through the Lander's cut-off to Idaho, Nevada, Oregon, and Washington. These territories had all been organized by that time and were receiving considerable immigration. It was at Pacific Springs that my route diverged from the telegraph line, which followed the southwest trail into Utah, and continued on the northwest trail. I passed immigrant wagons every day, often spending evenings around their camp fires. I was always a welcome visitor because of my knowledge of western life and western ways.

One day when about forty miles out on the Lander's cut-off, I overtook a party of Bannock Indians returning from a buffalo hunt on Wind River. They had to come east to hunt, as there had never in historic times been buffaloes west of the Rockies, except in small numbers. These Bannocks crowded around me and seemed very friendly. They talked "Chinook," a sort of gibberish made up of French, English, and Indian. I had never heard Chinook before, and of course could make little out of it. After we had traveled together for a short distance our courses diverged, and I kept on down the trail that followed the New Fork.

There is no language adequate to describe the beauty of the country which surrounded me. The cottonwoods with leaves glistening and quivering in the soft sunlight, the sloping valleys, the dark green underbrush, the majestic grandeur of the mountains, snow-capped in the background, and the vividness of the many-hued flowers left an impression on me that time has not even blurred. I can see the picture as it was almost sixty years ago — the peaceful Indian camp, the children playing, women busy at their duties about the camp fire, the horses grazing nearby, and the clear silence that hung over all broken only by the barking of the dogs and the rippling of ice-cold water down the mountain side.

I crossed the Little and Big Sandy and went westward until I reached Green River, a turbulent, roaring torrent hemmed in by walls of stone. I crossed the Green River on a ferry operated by a cable stretched from bank to bank. A man by the name of Duval and his young son tended the ferry. He had no guard, and there was little need for defense against the Indians. There never was much fight in the Indians west of the Continental Divide.

From the Green River my course lay to the westward toward Bear River, which I struck near the present town of Cokeville, Wyoming. The trail led westward instead of northwestward, for the mountains to the northwest were insurmountable. I followed the

Bear River in its westward and northward course till
its course turned south, near Soda Springs, then crossed
over from its north loop to the Port Neuf River which
I followed down. A ferry was in process of construction over the Snake. The location was on the site of
the old Fort Hall of early days and on the proposed
stage line from Ogden, Utah, to Virginia City, Montana. When I reached the place some men were engaged in tearing down what was left of old Fort Hall
and using the dobies, (sun-dried bricks), for buildings
nearer the landing. The bricks were much larger and
heavier than the modern pressed bricks.

My horse was thin and needed a rest, so I applied for
a job and was set to work on the ferry. I turned my
saddle horse loose with the extra stage horses. Feed
was plentiful and he did well. During my journey he
had had no time to eat except for a short period at
noon and at night. My job on the ferry was in consequence timely for him, and to judge by his actions, ap-
preciated. It was too easy for me, however, and soon
put me in a restless frame of mind. There was often
too much time between passengers with nothing to do
except wait, which was trying to one of an active disposition.

Fort Hall is about nine miles up from the mouth of
the Port Neuf, on the east bank of the Snake and about
due west of where Ross's Fork empties into the former.
The Port Neuf flows from the southeast and Ross's
Fork from the northeast. Up the Port Neuf about
twenty-five miles was Port Neuf canyon, where the
river ran swift and deep between almost perpendicu-

lar walls of stone. The stage road to Ogden, Utah, ran for a long way in this canyon, and while I was at work on the ferry at the Fort Hall crossing the stage was held up by highwaymen armed with sawed-off shot guns and robbed of $27,000. No one was hurt, but Jack Hughes was one of the passengers who lost his roll. Robbers usually went about with pick and pan, disguised as prospectors, and in this way aroused no suspicion. About a year later another robbery was committed in the same canyon, in which six passengers were killed and the seventh left for dead. The robbers made a haul of about $110,000, $60,000 in gold dust handled by the Express Company, and $50,000 from their victims. It was believed the gang was in touch with some one in the express office in Virginia City who kept them informed of large gold dust shipments. The danger from road agents was so great that Wells Fargo Company charged five percent for carrying charge from Virginia City to Salt Lake. Probably more gold at this time was transported by freighters than by express, as it was safer. The freight charges were $10.00 a hundred pounds payable in gold — which carried a high premium at that time. A part of my duty while working on the ferry was to help transfer the express from one coach to another. At one time a banker by the name of Millard from Omaha was a passenger, and when I helped him lift out his bags and manifested surprise at their weight, he told me they contained gold dust.

The ferry on which I worked did not have a monopoly on the transfer business by any means. About fifteen miles above our station was a ferry run by a Mormon named Meeks, and fifteen miles further up stream was still another, known as Connor's Ferry and operated by a little band of General P. E. Connor's soldiers stationed there. General Connor had his headquarters at Salt Lake and held military control over a large territory known as the Utah district, with many small detachments of troops widely scattered over an almost unroaded country. These two upper ferries were not on stage lines; their business consisted entirely in setting immigrants across. Some days I had little to do and my boss set me to work on moving the dobies from the old buildings to the new ones under construction. I often found names and dates on some of these old bricks. On one I found a bear track, which had evidently been imprinted by the bear before the brick had hardened.

In order to meet the competition of the up-stream ferries, I was often sent eastward along the trail to meet immigrants and direct them to our place, using the good talking points that our camping ground was best supplied with wood and water. On one occasion I rode back on my pony and met a large train of immigrants, mostly from Kentucky, Missouri, and Kansas. I stopped and talked with them. Their first question was, "Where did you come from?" When I had told them, they asked, "How is the grazing?" to which I replied, "Excellent," and added, "We also have plenty of wood for your camp fires." I then went on farther back, and on my return to the camp in the evening was pleased to find the party I had met in the morning in camp at our crossing.

One of the grizzled old fellows said to me, "Say, young man, I've got a crow to pick with you. Come here." I rode over to his wagon, expected a berating for some fancied mis-statement. When I neared him he pulled out a jug and a dark looking bowl, and asked, "Do you ever drink?" I told him, "No, I hadn't learned the habit yet," and he nodded. "It's just as well," he said, "you're better off without it." Then after he had helped himself to a drink, continued, "You're the first man who has told us the truth about camping places since we left the Missouri River. We've been robbed at every slough, mudhole, and creek all the way from Missouri." He looked me over meditatively, until I became rather embarrassed by his scrutiny. "You're a truthful lad. I haven't a chick or a child. Thar's all I have left." He pointed a bony index finger towards his wife. "I lost everything I owned in the war, first pillaged by the Confederates and then by the Yanks. Couldn't sell my land, so just took what little stock and money I had left and started out to look for a place where I can live in peace. I'm bound for Williamette, Oregon, and you'd better come with me."

Sensible of his tribute though I was, I told him I was restless and couldn't stay long in one place. With a far-away look in his eyes and a wistful voice, he said, "I'm sorry. I'm looking for some one who can stay with the old woman and me." The next morning we

ferried the whole train of fifty wagons across the Snake
River.

Just over the river a short distance is a fine spring
known as Lander's Spring, after the explorer Colonel
Lander. At this point the emigrants always stopped to
shoe their horses, repair wagons, set tires, etc., before
setting out on the next lap of their long journey.

My mate, Teddy O'Neil, a fellow countryman of
mine, and I had a camp, consisting of a wagon box
with bows over which a tarp was stretched, up near
where the boat lay at anchor. This wagon box served
us only for sleeping quarters, the cooking being done
on an outside camp-fire. One evening we had boiled
beans and bacon, and left the dutch oven on a bed of
coals to bake slowly until the embers died out. The
ground under a camp fire, at least in mild weather,
holds enough heat to keep a pot warm all night. We
were both inside our wagon cover, O'Neil reading
while I lay on the bed, when we heard a noise as if
something was pushing off the dutch oven lid. I lifted
up the wagon cover and peered out into the gathering
darkness, and there stood a grizzly bear raking out our
beans and devouring them as fast as he could. O'Neil
grabbed his gun and made ready to shoot, but I laid
my hand on the gun barrel and said, "No you don't,"
and to his indignant "Why?" answered, "Your old
muzzle loading smooth bore couldn't hurt him, and
besides you couldn't hit a wagon box. If you shoot,
I'll cut a hole in the wagon sheet and run." "Well,
have it your own way," said he, setting down the gun.

In the meantime the bear had cleaned out the dutch

oven, licked his paws, and departed in peace, with no expressed objections from us. Had O'Neil fired his smooth bore into the bear, he might have resented the insult; as it was, we quit friends. A grizzly is harmless if you let him alone, but it is better not to start anything unless the advantage is on your side.

CHAPTER XII

WITH the coming of fall, immigrant travel began to dwindle and consequently the business on the ferry fell off. We had the regular daily stage and frequent freighting outfits to or from the Montana gold fields, but the most of our business was from the immigrants who came in trains during the summer season. I spoke to my boss, and he consented to my quitting at an agreed future time. I had the gold fever and made up my mind to go to Virginia City, where gold had been discovered about two years previous.

But before I left the ferry, I had a number of interesting experiences. One day an English cockney, recently arrived in this country, came to our landing and stayed several days. It was soon apparent that he had enough bravado and bombast to shame the most arrogant lord. Nothing in America met his approval. He condemned the weather, the size of the country, the occupations, the manner and the breeding of the people. Nothing looked good to him. In spite of these drawbacks, however, he was bent on going hunting, and wanted someone to go with him. Failing to persuade anyone at the stage station, he was reduced to an appeal to us at the ferry. He was used to hunting big game in "h'Africa," he said, and asked me if there was a chance of his getting one of "those bloody h'animals you call a bear." I told him there was an old dog at the Fort all scarred up from encounters with wild animals. "Old Tige will surely find you a bear if you take him out with you," I told him, and added the caution, "Look out, for when he finds a bear, he will make a bee line to you for protection." His face wreathed in smiles, he thanked me; "H'I'm much obliged to you for the h'information," he said, and put off at once at his best walking speed to get the dog.

Now old Tige was a large dog, and in his prime had been a worthy antagonist for many of the wild animals of the forest and bore many scars as a result of former encounters. But by this time he was old enough to have a sleepy look in his eyes, and his teeth were worn down to blunt stumps. Although he had lost much in agility, when anyone took a gun, however, and called to him, the memory of his former exploits made him feel "as much of a dog as he used to be."

The Englishman set out bravely with dog and gun to "hunt bear." About two hours later, old Tige came in, tired and panting. This was unusual, as Tige was never known to forsake a master on a hunting trip before. Some one spoke up, "Where is the Englishman?" to which the answer came, "Never you mind, he'll come in loaded with glory."

Although we dismissed the matter so lightly, the dog kept looking back, and seemed to say as plainly as his dumb lips could, that he wanted some one to go back with him and bring in the Englishman. So we let him lead the way and followed for some two miles to a large cottonwood tree where we found the Englishman seated in a fork about twenty feet from the ground while his gun lay at the foot of the tree. One of the men was unkind enough to ask where his bear was. He said, "H'I don't know, 'e was 'ere a moment ago." "Why didn't you get him? You had a gun," asked another. "The bloody dog and bear were both on top of me before I knew it," said he. "H'I just 'ad to climb this blooming, blarsted tree."

The bear had tamed the Englishman. He climbed down and picked up his gun, loaded and with full magazine, and stalked away, insulted by the merriment of the bystanders. This was the last we heard about hunting in "h'Africa."

It was while I was working here that Mrs. Slade crossed our ferry on her way to Salt Lake City with the body of her husband, as I have already narrated.

The mining camps at Bannack and Virginia City, where gold had been discovered about two years earlier, were receiving a great influx of miners and those who prey upon them. Most of the influx came over the Oregon Trail to Fort Hall and northward, but a large number came by way of the Missouri River to Fort Benton and thence overland. A few were convoyed across the hostile Sioux country from St. Paul by Gen. Alfred H. Sully and Capt. James Fisk.

When I left work at the ferry, I was offered a job by a freighter named Alex Toponce, who was hauling butter, vegetables, eggs, and flour from Richmond, Utah, to Virginia City, and I engaged to him. As it was getting late in the fall, he was anxious to get over the mountains before snow fell. Our route led us up the Snake River for forty or fifty miles to the mouth of Camas Creek, up this creek to its head, and over the divide and down the Beaverhead. Our first snow caught us after we had crossed the divide. One night we were compelled to keep up a fire all night, with the smoke blowing over our potatoes to keep them from freezing. The next day we hitched up bright and early and made quite a descent during the day, finding the weather much moderated in consequence. We heard later of a man who tied his mules to his wagon when caught in this snow storm, and two of them chilled to death. A mule deprived of the chance of walking around cannot stand much wet snow and cold wind.

After we got down the mountain on the north side, we found road ranches established every fifteen or twenty miles who took care of immigrants and freighters. We arrived in Virginia City without mishap, except considerable fatigue from our long forced march. We went to bed without even making a circuit around town, as we knew there would be plenty of opportunities for that ahead of us.

CHAPTER XIII

In the Land of Gold — Virginia City — Helena

THE NEXT morning, which was Sunday, after our camp work was finished, I strolled down town. I had never been in a mining country or a mining town, and was not a little anxious to see the sights. On the corner of one of the main streets stood a man preaching the gospel with much fervor to a small audience, and I listened to him a while. He was the first preacher I had heard, or had an opportunity of hearing for over a year. On the opposite side of the street, crying his wares in opposition to the preacher, stood a Jew peddler selling red flannel shirts. Up and down the middle of the street rode a man on a poor shaggy little pony, seeking to auction him off by extolling his gentleness, endurance, swiftness, and easy keeping qualities. In the back yard behind one of the saloons a fist fight was going on, with much noise and some bloodshed. Most of the buildings were saloons — all wide open doors through which could be heard loud singing, the click of poker chips, and the clinking of glasses at the bar. Gold dust, while not the only medium of exchange, was the principal one. In the bank windows gold nuggets and dust were displayed in basins and pans.

Now that my previous job had ended, I began to look for another one. I met a man whom I knew, who proposed that we go in together to work a mine owned by a doctor in town. My acquaintance had a cabin which I was asked to occupy with him, so we joined forces and went to work. The mining at that time was all placer, or poor man's mining. A man with only a shovel and pan could take a claim and go to work. Placer mining is always the first gold mining, but placer deposits are soon worked out. For washing and separating the gold we got a rocker into which the sand and gravel were thrown. The sloshing of the water slopped out all earth and stone particles while the gold, being heaviest, stayed at the botton. When enough was concentrated it was taken out and weighed up. When the weather got cold enough to freeze the ground and the sand bars, we could no longer work on the placer deposits so we parted company, each taking his share of the gold dust in a buckskin pouch.

Much dirt was panned over that proved not to be "pay dirt." In fact, placer mining is always confined to a comparatively small territory. During the ages, rains and frosts have disintegrated the gold bearing stone. The lighter earth and stone particles have been washed away, while the gold, being heavier, is concentrated on the bottom of the mining floor, called the bed rock. Placer mining is always carried on in an old creek bed or gorge where the gold has been concentrated by time. Gold is widely scattered in nature, and without the help of nature in cencentrating it there would be no placer mining.

One evening on the streets of Virginia City I met a

ranchman from Stinking Water [1] who invited me to go out to his ranch and spend the winter with him. I gladly accepted. By the terms of our agreement I was to buy my share of the winter's provisions. After a few days in which I made the necessary purchases we went out to the ranch, about fifteen or twenty miles southwest of Virginia City, and made ourselves comfortable for the winter. The buildings, consisting of three cabins and several small barns, were built of rough logs. The ranch was located on the main trail to Silverbow mining camp, and travelers passed along the trail almost daily. Sometimes during the winter we were alone, sometimes overcrowded, with even the dirt floor of the cabin covered with bed rolls. Very few horses were used on the trail because of the difficulty of getting feed. Everyone who traveled over the mountains carried a pack consisting of bedding and food. Prospectors (and most of them were prospectors) carried in addition a pick, a shovel, and a gold pan for washing out the dirt. The rancher with whom I stayed made his living by sending out live cattle to the various mining camps to be killed and sold.

When my agreement concerning provisions was made with the rancher, I fortunately laid in a good supply of flour. About February the shortage of flour became very apparent. Only a few merchants had any to sell or a supply for their own use. Although it was not generally known, an old Frenchman named Beau-

[1] Called in Shoshone, Pasamari — which means stinking water, although it is a beautiful mountain stream. This stream was called Philanthropy River by Lewis & Clark (Coues Edition, p. 459).

vais had a considerable stock of flour which he had *cached*. His practice was to bring out a sack at a time, always insisting that this was the last. Flour went to $20 a sack and kept on climbing till it reached $140.

There was no law in this country except the miner's law. This was supreme. A miner's meeting was called and a committee appointed whose duty it was to search out places where flour might be secreted. A considerable supply belonging to Beauvais was found hidden under a haystack, and all of it was confiscated by the committee and distributed among the women and children. If they were too poor to pay for it, the miners paid for it by contributions. But instead of $140 a sack, Beauvais got $80. A train of freighters bringing in flour had been expected almost any time, but it was later learned that they had been caught in a snow storm while crossing the mountains and had lost their teams. This news reached Virginia City from men who came in on snow shoes.

It seems almost incredible that the population around Virginia City — all transients — had grown to over 10,000. Prospectors had worked out in all directions from Virginia City during the winter, a few losing their lives by exposure in the mountains while feverishly searching for dirt that would "leave a shine in the pan." Around a mining camp work is always slack in the winter season, and the discovery of gold in the Last Chance gulch, where Helena was later built, and at Grizzly Bear nearby in the late winter of 1864 sent a mob of men from Virginia City hitherward. I was one of this mob. With several other men, I joined forces with a man in Virginia City who had an old crowbait of a team. It was so poor and feed was so scarce along the way that we barely crawled along; but it was the best we could do. What grub and bedding we could rake together were put into the wagon, but to relieve the poor team as much as possible we all walked and in addition carried large packs on our backs. The road all the way to Helena was jammed with outfits similar to ours.

When we reached Helena, the town was a month old. Streets were laid out along the Last Chance Gulch, and a number of log buildings were under construction. Two or three general stores and as many more shacks in use as saloons and dance halls were completed and all doing a noisy and apparently a profitable business. Day and night the hurdy-gurdys, concertinas, and rolette wheels were going. The saloons never closed, and not a few of the mob, either having no money to pay for a bed or finding no place to sleep, took advantage of the refuge they offered. At any hour one would find some nodding from the rude wall benches or sleeping, curled up on the floor in the corner.

Like most of the throng, I was looking for work — just anything that would insure something to eat. I could not stand mining underground or even on the surface where one had to slop around in water, so I took work turning a windlass by hand at three dollars per day. The pay was low, but beggars can't be choosers. All my small wage was required to pay for meals of the plainest and coarsest food, and even then I went hungry most of the time. Meat was the only article of food that could be had in desired quantities, and consisted largely of wild game such as buffalo, elk, deer, antelope, and bear, supplied by market hunters. Flour, beans, rice, and dried apples were the standard articles of diet in addition to the meat, and when purchasable commanded a high price. Potatoes and other fresh vegetables were unknown in this locality the first season.

I continued turning the windlass until April, when I went to work hauling dirt by ox-team from Holmes Gulch, which was dry, to Prickly Pear Creek about four miles away, where we washed out the dirt. Our dirt netted about $8.00 a load by the crude and wasteful method used in washing. To record a mining claim cost but $1.00. Every claim had to be recorded, as the discovery alone did not protect one in the ownership. I staked out a claim and washed out some gold, but changed my mind and did not record it. The claim I gave up filing on was located where White Hall now stands, and afterwards proved to contain a rich vein of quartz.

Helena was closer to Fort Benton, 140 miles away, than to any other freighting point. The freighters got $8.00 per hundred from Fort Benton to Helena and to Virginia City $11.00. Goods were transported to Benton by steamboat when the water was high enough in the Missouri to permit it. In case of low water, goods were unloaded at points lower down — even as far away as Fort Union at times, in which case it was necessary to make a haul of 500 miles overland. Even then the distance was less than from Salt Lake. In order to relieve the scarcity of flour at Helena, a man by the name of John Grant,[2] on one occasion, went to Fort Benton with a string of pack horses and brought back ten sacks. He sold out at once for $1.10 a pound, and I parted with $11.00 for ten pounds of the precious stuff. We used the flour in making pancakes, the batter consisting only of water, flour, and salt — a sort of paste which was fried in bear's grease. This batter had one virtue — it could be made thin, and the thinner the cakes the longer my scant supply of flour would last. I have looked in vain through the Washington Cook Book for this recipe, which an enterprising publisher should not have overlooked.

The route from Helena to Fort Benton passed over what was known as the Mullen Road, which was built from Fort Dallas, Oregon, to Fort Benton, Montana, at government expense, primarily as a military road. It reached Fort Benton in midsummer 1860. Between Helena and Fort Benton this great highway followed the Missouri River and crossed Sun River where the city of Great Falls is now built.

People were coming into the mining region almost every day, mostly on foot. A man blew in one day and told an incident of his trip. He hailed a ranchman by the wayside and asked him if there was a chance of getting something to eat. The ranchman replied,

[2] John Grant was an old time Hudson's Bay employe who had previously for thirty years been located at old Fort Hall, Idaho. In 1862 he moved to Deer Lodge, Montana, where he engaged in raising and buying cattle and supplying beef to Bannack, Alder Gulch, and later Helena. He also brought in provisions and supplies which he sold to miners.

"Why, yes, the chances are good," and handed him a
fishing rod and line. Game and fish foods were plentiful for some years after settlers began to pour in.

It was hard to do much mining without getting wet
feet, and my ailment required me to keep out of water
as much as possible. Consequently, in May, 1865, I
gave up mining and took work with a large freight
outfit, owned by Jerry Mann. Having had much experience with horses and live stock in general, I was
pleased with the opportunity. At first I was given the
job of night herding about 400 oxen, six yoke being
used to each of the thirty freight wagons and the remainder driven loose and used to replace those which
became footsore or out of condition for work. From
Helena the outfit went straight north on the west side
of the Missouri River. Our route took us over Prickly
Pear Creek and over the mountains by the same name;
across Sun River, which has its rise in the Glacier
National Park, and thence to Fort Benton. As a rule
our trip was made by easy stages, the outward trip
being for the most part empty. On the return trip the
wagons were loaded to capacity with all sorts of provisions and mining machinery. The boats had not yet
reached Benton from St. Louis when we made our first
trip of the season, but we loaded up our wagons from
goods unloaded the fall before. On reaching Helena
again, we learned that the Civil War had closed and
that Lincoln had been assassinated. Many of the
buildings, but not all by any means, were draped in
black. There were some who felt a deep and genuine
sorrow on the death of Lincoln, but almost as many

rejoiced inwardly, and not a few outwardly. Many Southerners had come into Montana in the early days, and politically it has been consistently Democratic since its organization. The names of the gold mines — "Confederate Gulch" and "Jeff Davis" — are sufficient to indicate the political leanings of the owners. Street brawls brought on by sectional feeling were an almost daily occurrence. To shout for Jeff Davis or Lincoln either was an open invitation to hostilities and one which was usually accepted by someone within hearing.

On our return from Fort Benton, we learned that the miners at Virginia City, on the verge of starvation, had fitted up teams and gone out to get the food not spoiled by freezing from the pack train which was snowed in early in the winter on its way to that place, as I have before stated. I also found out that barley was being grown in small quantities in the Bitter Root Valley and that a small flour mill was in operation. The flour was of poor grade, but it was better than none.

Our long train of "bull wagons" set out for another trip to Fort Benton where we expected to arrive in time to meet the first up-river boats. Anticipating an urgent need for supplies, the miners had "chipped in" $1000 which they offered as a prize to the first boat to arrive at Benton. It was not always possible for steamboats to reach Benton, and in case of exceptionally low water, impossible. There were some difficult places to get by, such as Cow Island, Dauphin, and Dead Man Rapids. In the latter a large post had been sunk in the ground, called a dead man, to which cables could be fastened to pull boats over the rapids. In case a boat got stuck on a sand bar below Benton, the teams would go right on down the river to load up the freight from the distressed boat, as there was no possibility of its being able to get higher up the river before another year.

As soon as the boats began to arrive at Fort Benton, the road from Helena and Virginia City was lined with teams. Gad E. Upson was Indian agent and G. W. Baker was in charge of the American Fur Company at Fort Benton at that time. In making our second trip, we lay over to rest our cattle a day or two, and by so doing lost the opportunity of getting the freighting of two cargoes which went to outfits that passed us while we were resting. So, after our outfit went into camp at Fort Benton, Jerry Mann rode back to Helena and telegraphed parties at Virginia City who had goods unloaded at Fort Union, D. T., with the hope of getting a contract to go there after them. Mann got the contract and returned to our camp where we were waiting for him. As the contract covered more freight than he could haul with his outfit, he got two other outfits of sixty wagons owned by Matthews Brothers of Red Oak, Iowa, that had no freight in sight, to join him. The combined outfits made a train of ninety wagons, six yokes of oxen to a wagon. In addition we had about thirty extra oxen to take the place of any that might play out on the trip. Thus our outfit had over 1,100 oxen in all.

Just ahead of our combined outfits of Mann and Matthews Brothers was the outfit of my old friend

Alex Toponce. He had forty wagons with six yokes of oxen to the wagon which, with the extras, made over 500 in his outfit, or with the four of us together a total of 130 wagons, about 150 men, and 1,600 oxen — all bound for Fort Union to bring freight back to Helena, 500 miles away.

Toponce borrowed two government mountain howitzers at Fort Benton which he trailed with his outfit, charged with grape and cannister as an added protection against Indians, who at this time were getting quite ugly. Most of the bull whackers were either deserters from the army or were ex-Confederate soldiers captured on Southern battle fields and turned loose on parole, and some of them were skilled gunners. Since they were not free to re-enter the Confederate army and their Southern homes were over-run, they had come west to remain at least until the war was over. Each teamster was equipped with a Henry repeating rifle with a magazine carrying sixteen shots.

The pay of all bull whacker employees continued during delays on the road of less than ten days; in case of longer delays their pay stopped, but they were allowed their board.

We followed the Missouri River on the north side or the divide beyond it. The three trains were kept about five miles apart so as not to be in each other's way, the wagons in each outfit keeping in as compact line as the nature of the road would permit. The road along the Missouri River to Fort Union was good for the most part, laid out as it was for some distance on the bottom plateau between the stream and the bluffs, far enough away from the timber on one side and the bluffs on the other to afford us protection from ambush. The wagons traveled in two parallel lines a few rods apart, the best teamsters in the lead acting as pace-makers. In case of danger by a system of pre-arranged signals the parallel lines were immediately thrown into a circular corral for effective defense.

I didn't get to see much of the country as I was a night herder; in the day time I rode in a wagon and slept.

On this trip we ran out of flour and were without for a period of seventeen days; and for a shorter time were entirely out of salt and sugar. Meat was always to be had. Buffaloes were numerous. A hunter could be sent ahead and almost without fail could kill one near the trail and have it skinned out by the time the outfit got there. Before camp was made some one was de-tailed to gather up wood for the camp fire. Then, gathered around the long fire of logs, every man had an opportunity of cooking his own meat to suit his taste — a sort of cafeteria style. Each could also take his portion from the cut of beef he liked best. If his taste called for liver, a kidney stew, or a hump roast, he could usually satisfy it. The hunter always tried to kill a fat, dry heifer or cow, as their flesh was more tender and toothsome than that of a bull. The hump was the choice part of the animal. Plainsmen all agree that one tires less on a long-continued diet of buffalo meat than on a diet of any other animal, fish included. It is also agreed that one can do without bread when on a buffalo meat diet and miss it less than when confined to any other meat. The animals were so fat, however, that we couldn't eat much of their meat without salt.

We saw few people other than Indians after leaving Fort Benton. One whom I recollect meeting was Thomas Campbell, who was on his way up to build a trading post where Poplar River Agency now stands. We bought a little flour and sugar from him. The flour was in bad condition and the sugar was dark brown and badly caked; but we were grateful for them, even in such condition.

Dutch John, our hunter, who had been working at Fort Benton for the North American Fur Company, was married to a half-breed Arikara woman of quite fair complexion. They had a little girl about eight years old, which he, Dutch John, was now taking with his wife back on a visit to her people at Fort Berthold. They always camped with us, but carried a tent of their own.

One day a party of thirty Crow Indians pitched their camp near ours. They were sociable and friendly. One of them had a silver medallion, worn about his neck on a buckskin string, on which was engraved the profile of President James Monroe. The dates were worn off, but the words "Council Bluffs" were still decipherable. We all gathered about the Indian to look at the pendant, and the wearer told us that his father had attended the great treaty at Council Bluffs [3] to which all the plains Indians were invited. The treaty referred

[3] The treaty of Council Bluff when the medal was presented was undoubtedly in 1819.

to must have been held during Monroe's administration between the years 1817 and 1825. While we were engaged in this interesting diversion, an Indian motioned our cook over to him to trade. The Indian had a fifty dollar bill which he gave the cook for a cup of sugar. We never learned where he got the money. He could not read and did not know the value of it. To him the bill was a souvenir or token, and the cook made no effort to enlighten him.

One of the most interesting sights of the Indian camp was a huskie dog hitched to a travois loaded with moccasins and rawhide ropes.

The Crows, after accompanying us for a few days, left, going in a southerly direction. They told us in sign language that they were going on a horse stealing expedition against the Sioux, their mortal enemy. The Crows were not well prepared for a fight, as most of them were armed only with bows and arrows; a few had not even these but carried instead spears with handles five feet and blades two feet long.

A few years later when delivering beef at the Grand River Agency I noticed a Sioux tent [4] on which was drawn a pictograph representing the killing of thirty Crow Indians. On inquiry I learned that this was the last chapter of the history of the little band of Crows that had just left us so hopefully. The Sioux exterminated them at Rosebud Hill.

We pushed on as fast as possible so as to reach Fort

[4] The Humkpapa "Winter Count" seems to indicate that the thirty Crows were killed as shown by the pictograph in 1862, instead of in 1864, and undoubtedly referred to a different "killing" than the band Arnold fell in with in 1864.

Union before extremely cold weather should set in.
The last stream we crossed, about thirty miles west of
Fort Union, was the Little Poplar. It was solidly
frozen over, as this was after the middle of December.
We looked forward to Fort Union, sugar, salt, butter,
and hot biscuits. What joy awaited us no one can tell
who has never done without bread for a month. The
wind was cold and seemed to blow continuously toward
the end of our journey. Grazing was also getting poor
as we approached the fort, because the Indians who
hung around or came to trade there always had large
bands of horses with them.

At last Fort Union was sighted. It was situated on
the north, or left, bank of the Missouri on a level flat
of table land that extended back from the river for a
mile and ended in a succession of ridges and buttes, or
badland hills. There was little timber within a mile of
the post, and the north winds came across the level
flats with a piercing sweep.

CHAPTER XIV

The Blizzard Tragedy

Fort Union was the best known and the most important fur trading post on the upper Missouri, and one of the oldest. It was not a military post but a fur trading post only, although soldiers had been stationed there for a short time. When we arrived, there was but a quartermaster and a guard of six soldiers. The fort consisted of a stockade inclosure with a river front of 220 feet by a depth of 240, within which were the trading store, warehouses and fur storage rooms, blacksmith shop, employees' residences, hay stacks, stock barns, and corrals. The stockade had two gates. The one on the north, away from the river, was used mostly by hay wagons and for bringing in and taking out stock. The other opened on the south side of the stockade but a few yards from the steamboat landing, and was used by freighters' wagons and the trading public. The gates were all locked and barred at night as a precaution against theft, incendiarism, or possible Indian attack. Two diagonal corners of the stockade were surmounted by blockhouses with port holes, in which night guards were placed. The steamboat landing was but a few yards from the south gate.

Freighters and their teams had to camp outside the stockade. While seven or eight wagons could be admitted at one time for loading, they were taken outside as fast as the clerks could check out the goods and the teamsters could load them. The teamsters with the loaded wagons pulled out on the trail, toward Fort Benton, and away from the fort, where grass was much better and camp could be made to await the remainder of the train and the order for the outfit to move out on the return journey. We loaded with goods consigned to Helena merchants, the name of the one receiving the most was Hanauer. The water was low and the steamboat captains, not wanting to risk getting fast on a sand bar by going further up stream, had unloaded the goods at Fort Union and notified the consignees to come and get them, and this was why we had been sent to this distant post.

Alex Toponce with a large outfit had come down from Helena, as I have said, a little ahead of us, and we camped just far enough apart so that our cattle would not get mixed when out grazing, yet close enough to give each other assistance in case of attack. He arrived ahead of us and loaded first with government goods which he had bought. Soldiers temporarily located at Fort Union had been transferred a short time before to Fort Rice, but it had been impossible to move the supplies before the river closed with but one small boat, the *General Grant*, which was at their disposal. Consequently these goods were offered for sale, Major Pease and Alex Toponce being the successful, and, I think the only bidders. The goods were divided between them on a pre-arranged basis, Toponce taking the sugar, coffee, and other articles which were most in demand at Helena, and Major Pease taking the remainder. Both outfits were just about ready to start on their 500 mile journey when a delay was brought about in an unexpected manner. Al White was Mann's wagon boss and Calenses Hawkins was Toponce's. Orders had been given by them to move out, but two of Mann's teamsters, both Mexicans, got drunk and attacked a man named Holmes, Mann's night-herder who had been my pal on the trip. Holmes killed the two Mexicans in self defense with a double-barreled shot gun. They were buried at Fort Union. Holmes was tried for murder and was acquitted. Major Pease, who had been running the Indian trading store, acted as judge.

So, on January 2, 1866, the outfits both pulled out — but I remained in Fort Union. Having been a child of nature since my boyhood days, I either could, or thought I could, estimate the sort of winter we were going to have. As a matter of fact, one could not go far wrong in predicting a cold winter at Fort Union, as mild winters were an exception. Even before our outfit reached Fort Union, I had made up my mind not to return with it, for at best the trip would be perilous at that late season.

I had known Toponce for over a year, having met him the first time when he crossed the Snake River ferry with a line of freight wagons while I was working there. Later I met him at Virginia City, and still later at Helena. Both he and Mann were resourceful and full of energy, tireless and fearless. As I look back now, it seems foolhardy for them to start out on a 500 mile journey in January, heavily loaded, with no feed for their live stock except grass and no protection for themselves but Sibley tents — and this in a country where high winds from the northwest prevail, where wood is scanty and snow sure to be deep, and where no settlers had located. Had the venture succeeded they would have reaped large profits.

As I did not return with the outfits, my story of their experience necessarily comes from friends [1] who did start back with them. Toponce's outfit took the lead, trailed about five or six miles by Mann's. About the 3d or 4th of January, when Mann's wagons had reached the mouth of Quaking Asp where it empties into the Missouri and Toponce was about six or seven miles up this stream, a severe snow storm struck them. It was impossible to go further. Toponce left his wagons and dropped southward to the Missouri River, where the Indians had many cords of wood prepared for future use. For the next fifteen or twenty days the cold was so intense that only part of the company could go to bed at once, the others remaining up to keep the fires going, not only inside but between the Sibley tents as well. The cold froze the cattle's horns until they bursted, and their legs and tails also froze. Some of the cattle were even found standing humped up in their tracks dead. The buffaloes drifted in from the north, and all that did not get shelter in the timber died from the extreme cold. Buffalo skeletons strewed the ground

[1] See Alex Toponce, for an extended narrative covering the blizzard and the breaking up of the ice gorge. The hardships and losses on this freighting trip can hardly be exaggerated.

in every direction. All the live stock in both outfits, about 1,600 head, perished, except two small mules that were kept inside a tent and fed cottonwood bark and buffalo meat.

As soon as possible Mann and Toponce set out on the mules in deep snow for Helena to get more cattle. They arrived there in March, and after buying the necessary horses and cattle started back with two loads of provisions and about twenty new men, 600 head of oxen, and forty saddle animals. But the Indians ran off all the saddle animals before they reached Fort Benton, and they lost all their provisions in crossing the Marias River. Three of their men were killed by the Indians, and two got into a fight with gun and knife and died as a result. They had to make the balance of the journey, 300 miles, on the meat of such poor buffaloes as had survived the hard winter, and they had no salt even for this.

When they reached the winter camping place of the two outfits, they found that Toponce had left, out of forty wagons well loaded, only the front wheels of one, lodged in a tree; provisions, ox yokes, and chains were all gone. Mann's outfit had lost almost as heavily. The ice was so thick that when it broke up there was a jam that forced the water out over bottoms sixty feet above low water mark. The stockade and building were all swept away. Four of Toponce's men were drowned and some of the rest remained in trees for sixty hours before being rescued by friendly Indians. Fifteen men were crippled and were sent down to Fort Union and later to Omaha for treatment. It was from the latter that I learned of the hardships and casualties suffered by the two outfits. Mann did not lose any wagons, as the ice gorge was not as bad at the point where he was camped, but he did lose 20,000 pounds of sugar and as many pounds of coffee, besides some flour and other articles.

Mann's outfit had started with all the goods that had been unloaded at Fort Union and consigned to Helena except some quartz-mining machinery, which was left on the bank of the river in front of the fort. The current undermined the bank so that it caved in, carrying the machinery with it, and the machinery was never recovered.

CHAPTER XV

FORT UNION — ICE GORGE

FORT UNION was a busy place when we arrived there and all during the winter. Here I saw my first Red River carts, used by the Red River French half-breeds who had come to Fort Union to trade. These half-breeds were also caught in the blizzard, were snowed in, and had to remain at Fort Union till spring. There were also many Canadian half-breeds, and Cree Indians, and four or five Mexicans. Huskie dogs were more numerous than horses there. Traders came and went on snow shoes from all directions, often accompanied by dog-drawn travois.

After the two outfits had gone, as I have already narrated, Jerry Mann found that the bills of lading given him did not correspond with the goods held by Major Pease. Major Pease thereupon offered me $500 to escort him to Fort Benton on horseback that the correction might be made, but I did not dare take him at his offer as bronchitis was giving me a great deal of trouble. I told him, however, that if he had any teaming to do I would be glad to take the job. He hired me to do the teaming, and during a short delay set me to tending the cattle herd. I had always done a great deal of riding, and in keeping with the custom of the times, especially in the winter season, wore *chaps.* As some of my readers may not know, *chaps*, unlike trousers, are made with each leg entirely separate and fastened only on the belt that encircled the body. A few days after starting work I came into the bunkhouse at the trading store, pulled off my *chaps*, which were wet, and put them in the kitchen to dry. Now this kitchen was presided over by a black mammy from Missouri. Some days afterwards I went into the kitchen for my *chaps*, and not finding them, asked Aunt Hannah if she had seen them.

"No, suh," said she.

Thinking that she did not know just what I meant by *chaps*, I added, "They were here — the leather breeches."

"What, dem ledder britches wid de seat all out?" said she.

"Yes," I replied.

"Law, chile, I di'n't see how I could put a new seat in dem, and I done burn dem long ago."

Shortly after this Major Pease sent me down the river about twenty-five or thirty miles to the mouth of the Muddy, where the Northwest Fur Company had an outpost, to take supplies and bring back furs bought from the Indians. Packineau,[1] a very old Frenchman who could talk but little English, was the post trader. He lived in a large double-room log house with an open fireplace, and was at this time about sixty-five years of age and had lived along the Missouri all his life. Be-

[1] Chas. Packineau a resident on the Missouri River from the early 40's till his death about 1872. He was at this time about sixty-five years old. His name is variously spelled Patenaud, Paquenaud, Packenau, Patineaude.

cause of his unusual height the Indians called him
Wasicu Hanska, Tall-White-Man. In addition to his
other accomplishments he could speak several different
Indian languages and could converse fluently in the
sign language.

A large band of Assiniboine Indians were camped
there under Chief Red Stone, after whom the customs
house north of this post in Canada is named. Red
Stone's people were mourning the loss of a score or
more children from an epidemic of measles. When the
Indian women wailed, the huskie dogs, of which the
camp had many, would set up a chorus even more
noisy, and the coyotes which hung around the camp in
great numbers answered in a succession of yelps ending
in a dismal howl. I had heard much wailing before,
but none half so dismal as the combined clamors of the
bereaved women, the dogs, and the coyotes, which
smote the frigid, starlit air of this timbered post at the
mouth of the Muddy.

When I drove down from Fort Union with supplies
for the store, I carried a little oats, but having no hay
was obliged to turn the team loose to eat cottonwood
bark for roughage. All horses here have the bark habit.

Major Pease had a number of woodchoppers stationed at this post, practically all of whom had deserted from Fort Rice, while Colonel Dimon was in
command. The latter was a Union officer but his men,
as well as the deserters mentioned, were known as
"galvanized" Yankees, because they had been Confederate soldiers who had taken the oath of allegiance to
the government on being captured and held as pris-

oners of war, and had been sent to this frontier post on
parole. These woodchopper deserters claimed that they
had fled in terror from the scurvy which was prevalent
at Fort Rice. They gave the report that fifty had died
with the disease, and more were expected to die. As a
matter of fact, these southern men didn't know how to
take care of themselves in this cold climate. It was
later learned that over a hundred died that winter.
Major Pease, being a North Carolinian, naturally felt
sympathy for these deserters and gave them jobs cutting cordwood to sell to steamboats. But all they cut
went out with the ice gorge and flood that committed
such havoc with us and with the outfits of Toponce and
Mann.

Ordinarily I brought to Fort Union furs and robes
the Indians had traded in, but one of my loads back
from the Muddy consisted of 1,100 buffalo tongues,
salted and smoked for shipment down the river in the
spring. Most of the buffalo tongues were shipped to
St. Louis and eventually distributed throughout the
east, where they were considered delicacies. I hauled
from Fort Union to the trading post such articles of
merchandise as Packineau ordered me to bring for use
in the Indian trade. By the time I had made several
round trips with a wagon, the snow had become so deep
that the road was practically impassable for a loaded
wagon, and I had to give up teaming.

When I was at Fort Union the winter of 1865-6 a
large oil portrait of Pierre Chouteau, Jr., hung within
the arched entrance to the fort, painted by George
Catlin, the Indian painter who had come up the Mis-

souri on the *Yellowstone* in 1832, accompanying Chouteau in the first steamboat to reach that point. I have never heard what became of the portrait, but presume it was destroyed when the fort was torn down some two years later. At the time when I saw the portrait it had been painted over thirty years but I cannot say whether it had hung beneath the arch all those years or not.

Several other men at the post and myself, all of us temporarily out of employment because of the blocked roads, planned a little venture on our own account — that of taking wolves by trap and poison for their fur, cutting cordwood and putting up ice for the future steamboat trade. A large gray wolf skin, or buffalo wolf as it was often called, was worth about two dollars, and a coyote's skin was worth from a dollar to a dollar and a half. The place selected for our headquarters was on a point of land between the Yellowstone and the Missouri at the juncture of the two rivers, where there was an old deserted log trading post which Tom Campbell had occupied and abandoned because he had found his post too close to Fort Union to be profitable. The post consisted of two log houses standing some yards apart and parallel to each other, with a stockade connecting the ends to form an open court between the two buildings.

Our party occupied one of the houses, and a short time later Dutch John with his wife and child, another woman whose name I do not recall, and a Mexican called Sport occupied the other. The weather continued unbearably cold, and every few days a little snow was added to what we already had. The wind, which seemed to blow almost continuously, carried the pulverized snow and smote with blinding sheets of peril any who ventured far from camp. Occasionally a let-up in the severity of the weather would allow one or more of us to go up on the ice of the Missouri to Fort Union to bring back in packs on our backs such articles as we required — sugar, coffee, flour, and tobacco.

The wolves we poisoned were usually frozen stiff when found. We removed the entrails and piled up the carcasses like so much cordwood to await the thawing weather of spring for skinning. We also cut steamboat wood and put up ice at times when not occupied in stringing poison baits and walking the trap lines. Our plan was to kill buffaloes and preserve the meat in an ice house which we built and filled with ice. The ice was three feet thick on the river, the thickest I have ever seen it.

The cold weather moderated in March, and we began to skin out our wolves. Dutch John and Sport made arrangements to go up the Yellowstone about ten miles, where Gen. Alfred H. Sully had built a hunting camp to hunt elk a year or two earlier. They got off about the middle of the month, but left their women with us. Shortly after they returned a blizzard came up and continued in sustained fury for three days and nights. Neither man nor animal could make headway against the gale or see through the blinding sheets that filled the air, carried by the sixty-mile wind. A howitzer six-pounder that had been left at the post by some one who preceded us, came into good play after the storm started, as we fired it to guide the Mexican, who was out on a trap line, home safely. A poor buffalo bull drifted to the leeward side of our stockade and stood humped up there during the storm, never leaving the protection to pick anything to eat until after the storm had abated. We did not molest him, although we were making our living in part by killing these animals; but to take advantage of his extremity was too much for us. When the storm was over we saw buffaloes, white-tailed deer, and elks walking on the drifts of impacted snow and browsing on the tops of the willow branches which protruded above. I cannot recall another winter since that time as severe as this one was.

Within a few days after the storm ceased the snow began to melt. The Indian women were kept busy tanning buffalo, deer, and elk hides for moccasins, mittens, caps, and leggings.

When the thaw was at its height an Indian, a relative of Dutch John's Ree wife, came riding up through the slush. He told Henry Nelson, a galvanized Yankee from North Carolina who was in charge of the camp, to move out or we would be swept away by high water. He could not talk English, but he conveyed this information in sign language. Nelson replied in sign language that we would get out as soon as the water got high. The Indian replied, "When the water gets high you will not get out," stooped down, picked up the Ree woman's little girl, lifted her in front of his saddle, and rode off in the gathering dusk, saying as he did so, "I'll save her anyway."

As I have already said, our camp was in the forks of the Yellowstone and the Missouri. The bottoms were two or three miles wide on either side of us. But we were busy with our wolf skins and gave the warning little consideration. When I stepped outside just as we were preparing for bed, I heard an unusual noise of rushing waters and the crunching and popping of ice. I returned to the room and reported what I had heard. One of the men dismissed it with "Aw, that was just the wind in the cottonwoods," and we went to bed. In spite of the confidence of the others, however, I was a bit nervous and could not sleep. Our bed had an upper and a lower berth, the framework being made of poles shaped and driven into augur holes in the logs of the wall and the outer ends supported by upright posts. Two men occupied each berth, I being in the lower.

Within a few hours after we had lain down, I was aroused from a half slumber by the sound of water splashing against the house and running under the door. I yelled, "Here's the water now," and stepped out in ice cold water up to my ankles. I lit a candle, and we got dressed as well as we could. There was no time to plan anything. We threw together all the bedding, consisting of a few blankets and tanned robes. Henry Nelson proposed that we try to wade out, and I immediately agreed, without stopping to think of the impossibility of our being able to do so. Besides what I wore I took nothing with me except a blanket, even leaving my gun behind. I wore only moccasins on my feet, and a fur cap on my head. Henry carried a five-shooter pistol, which came into good play a short while afterwards. In the darkness we felt and splashed our way out through the gate, taking, as we thought, the direction towards the nearest high land. Not until we had gone some distance in the timber did we recall that there were several low channel beds between us and the high lands we desired to reach. After a little consultation we agreed that it would be impossible to reach the high land, almost two miles away, without passing through swimming-depth water. In addition to the darkness there was a heavy fog. Neither of us knew the direction of the stockade we had left but a few minutes before. The water was rising; the large cakes of ice striking against the trees, breaking off dead trunks and grinding against each other, gave anything but a pleasant sensation. One who has never witnessed an ice gorge and the plowing of the masses of ice through the timber like a great gunboat can form little idea of their power. Many trees are torn up by the roots as if they were frail garden weeds.

By this time the water was up to our waists and as cold as ice could make it. While there was not much current, we had to keep our hands before us to ward off the small chunks of ice and driftwood floating on the surface. We had not only to contend with the darkness but with a fog which added to the gloom and reduced the chances of our finding our way back to the house. Each of us realized that we were in dire circumstances, the distance to the fort and the rapid rise of the water making haste necessary. Not knowing where we were going, any step might precipitate us into the channel of the river beyond our depth. Notwithstanding our exertions our legs and hands were becoming numb, and we were not slow to understand what that meant.

I have been many times in battles, heard the screech of shells, the whistle of bullets, and felt the dirt thrown into my face by them; in fact, I had faced dangers in many forms and not been awed by death. But the idea of slowly and gradually freezing to death, wandering around in ice water, lost, stumbling into holes, with the constant fear of going over the river brink, was a new and terrifying thing. Henry and I were but a few yards apart, struggling with every step yet saying nothing. Finally I spoke up, "Henry, we are lost." "I'll try my gun," he muttered. "There's a chance." He fired his pistol into the air with stiffened fingers. No sooner had he done this than I asked him, "Save one of those shells for me. I don't want to freeze to death. If we've got to go, I want to go instantly."

Then suddenly a distant light flared up. We floundered over to it, and found that our two companions had clambered up to the dirt roof of the cabin and had started a fire there when they heard our shot. They helped us to the roof, where we found bedding, an ax, some nails and ropes, which they had shoved up through the chimney hole. We wrapped ouselves in dry blankets and sat by the fire, with limbs numb and teeth chattering. Across the courtyard we could see the occupants of the other cabin, consisting of two

Mexicans, two Indian women, Dutch John, and a Frenchman named La France, also building a fire. The men tore off the puncheon boards from the gable of the building and used them for fuel. Our neighbors had also rescued all the provisions they could in the confusion, and were now making coffee and pancakes to warm themselves, as the night air was damp and extremely raw and biting.

The distance between our roof retreats was not a great one, yet we had to yell at the top of our voices to be heard above the roar of the river torrent, the breaking of ice, and the crashing among the trees. The stockade posts were set deep in the ground and the earth tamped in around them was solidly frozen; otherwise our buildings might have gone too. No large cakes of floating ice had reached us, but we knew the ice gorge had not yet broken. The whole night long the swirling waters swept just under the roof of the house, which would have floated off except for its mooring to the posts in the frozen ground. But, and we were almost afraid to ask ourselves the question, how long would the ground remain frozen when covered with water?

When dawn came and the fog arose there was revealed to us a picture of such desolation that our hearts were sick. Water extended for over two miles on all sides of us; the Yellowstone was backwatering and the Missouri slowly rising. All our cordwood, representing the labor of most of the winter, had gone during the night; our oxen and a pony owned by La France were drowned; all our buffalo, elk, deer, and antelope hides, wolf and beaver skins, were swept away; and the ice house was shaved off at the ground, and with its contents was probably many miles down the Missouri.

The dog which we had with us on the roof was making things even more hideous with its plaintive howls. He had enough to make him howl, for in addition to the troublous aspect of the water, his head and eyes were swollen and festering from quills he had received in a recent encounter with a porcupine. But, although we sympathized with his complaints, we were in too wretched a state ourselves to stand the clamor, and I threw him overboard, expecting shortly to follow him. But Dutch John, who was a resourceful fellow, started ripping up the puncheons and the ridge logs from the roof of the house he was on, to build a raft. The other cabin was to the west of ours and in all probability would be struck first when the ice began to flow freely. We followed his example, intending to launch the raft only when compelled to do so by necessity. When it was finished, we anchored it with ropes to the corner of the house.

As soon as the fog lifted, the sun came up warm and brilliant. We knew no one could reach us — all we could do was to wait. On a high ridge north of the Missouri we could see Indians looking, probably to see if we were still alive. They saw us, and as we learned later, reported to Fort Union that we were on the roofs of our houses.

By nightfall the slush ice began to grate ominously against the sides of the houses and scrape off the rawhide and wolk skins tacked on them. We kept a candle burning with a windbreak around it, taking turns watching and trying to get a little sleep. Just before daylight we heard the roar of a cannon fired at Fort Union and took courage from its message, hoping for rescue from our perilous situation.

CHAPTER XVI

Our Rescue — Down the Missouri on a Mackinaw

OUR SPIRITS rose with the prospect of rescue, and we waited rather impatiently. By this time large cakes of ice were going by. An extra large one struck the house Dutch John and his party were on, and moved it off its foundation. Expecting it to go down stream, they jumped upon the raft they had constructed and with long ridge poles tried to pole it back away from the Missouri into the backwater of the Yellowstone. They succeeded in drifting in among the cottonwoods where their protecting trunks broke the heavy ice flow. Here they secured the raft between trees, caught some driftwood and built a fire to keep warm through the long, chilly night. In their haste in getting onto the raft they forgot to take any provisions with them, but on the day following, La France caught a porcupine that had taken refuge in the cottonwoods to which they were anchored, and roasted it. He also shot a wild goose, but it floated by just out of reach.

Another day went by, with still no sign of rescue. We were exhausted; worry, short rations, and little sleep were beginning to tell. The third day I helloed over to La France, "How are you fixed?"

"Seventeen feet of water and nothing to eat," was the cheerful reply.

"Shall we come over where you are?" I asked.

"Stay where you are till you're washed off. You can't make it. There's a current between you and us that would carry your raft down and it's too deep to pole."

All through the day we could see elk floating down on big cakes of ice. Whole bends of the river rose and with much creaking and straining slowly moved away, carrying timid rabbits, bobcats, and white-tailed deer. On one large cake of ice stood four buffaloes; I suppose they had been trying to cross the river when caught by the torrent. Of all the animals carried down on the ice the elk seemed to be most numerous.

The compact flow of ice continued until the fourth day when some open spaces began to appear; we again looked forward hopefully for a rescue boat, which might now reach us without being crushed between the grinding ice cakes. We kept a sharp lookout. Of a suddent the cry went up, "The boat's coming!" and up the river we could see a mackinaw boat, bearing the stars and stripes, coming to our rescue. The boat had two oarsmen, and our old friend Packineau was steering. Major Pease, who owned the boat, was waiving from the stern. A mackinaw boat is generally built about thirty to thirty-five feet long to carry bales of furs to St. Louis. They first picked up the occupants of the raft and then took us from the roof of our house. We landed on the north side of the Missouri, just about where Fort Buford was afterwards established.

Major Pease told us that all who wished to go back to Fort Union might do so, and he would give them employment; or those who wished could go on down the river with him, as he was on his way toward Sioux City to meet representatives of Durfee & Peck, the new purchasers of Fort Union, on an up-river steamboat, to arrange about the transfer of the property. The two Ree women went back to Fort Union to join their tribe, and Nelson, La France, and the two Mexicans also went to Fort Union. My two galvanized Yankee companions of the winter and I accepted Major Pease's offer and went down the river with him. In the party were also Packineau, a man by the name of Jack Kane, and an Indian and his two wives destined for Fort Berthold. Within an hour after Major Pease's announcement we were on our way down the river.

We camped at the end of the first day at the mouth of the White Earth River, where, as Packineau told me in broken English, there had formerly been a trading post called Fort Williams. We built a rousing campfire and enjoyed its welcome blaze. It was a gratifying change from sitting all curled up on top of a log shack surrounded by water, which had been our portion for some days.

Two years later while I was at Fort Rice, Durfee & Peck, the purchasers of the Northwest Fur Company's posts, brought up some Missourians to cut cordwood and stationed them just below the place we camped that night. These Missourians, being unacquainted with western ways, mistook the signs of friendship of some Ree Indians who had furs to trade for sugar, coffee, and flour, and fired on them. Two of the most prominent Indians, Tasunka Hinsa (Red Horse) and Wamani (The Thief) were killed. Whereupon the Indians attacked the white men, remaining out of danger as much as possible until the latter had used up their ammunition, then climbed the house, tore the puncheon boards off the roof, killed all five of the occupants, and took all the provisions, clothing, and blankets they had.

About the same time the Indians found a Frenchman nearby with a Sioux wife whom they killed. Out of revenge the Frechman went down the river to a point where the smallpox was raging and brought up some infected blankets. He sold them to this band of Rees, and nearly all of them died of smallpox as a result.

We sat up late that night at the mouth of the White Earth River with our boat anchored safely while the glowing fire reflected on the river whose icy waters were burdened with mud and driftwood, while the water ground by with its icy burden. We all took turns telling stories. When it came Major Pease's turn, he asked us if we had heard about the killing of Charley Carson, a nephew of the famous frontiersman, Kit Carson, up near Fort Benton.[1] Not one of us had heard the story, as we had been shut off from outside news during the winter. All of us except the two deserters from Fort

[1] This story of the killing of Charley Carson is given as related by Major Pease. There is little data on the matter. Superintendent David Hilger of the Montana Historical Society sent the author a contemporaneous clipping from a Helena paper where a hearsay account was given that differed somewhat from the above. Carson was probably buried near his ranch on Dearborn River.

Rice knew Charley and we were shocked to learn of his death.

When I was freighting between Helena and Benton I saw Carson quite often and had a high regard for his manly qualities. He was a market hunter and served fresh meat to the bull trains that freighted between these two points. It seemed that he and a man named Schultz were hunting buffaloes on the Dearborn River, and while so engaged ran into a war party of fifteen or twenty Blood Indians. Carson and Schultz had made camp and turned their horses loose to graze when attacked, and no escape seemed possible. Whatever was to be done had to be done at once. Carson said to his companion, "One of us can stand them off while the other gets away. There is no need of both of us being killed. You can't shoot; make a run for your life while I keep them back. Go."

Schultz did as he was told and managed to reach Fort Benton safely while Carson stayed to face certain death.

A party was at once organized and set out to the Carson-Schultz camp where they found poor Charley killed and three dead Blood Indians to attest the accuracy of his marksmanship. He was a cool brave man, reliable in a conflict and a wonderful shot. I hold him one of the bravest men I ever knew. I have heard many heated arguments around the camp fire as to whether Schultz should not have staid and died with his pal. Carson thought otherwise. In all my experiences in western tragedies I have never known of a sacrifice more complete, more certain, and more unselfish than that of Charley Carson, who laid down his life for his friend. I am told no monument marks this dead hero's grave, and whatever rewards he gets for his unselfish sacrifice will be on the other side of the Great Divide.

The next morning before breaking camp, the Indian who was with us discovered a band of elk on a nearby point of an island, and shot one. This band had taken refuge from the floods on high land, now made into an island by the height of the water, and were afraid to swim out. The remainder of the band watched us skin and dress one of their number without much concern.

When we put off down the river for Fort Berthold, we all had to take a hand in poling off the large cakes of ice which might otherwise have crushed our craft. The river was so high that we did not find it necessary to follow the channel but often made short cuts across bends that were open prairie in ordinary stages of water, but now water extended from bluff to bluff. We saw many beaver that had been drowned out of their homes sitting disconsolately on chunks of ice; but we had no desire to add to their misery and passed by without molesting them.

Not until late in the evening did we reach Fort Berthold, where we found difficulty in effecting a landing owing to the swiftness of the current next to the shore. Finally, when we had made a good anchorage with ropes, a few of our party went up to the trader's store with Major Pease, the rest of us remaining on board to protect the property. The Indian passenger got off with his two wives, and in his place we took on a lieu-

tenant and his mixed-blood wife who desired passage
to Fort Sully.

Early the following morning we put off again and
in about four hours reached the mouth of Knife River
— the old site of several Indian villages. Packineau
pointed out the site of old Fort Clark,[2] named after
William Clark of the Lewis and Clark expedition.
From Fort Berthold down to Fort Rice there was no
visible sign of human habitation. In fact, the Indian
population, especially of this region, had never recovered from the terrible scourge of smallpox during the
years 1837-38. The Mandans, Hidatsa, and Arikara
who dwelt in villages along the river, suffered most
because of the compactness of their population. The
Sioux, being more widely scattered, suffered least.
Many of those who survived the smallpox epidemic
were disfigured by hideous scars. A number of Indian
women were out in their bull boats, but they were
careful to keep reasonably close to shore.

Traveling on the west side of the timber that skirts
the river-channel near the second bench we arrived at
Fort Rice. The fort was garrisoned by several companies of the 13th U. S. infantry under Lt.-Col. J. N. G.
Whistler. We did not remain long at Fort Rice, but
continued on our downward voyage. The two deserters
who were with us had come from Fort Rice, and for
fear of apprehension went into hiding until we were
ready to resume our journey. Fort Rice had been built
by Gen. Alfred H. Sully in the summer of 1864. We

[2] Fort Clark was on the west bank of the Missouri about a mile
north of the present village of the same name.

were told when we landed that Major Chas. E. Galpin, his son, Sam, and Horatio H. Larned had left the day before in a skiff on a down-river expedition to Sioux City to buy cattle to replace the post beef herd that had been run off by the Indians. Galpin was post trader under the firm Gregory, Brugier & Goey of Sioux City, Iowa, but the cattle were to be bought for the soldier garrison to supply them beef. Larned was clerk of the trading post under Major Galpin at the time.

We soon overtook Major Galpin's party, and they were glad to transfer their bedding, provisions, and oars to our mackinaw boat, as their skiff was small and unsafe. They tied the skiff to our mackinaw and towed it behind. Major Galpin and Major Pease were well acquainted and took advantage of the chance meeting to learn the news from each other. We saw no white men's habitations between Fort Rice and Fort Sully. Fort Pierre had been abandoned and torn down and nothing remained to mark the place but standing chimneys. Most of the building material in Fort Pierre had been used in the Fort Sully buildings. Just above old Fort Pierre we passed the ruins of Fort La Framboise, the crumbling, old-fashioned stone chimneys still being visible. Just before we reached this point on the river Major Pease pointed out on a high hill on the west side of the river a wooden cross that marked the burial place of the French fur trader Dorion.[3]

Fort Sully was situated on the east bank of the river about five miles below the present site of Pierre, S. D.,

[3] The Dorion mentioned is probably a half-breed son of Pierre Dorion, Sr., who was interpreter for Lewis & Clark for a time.

opposite the north end of Farm Island. We stopped at Fort Sully to allow the lieutenant who had accompanied us from Fort Berthold to land. His Indian wife went on down with us to Crow Creek, where she had relatives.

The first up-river vessel we met was the *Deer Lodge* [4] on April 18. The next day we met the *St. John*, a large 300 ton side-wheel boat belonging to LeBarge Bros. of St. Louis, and that night the *Jenny Brown*, under Captain Horn, a boat belonging to the new fur company, Durfee & Peck, of Fort Leavenworth, Kansas. We had hailed the *Deer Lodge* and they had told us that we would meet Durfee on the *Jenny Brown*, which we found anchored to the bank and the crew fast asleep. We rowed alongside between the boat and the shore and climbed in. No rougher looking set of pirates ever boarded a vessel than we. The watchman was surprised to see such a motley group, yet made us welcome. He had just come from St. Louis, and to him, accustomed to civilized life, our buckskin suits, long hair, and unkempt shaggy beards must have been rather a terrifying sight.

The cook of the boat gave us a square meal, including vegetables, which we had not tasted for months. Then Larned and Sam, Packineau and myself resumed

[4] Mr. Larned thinks that Durfee came up on *The Miner*. The records of boat arrivals at Fort Benton show that the *Deer Lodge* and the *St. John* were the first to arrive the spring of 1866. *The Miner* did not reach Fort Benton until a month later. The *Jenny Brown* belonged to Durfee & Peck and it is reasonable to believe that Durfee would come up in one of his own company boats. Hawley, the managing director of the Northwest Fur Co., came up on *The Miner*. (Larpenteur, vol. 2-436).

our journey down river, leaving Major Galpin and Major Pease to accompany Durfee back up the river to Forts Rice and Union on the *Jenny Brown*. We now met steamboats daily, laden with goods consigned to up-river points. We landed at Fort Randall and took on a soldier and his wife bound for Sioux City.

Our next landing place was the Yankton Agency where Dr. Burleigh[5] was Indian agent. We stopped for only a few minutes, then oared ourselves on down to the village of Yankton. We stopped for breakfast at the only hotel, run by Henry Clay Ash.[6] The well-known Miner Bros. had a small store there. Yankton had only a few dozen buildings, mostly constructed of logs, but in spite of its insignificance was aspiring to be the capital of Dakota Territory. In fact it did become the capital and remained so until Bismarck took the honor away from her in 1883. The population of Dakota was so sparce that it could muster up only one militia company, whose captain was one of the Miner Bros. above mentioned.

Our next stop was at Vermillion. Here the river was so high that we rowed right up to the hotel steps and got out. This experience with high water induced the growing city of Vermillion later to move to higher ground.

Packineau and the wife of the soldier who was with

[5] Dr. Walter A. Burleigh was a member of the firm of Burleigh, Hedger & Bogue at Yankton and had held a number of official positions among them being member of Congress for Dakota Territory. Burleigh county, North Dakota, was named for him.

[6] Henry Clay Ash is the father of the well-known Ben Ash who is at this date still living at an advanced age in Sioux Falls.

us abandoned our boat and took passage on the stage to Sioux City. I think they were influenced in doing so by the fact that some of the boys had got a jug of whiskey, and over their cups had insisted on rigging out the boat in sails, which would make the trip dangerous if we should strike a snag or a submerged tree trunk. As it turned out the wind was at our back and the sail worked well, allowing us to move along as rapidly as safety would permit with only an occasional resort to the oars.

We neared the end of our journey toward night, and secured the boat under a high bluff. I climbed the bluff and could look across and see the lights of Sioux City not over three miles away. We reached the city early the next morning after an hour's sailing.

While we were waiting for the rest of our party to pull in, we watched the arrival of a steamboat from Rock Island, Illinois. It was bearing Santee Indian prisoners from that point to be placed on a reservation near the mouth of the Niobrara River in Nebraska.

Those of our party, however, who had taken the stage at Vermillion had a terrible time. The stage wallowed along through the water and mud all of two days and nights and did not reach Sioux City until the morning following the day of our arrival. The stage crawled in covered with mud and gumbo with the passengers likewise be-smeared, as they had to push in the difficult places to help the played-out horses. On the outside of the stage was painted in large letters, visible through the incrusted splatters of mud, "Weakly Stage."

CHAPTER XVII

SIOUX CITY AND BACK TO FORT RICE

ON THE way down the river I had sold my gun to one of the boys for $25, expecting Sioux City to be a large place where a gun would not be necessary. I was very much surprised and disgruntled, therefore, to find that it was little more than a town. It had one hotel, the Wauregan House.

The thing which we enjoyed most in our visit to the city was eating. Personally my diet for the past three years had been chiefly buffalo meat, often with nothing else to break the monotony of the bill of fare. Not only was there little variety in the food but even less in its preparation. A diet of buffalo meat cooked on a buffalo chip fire, three times a day, without fruits or vegetables of any sort and often without bread, or even salt, presents little appeal to an appetite not sharpened by the most active outdoor life. One of the customary methods of making bread was to mix the dough — flour and water — without either soda or baking powder, plaster the end of a green stick with all the dough it would carry, then bake it by holding in the blaze of the camp fire. The meat was often cooked in the same way. So, although the pangs of hunger will give a relish to the most undesirable and ill-prepared food, a

136

chance to fill up on the delicacies of civilized life was a blessing of which we took full advantage.

When in Sioux City I met a man by the name of Tom Powers,[1] who was well acquainted with the upper Missouri River country. He told me that a man who wished to work for wages should not come below Fort Randall. The Civil War was now over and the financial distress brought about by the waste of the long conflict was becoming gradually more acute. He said that the farther east one went the harder it was to get employment and the more demoralized conditions were becoming.

Brackett's Battalion,[2] under General Sully, was stationed in Sioux City and was being mustered out. In consequence soldiers were selling their horses and arms, and I bought a six shooter. General Sully had conducted two military expeditions up the Missouri and had located and built Fort Rice. He was well known to me by reputation, although I had never met him. A friend said to me, "Ben, let's go over to General Sully's tent." General Sully, we were told, was on his way to Washington and had stopped in Sioux City temporarily. I assented readily enough, and we went over. He received us cordially, and I was introduced. In person General Sully was a tall, military looking man

[1] This was the Thos. C. Powers who afterwards became one of the most prominent figures in Montana. He made his home in Helena but had a line of mercantile stores in most of the cities in the state, conducted under the title of the Powers Mercantile Co. His death occurred March 16, 1923.

[2] Maj. A. B. Brackett commanded a cavalry battalion under Gen. Alfred H. Sully in his two expeditions through North and South Dakota in 1863 and 1864.

with a florid complexion and thin hair well tinged with gray. We talked for some time on the treaties either proposed or recently entered into with the Indians and the appointment of Indian agents in the up-river country. Suddenly General Sully turned to me, and said:

"Don't you think military agents would be more kindly received by the Indians than civilian agents are?"

I replied, "Yes, I am sure they would be, and in case of trouble they would be able to manage things better."

The general, who seemed to feel rather strongly on the subject, added, "Yes, and an army officer can perform his duties without political influence because his pay would go on just the same. If a military agent didn't perform his duties satisfactorily, he could easily be replaced and in case of malfeasance could be punished by court martial. Besides, now that the war's over, many good officers will be available for the Indian agency service."

He then pulled out a note book to make some notations of the conversation, and we took our leave.

While in Sioux City I met a man whom I had known back in Ohio. He recognized me but I couldn't place him until he had explained who he was. I told him I had changed my name to Ben Arnold. I don't know whether he ever wrote home that he had seen me or not. In all my western travels I never met another man whom I had known in Ohio, so completely was the past blotted out.

The country was just beginning to feel the depress-

ing effect of the great Civil War. There was no gold
or silver in general circulation. The money most generally seen was fractional paper currency known as
"shin plasters." The army had been rapidly disbanded
and the soldiers were looking for employment. There
was little capital available for new enterprises and
work was hard to get, even at wages far below those
prevalent a few years earlier.

By this time Larned and Sam Galpin had gathered
a herd of cattle together, bought west of the river in
Nebraska. These they were to drive overland to Fort
Rice for the post-traders, Durfee & Peck, who had con-
tracted to furnish them for the military authorities at
that post, as has been mentioned. Larned asked me to
accompany them and gladly I agreed to do so, as I was
anxious to get away from Sioux City where work was
so scarce, back to the raw frontier.

From Sioux City we struck out with our 100 head
of steers, and a few cows which we were taking back to
supply some of the civilians around the post. Among
the civilians was Larned's father, who had remained
at Fort Rice after his return from Fort Dilts [3] with the
Captain Fisk party, escorted by a regiment of Sully's
soldiers. Our route was east of the river on a trail well
up toward the divide, where the traveling was better.
It was now about the middle of May, and the grass was

[3] Fort Dilts is located about seven miles east of the present city of
Marmarth, N. D., on the Bowman-Slope county line. It was constructed by Capt. Jas. L. Fisk's party in September, 1864, when attacked by a hunting party of Sioux, and marks the end of their
journey towards the gold fields in Montana. After the rescue of
Fisk's party they were brought back to Fort Rice.

fine. Our outfit consisted of one yoke of oxen hitched
to a wagon and one saddle horse. I was better schooled
in handling oxen than Larned, so I drove the team
while he rode horseback and drove the cattle. We saw
no white settlers between Fort Randall and Fort Sully
except a few Frenchmen, one at Bijou Hills and some
at Crow Creek.

When we arrived at Fort Sully, Major Galpin was
there,[4] and had us butcher three head of beeves for
passing steamboats desiring fresh meat. Boats were
coming and going on the river every day, and travel
was safer by boat than by overland trail. One of the
three boats that landed while we were at Fort Sully
carried Father De Smet, a Belgian missionary priest
well known in the northwest. General Harney was
also on his way up river to locate some new military
posts. His boats were government chartered and, in
addition to him and staff, carried soldiers to construct
and garrison the new posts when located.

Before we left Fort Sully it was felt safer for us to
engage an Indian to help us through. Since there were
only three of us with the beef herd, we would be at the
mercy of any marauding band of Indians we might
meet up with. Consequently a reliable Sioux named
Porcupine was hired by Larned to go with us as an
added protection against Indian depredation.

Only two years before our journey General Sully
had come up the river on a military expedition. Among
his men he had a topographical engineer and naturalist

---

[4] Mr. Larned thinks this is an error, as according to his recollection
they did not see Major Galpin until they arrived at Fort Rice.

named John Feilner who was in the habit of going out alone to make observations and gather specimens. He and two companions while detached from the command were attacked from ambush by three Cut Heads on the Little Cheyenne east of the Missouri, and Feilner was killed. Within a few minutes a detachment of soldiers under Captain Miner came up, struck the trail of the Indians, and after a chase of about fifteen miles over-hauled and killed them. By General Sully's orders their heads were cut off by Joseph La Framboise, the guide and interpreter, brought in, and placed upon high poles where they remained until natural agencies brought them to the ground. When we passed the place the poles were still there but the heads had been buried. We camped the following night at Swan Lake Creek, where we saw buffalo but did not try to kill any.

I drove the ox team at a leisurely gait, half asleep, while Sam Galpin dozed in the wagon box on the bedding and Larned drove the herd, occasionally lash-ing with his drover's whip some laggard that persisted in dropping too far in the rear. Porcupine was always taking observations from high points. Sometimes he would leave us and be gone for some time. One night when we were camping on Blue Blanket Creek he went away and did not return until after two o'clock, carry-ing a young antelope on his back. Sam Galpin and I were asleep, and Larned who was on guard gave Porcu-pine his supper. The Indian made no explanation of his absence, and it was only by chance that we ever learned the reason. A year later Larned learned from hostiles who came to trade at Fort Berthold where he was clerk, the nature of Porcupine's mission.

Black Cloud said to Larned, "I was going to kill you once." "When was that," asked Larned, startled. "The time you and two other fellows were bringing up some cattle to Fort Rice," was the answer. Black Cloud said he was a member of Drags-the-Stone's party which had been following us all one day, waiting for a favorable opportunity to attack. That night when we camped in the Blue Blanket bottoms, Porcupine had come to him and said:

"I have promised to see that these white men reach Fort Rice in safety. I am going to be as good as my word. His son is part Indian, and he is one of the party. If you kill these white men you must kill me first." Black Cloud said he had a long argument with Porcupine, but the latter under no circumstances would permit him to molest us.

"They are my friends," insisted Porcupine. "They shall not be killed."

But for the fact that Larned worked for Durfee & Peck for several years and learned to talk the Sioux language, he would not have learned of Porcupine's good offices in our behalf. Larned wrote me fifty-five years later and told me how narrowly we had escaped death that night. Porcupine knew the Indians had been following with hostile intent, yet never mentioned a word to us either of that or of the rescue. I met Porcupine several times afterward on the Platte River, even camped with him, but he never spoke of what he had done for us. Larned tells me that he met Porcupine years afterwards and talked with him, and when he asked him why he did not tell us that Black Cloud intended to attack us, Porcupine laughed and said:

"You are alive. You did not die. It was best that you did not know. Had I told you, you would have been afraid. When I kept silent you had no fear. It was best so."

But to return to our journey. Unaware of the danger we had escaped, we continued our journey until we struck Long Lake Creek, opposite Fort Rice. There was no way to get the cattle across except by swimming them. The fort sent us help. We tied long ropes around the horns of some of the gentler animals and passed the ends of the ropes to men seated in small boats. When the oarsmen started across the led cattle were forced into the water and the others, pushed from behind, followed the leaders. No cattle were drowned.

By agreement with the post commander the cattle were given a week to rest and fill up before being turned in. There were no live-stock scales at Fort Rice, consequently it was impossible to weigh them. So three average animals were cut out, killed, dressed, and weighed on steelyards and the whole herd was turned in at the average weight of the three. Durfee & Peck received ten cents a pound for cattle, or about $108.00 per head. As they had cost in Eastern Nebraska less than $30.00 per head the venture was quite profitable. The company gave Larned $500 as a reward for the success of the trip, and this money he sent for deposit to the Weare & Allison bank, Sioux City, Iowa, then the nearest banking institution.

In the fall of 1865 regular soldiers were sent to the various western posts to take the place of the galvanized Yankees, as the war was then over and they wanted to go to their southern homes. On July 31, 1866, a Sioux war party made a swoop on the beef herd, killed the herder, and drove off all the cattle. The alarm was given to the garrison, but as it was composed of infantry, nothing could be done. The infantry attempted to follow the attacking party, but the Indians merely played with them. They would move slowly until the soldiers were almost within shooting distance, then whip up for a mile or so and slow down again, attempting, so the soldiers thought, to lure them into an ambush. This ended the beef herd for the winter.

I helped on the construction of a house for Major Galpin, and when that was finished engaged to Durfee & Peck to put up hay. There were two other men working with me, and an Indian was employed to sit on the hill as lookout for us while we cut hay. The Indian boy told us to keep hidden, that all the Indians wanted to do was to deprive the soldiers of their beef herd, and as we were not soldiers they wouldn't bother us. The body of the herder who had been killed, when found was riddled with arrows.

In October, 1866, an old Frenchman named Merswyne and I bought a boat and went down to Fort Sully, where we got a job cutting cordwood for Lt.-Col. John Pattee, a brother-in-law to Samuel J. Kirkwood, the famous war governor of Iowa. He had formerly been a soldier but had been discharged, and at this time had married an Indian woman and settled down to ranch, but he devoted most of his time to contracting cordwood for the steamboats. Lieutenant-Colonel Pattee was in command at Fort Sully in December, 1864, when Mrs. Fanny Kelly, a captive of the Sioux for some months, was delivered to the fort and later sent to her home in Kansas.

While working at the wood-yard I met a Digger Indian by the name of Baptiste. He had come back with J. C. Fremont on his return trip from California to St. Louis and from there on the steamboat *Yellowstone* up the Missouri. He was now quite old, and, although a Digger Indian, had learned to talk Sioux. He said that Colonel Fremont had promised to send him back to California but had not done as he had agreed. Baptiste had been adopted into the Two Kettle band of Sioux and lived with an Indian named Le Graw, or Chepa. I knew Chepa well. On one occasion he told me about finding gold on the Little Missouri, but I afterwards found his gold to be pyrites of iron.

In the summer of 1867, about seventy-five steamboats came up the Missouri River loaded with freight for the up-river territory. This serves to show the activity in the mining field. The number of boats, of course, called for more houses along the river and more men to cut wood to supply the boats. During the winter of the same year I built two log houses, one for myself and one for George Pleets and family. In the meantime, however, I got a job in a trading post on Farm Island, and Chepa, Mrs. Pleet's uncle, occupied

it. Chepa was well fixed for that time — had two
wives and about fifty head of fine horses. One of these
horses, a black curly fellow, high-spirited and swift, I
used to borrow occasionally to hunt deer on; and many
a one I brought in on him. Chepa was a generous, big-
hearted man, whose wholesome spirit is shown by his
taking two orphans, a boy and a girl, to raise. The
boy, who was just old enough to herd the horse band,
was named Crow Eagle.

There was another temporary member of Chepa's
family in whom I was even more interested — a niece
who had got separated from her own family in western
Wyoming and was spending the winter with him. Her
name was Itatewin, or "Wind-Blows-on-Her." She
was a fine-looking and industrious girl. I hired her to
make my mittens, leggings, moccasins, and hunting
suits from the skins of animals which I brought in. I
could not speak much Sioux at that time, but after
becoming acquainted with her made an extra effort to
acquire a speaking knowledge of the tongue. I was then
but twenty-three years old and bashful, but the inevitable result followed. We agreed to become man and
wife, and mutual consent was all that was necessary
among people in this country. Chepa gave us a nicely
tanned and decorated buffalo robe for a wedding
present.

CHAPTER XVIII

Cutting Wood for Steamboats

In the spring of 1867 I went to Ash Point to cut wood. After I had eight cords cut, a steamboat came along and took it all for $64. My wife's relatives, who were camping near us, were almost destitute; so I did not take a cent of money but took flour, sugar, coffee, and other provisions for the whole of the amount. Among the provision, whether by mistake or as a sort of gratuity I never knew, a barrel of ginger snaps was rolled out before the boat set out up the river. The Indians seemed to enjoy these especially. I divided all these supplies among the Indians in equal share, which measurably relieved their distress. Shortly afterwards they left for James River on a buffalo hunt and my wife went with them. I returned to Fort Sully.

Louie Luzerne ran the post store at Fort Sully. Here I met a man by the name of Nichols, who wanted to join me and go back to Ash Point to cut wood. He proposed that we buy an old team of mules, wagon, and harness from Charles Primeau,[1] who held the outfit at $200, although the wagon was an old rattle trap and both it and the harness were held together with ropes and rawhide straps.

[1] Chas. Primeau was a noted interpreter on the upper Missouri.

Before we made the purchase, however, Nichols proposed that I go up with him to Chantier Creek Island where he had an interest in a good amount of wood with Joe Wandell, Louie Frainier, and a man by the name of Lynch. He wished to bring the wood down and deliver it to a boat that had offered to buy it. There was no coal in use on any of the steamboats at that time and in season wood was in brisk demand. I consented to accompany him, and we went up to the Island. We got a skiff to ride back in after delivering the wood, and tied it by a long rope to the side of the steamboat to which we were making the delivery. The rope was somewhat weak in places and Nichols said he would ride in the skiff so that if the rope broke he could save it from getting away down stream. The waves from the steamboat threw water into the skiff, and as soon as Nichols jumped into it I saw that it would be sucked in under the steamer. To prevent such a catastrophe, I took the ax and cut the rope which fastened the skiff to the boat; but I was too late. Nichols and the skiff had gone out of sight, and the suction drew them under the boat. Instantly the cry "man overboard" was raised. By the time the boat had come to a stop, Nichols had swam out, leading his skiff; whereupon the steamer backed up and took both on board. Nichols had on his person $200 in greenbacks which I helped him to dry out. The boat was bound for Montana and carried a long list of passengers en route to the gold fields. We delivered fifteen cords of wood to them, and within a few days had disposed of all Nichols and his partners had, as the growing scarcity of wood higher up made all boats desirous of keeping their fuel space full.

We returned to Fort Sully in the skiff and bought the mule team and outfit from Primeau; we then loaded the skiff on the wagon and went back to Ash Point overland.

At this date there had been no treaty made with the Indians which gave the whites the privilege of entering the Indian country, much less of cutting wood on Indian lands. In the treaty of 1855 at Fort Laramie, all the territory west of this part of the Missouri was set aside as Indian lands, and all white soldiers, travelers, or settlers were prohibited from passing through. Contrary to the expressed terms of the treaty, the country was fast filling up with white people. Military garrisons, constructed from timber grown on the Indian lands, had been established west of the Missouri. White people were killing off the game and trapping in the Indian country. The Indians were deprived of their food, the buffalo robes, and the beaver furs which had been their chief articles of trade at the trading posts, and the timber which was their dependence for buildings and fuel in the winter season. Truly, the Indians were justly aggrieved at the encroachments of the whites on territory that had always been theirs and that had been specially and specifically confirmed to them by treaty but a few years before.

When we had cut about fourteen cords of wood, two small steamboats came along and we divided what we had, selling seven cords to each. Just as we finished the transaction, a large vessel, the *Wash Graham*, rated at six hundred tons and carrying a crew of forty which was bound for Fort Buford, stopped for wood. When they found us sold out, the captain gave us $2.50 an hour to drag dry logs onto the boat with our mule team. On leaving, the captain contracted for forty cords of wood at $7 a cord for his return trip a month later.

While talking with a little cross-eyed passenger of the *Wash Graham* named Sadler, who was bound for the gold fields of Montana, I told him that he could earn more money chopping wood for steamboats along the river than he could working in the mines. He took me at my word and hired to us. He was a good chopper and we raised his pay from day to day. Before long, however, he concluded that the work was too hard and asked for his time. He took passage on a boat for Sioux City. Within a few weeks he blew in again unexpectedly, dead broke and willing to chop wood again. All he had to show for the money we had paid him before was a pair of spurs, and his reason for buying them I could never quite make out.

While at Sioux City he had learned a new song, "Shoo Fly Don't Bother Me," with snatches of which he regaled us in an unmusical voice at any hour of the day and most of the night. Like many other ne'er-do-wells, he was frequently boasting of what he would do when he made a stake. He would build a large ranch, raise cattle and horses, and make good use of his money. Some years later when the Black Hills were opened he went in and by luck or otherwise made a fair stake, I understood. Whether he would ever have fulfilled his boasts is still a question, for he was killed and scalped by the Indians in 1876. He and three other men — "Gartner" from Dubuque, Iowa, Harrison from Wisconsin, and Texas Jack — were on their way out of the Hills when they were met by a small war party of hostile Sioux, who killed and scalped all four of them. They were buried in one grave along the Pierre-Black Hills trail by whites who came along a few days after the tragedy.

When we had about finished our work at Ash Point for the season, I went up to new Fort Sully, which was built on Okoboje Creek about twenty-eight miles above old Fort Sully and on the same side of the Missouri. While I was there, Durfee & Peck were unloading some goods for winter trading at their store. They had a yoke of oxen on the boat but no feed for them, and it was necessary to unload them. One of the Durfee & Peck employees asked me if I would not take the oxen overland to Fort Rice for the company, to be used in hauling wood. Durfee & Peck had a contract to supply the garrison with fuel. I consented to take the oxen over if my wife were willing. When I asked her she was only too glad to go, as she had hopes of meeting some of her relatives up that way. Bill Gill, a young Indian cousin of my wife, and a galvanized Yankee from Tennessee went along with us.

When we reached Fort Rice I turned the oxen over and engaged to chop wood for Durfee & Peck. I traded my Smith & Wesson rifle to an Indian for a big lodge made of tanned buffalo skins, which we pitched in the timber, and went to chopping wood for $1.50 a cord.

About nineteen others besides myself were chopping during the winter, three teams being required to haul the wood in to the fort as fast as we cut it.

Along about midwinter, when the three teams were on their way to the fort, an Indian came by. He passed the two lead wagons peacefully, but on reaching the last one, driven by Hugh Lock, turned and shot an arrow through the driver's body, the point protruding visibly through his clothes. The wounded man was hauled in to the fort, but no one seemed to know just what to do with the arrow. An old Indian, with more experience in arrows than we, came in and pulled the arrow on through the man's body. The strange part of it was that the man recovered and was given a job in Durfee & Peck's pool hall afterwards.

Among the wood cutters who worked for Durfee & Peck that winter were John Ramsey, Alex Laundry, and a negro named Isaiah, who could talk Sioux.

Toward spring we moved lower down on the river where the wood was of younger growth and easier to split. I threw in with a German who was an artist in making ax-handles, and he and I chopped six cords of wood daily for six weeks.

About this time my wife gave birth to a baby girl whom I named Marcella, after a girl with whom I attended school in Ohio in my young boyhood days.

Fort Rice was under the command of Lt.-Col. J. N. G. Whistler that winter and Jim Gayton[2] was clerking at the post tradership store run by Durfee & Peck.

[2] James B. Gayton is a well known trader at Fort Rice and other Missouri River points. He was the first white settler in what is now Emmons county, North Dakota.

In addition to their merchandising enterprises, Durfee & Peck ran a line of steamboats up and down the river, delivering merchandise to their various stores and taking furs, buffalo tongue, etc., in exchange down to market. The three boats owned and operated by this firm were the *Jenny Brown*, the *E. H. Durfee*, and the *Nellie Peck*.

After Durfee & Peck had filled their contract for wood with the garrison, they set seventeen men to work cutting wood for spring and summer sale to the steamboats. The men had picked out the best timber, cording it wherever it happened to be cut among the slashings up and down the river and on both the east and west sides. Laundry, Ramsey, Isaiah, and myself were set to work gathering this wood and stacking it at convenient places for loading into steamboats. When we got down as far as Standing Rock [3] we found a trading post that had been built by Durfee & Peck about two years before when the military officer commanding the department had ordered that all trader's stores be removed from the garrisons, under the belief that the Indians drawn to the stores to trade were demoralizing the soldiers. This order, however, had not been enforced and consequently the store erected at Standing Rock had never been occupied, or even completed. The Indian trade continued to go to Fort Rice. At any rate, at Standing Rock we had the free and unquestioned use of three empty rooms facing the river, as well as a large ware room in the rear and a

[3] Standing Rock Agency is at the present town of Fort Yates in Sioux county, North Dakota.

good boat landing just beneath the bank on which the buildings stood.

With an ox team we banked the wood on each side of the river where it would be most convenient for the steamboats to reach it.

Major Galpin had an interest in the wood in the vicinity of Standing Rock and shortly afterwards acquired the empty buildings from Durfee & Peck.

The buildings at Standing Rock had never been plastered or even roofed, and we were required to make these improvements. When finished Isaiah occupied the buildings as a residence. He was married to a Santee Sioux woman, but they had no children. Isaiah had been on the river for some years. In the winter of 1868 he had carried mail, making a trip each month on foot from Fort Rice to Fort Wadsworth — a distance of nearly two hundred miles. On such trips the mail and dispatches were wrapped in water-proof cloth and strapped with his bedding on his back. There were no settlements along the route nor even a road that could be followed, and he was obliged to carry enough bedding and provisions to take care of his needs in a meagre way for the period required to make the journey — about five days. It is difficult for us to conceive the hardship of such a journey in sub-zero weather, over an untracked prairie, without fuel and with a heavy burden on his back; camping where night or exhaustion overcame him. A man, whether white or black, who made such perilous journeys for the meager rewards of that day merited and should have our highest praise.

Isaiah was a good worker, faithful and reliable in every trust. After the winter of 1868 I never saw him again. Eight years later (when he was the personal servant of General Custer), he met his death with many other brave spirits on the Little Big Horn with the gallant Custer.[4] Standing Bear, one of the hostile Sioux, told me just a few years ago that he saw Isaiah's body after the battle and recognized him. There could be "no color" line with Isaiah.

One Sunday while we were at the wood camp and not working, a party of eight Indians on horseback came to us. Isaiah went out and met them, returned to the house, and took out a pot of mush with syrup poured over it, a pot of coffee, and some tobacco. The rest of us went out, "howed" to them, and shook hands. One of these Indians was Sitting Bull, a man of medium height, broad of chest, and in the prime of his young manhood. We probably manifested some fears, for they assured us that they had no use for oxen; all they wanted was a little tobacco. It was customary for traders to have tobacco for just such emergencies, and we willingly supplied their needs. Sitting Bull asked us for whom we were cutting wood and we told him for Major Galpin. He made no reply but seemed satisfied. They told us they were going down to Fort Randall.

A short time afterwards an up-river steamboat stopped to take on wood and gave us the information that a war party of Indians had caught the water-

---

[4] Isaiah was with Major Reno's battalion and was killed on the west side of the Little Big Horn before the command retreated to the hill on the east side of the river.

wagon driver at Fort Randall going down to the river for water, had killed him and got away with the six-mule team hitched to the wagon. The perpetrators of this deed were never captured. Could they have been the party of ten who visited us?

One day John Ramsey and I went out to hunt ante-lope. We found a herd, and Ramsey waited for me to go around and place myself just about where the herd would be supposed to run. I carried a double barreled shot gun loaded with buckshot. Ramsey fired, and, as we expected, the herd came straight for me. When they were within range, I arose and brought down two. We "pumped" the two I had killed, *i.e.*, disemboweled them and caused all the blood to flow out with a lifting and pumping motion of the animal's head; then we shouldered them and went into camp. Not until we reached camp did we notice that the half-burnt paper wadding from my shots had started a prairie fire. The wind was from the northwest and drove the fire direct-ly toward our camp. We fought it as best we could, but it got away from us, ran into the woods, and burnt four or five cords of wood before we could put it out. The smoke of the fire was seen from Fort Rice, a dis-tance of nearly fifty miles. Major Galpin thought we had been attacked by Indians and burned out, and had one of the boats steam up and bring down a detail of soldiers. When they reached us, in about two hours, they found us safe and the fire out.

When we had finished cutting wood at Standing Rock, Isaiah was left to sell and collect for the cord-wood while the other three of us went back to Fort

Rice with a team which Major Galpin had sent down for us.

At Fort Rice we learned that Father De Smet and Mrs. Galpin with a few Indians had been sent westward as far as the Yellowstone above the mouth of the Powder a month before, to talk to the non-treaty Indians, usually called hostiles, and to try to persuade them to come in for a treaty council which was announced for the summer of 1868 at Fort Rice. The anticipated treaty created great activity around the post.

CHAPTER XIX

FORT RICE INDIAN TREATY — 1868

As I HAVE stated, Father De Smet and Major and Mrs. Galpin had been gone some time in their effort to get some of the non-treaty Sioux to come to Fort Rice for the treaty council. The boat which was to bring in the commissioners and the Indian chiefs and leading men from the Platte was expected up from Omaha almost any day. Indians were already gathering in cavalcades from all directions and making camp as fancy or caprice dictated. Warriors and young men came on horseback; the old men, women, and children came by travois, wagon, and on foot, bringing with them their tents, bedding, dogs, dance costumes, medicine bags, and all other household plunder. Tepees arose as if by magic, while the ponies scattered out to graze and the dogs and children enjoyed themselves underfoot. The whole scene had an aspect of lively color once seen not soon to be forgotten.[1]

[1] There is little to be found printed relating in any way to this — the most famous Indian treaty on the Missouri River for a century. So far I have been unable to find in government documents even the mention of the treaty. The law providing for the treaty called it the treaty of Fort Laramie, but when the Indians did not go to Laramie the commission brought the treaty to Fort Rice. In the "U. S. Indian Laws and Treaties," vol. II, 1006-7, appears the names of the signers to the treaty without date or place being mentioned. I know of no other place where the name Co-kam-i-ya-ya appears in print, and but

All told, it was estimated that 1,500 lodges had assembled for the great pow-wow. Representatives came from all the central northwest agencies. Nebraska, Minnesota, Wyoming, Montana, and Dakota were well represented by the chiefs and leading men of the tribes. Santees and Cutheads, Yanktons, Ogalalas, Brulés, Sans Arcs, Minneconjous, Hunkpapas, Tetons, Yanktonais, Gros Ventres of the Prairies, Cheyennes, and Arapahoes mingled together on terms of amity, yet all tense with the great purpose of the meeting.

Sitting Bull, resisting all the entreaties of Father De Smet and Major and Mrs. Galpin,[2] would not come himself — not because he was too belligerent but because he was too intensely patriotic from the Indian standpoint to brook the encroachments of the whites; he sent Gall instead. The faces of three other great chiefs of the Hunkpapas were missed: those of Four Horns, Crazy Horse, and Lame Deer. They felt that a treaty had already been entered into. Why make another? Every treaty meant the relinquishment of more land. They were willing to keep what they had and let it go at that.

But with the exception of these the most important

for a chance note made some years ago when in conversation with H. H. Larned, frequently mentioned herein, the name of The-Man-Who-Goes-in-the-Middle would not have been associated with Gall. All the older Indians recall the above name of Gall. Pizi or Gall was the name by which he was commonly known. The material in this chapter has been gathered from many interviews with both whites and Indians. Only a few chance references to the treaty are found in print, and even then the name of Fort Rice is not used in an official way.

[2] See De Smet's *Life and Travels*, vol. I, 92-103, and vol. III, 908-920.

men of the Sioux Nation were there: Chief Two Bear, an upper Yanktonai interested chiefly east of the river; Running Antelope, the Hunkpapa, whose face adorns the U. S. Treasury $5.00 note, an orator and man of great power; John Grass, also an orator and leader of no mean ability. From the Platte River came Red Cloud, Afraid-of-His-Horses, Little Wound, Two Strikes, and Spotted Tail — five as great military chieftains as the century has produced. The Arapahoes sent Black Kettle, an outstanding leader; the northern Cheyennes sent Dull Knife, one of the greatest strategists of his time, either white or red; and Crow Creek sent White Swan. Each band of Indians brought its own interpreter, and here too the fame of the interpreters was in keeping with the dignity of the occasion and the standing of those who composed the commission. Among the interpreters were the well known Frank La Frambois, Basil Clement (or Claymore as the U. S. reports have it), Louis Agaard, Charles Primeau, and Nick Janisse, or Janis.

It is doubtful, too, whether any other Indian treaty commission had among its number so many men of outstanding prominence, certainly not of as great prominence in military lines. There were four with no lower military rank than Brevet Major-General — W. T. Sherman, W. S. Harney, Alfred H. Terry, and C. C. Augur — while John B. Sanborn was a Brigadier General. General Sherman did not attend the Fort Rice treaty although a member of the commission. He and other members had gone west to hold conferences with other tribes.

Among other notables present either as sightseers or to lend their good offices to the settlement of the vexed questions to come before the conference I shall mention only one name — that of Father Pierre Jean De Smet, the Belgian missionary who was more widely traveled, had a broader acquaintance, and exerted a greater influence among the Indians than any other missionary of that day on the continent.

This great conference was not only unique in the quality and standing of its leading participants, but also in another particular: it was held in the wilderness hundreds of miles removed from any city, town, telegraph station, or post office, and devoid of all the trappings of modern life.

All Indian representatives who came overland arrived ahead of the boat which was bringing the commissioners from Omaha and some of the Indians from the Platte regions. The boat had to take advantage of the June rise in the Missouri. It is only when the water is high that large boats can travel up in safety. The *Ben Johnson* had been chartered by the government for the occasion at an expense of $300 a day. Some thought the boat was "killing time" somewhere down the river.

But the impatient watchers did not have long to wait. One afternoon the smoke of a steamboat was visible for a long time in the same place, then the smoke wreathes approached. The *Ben Johnson* had been stuck on a sand bar for a while, but now hove in sight, quickly drew ashore, and put down the gang plank. Every foot of standing room on the banks was occupied by those anxious to get a look at the commissioners whom they had been awaiting.

A welcome belched forth from the throat of a cannon at the fort, the steamer echoed a shrill response, dogs howled and fought, horses neighed, Indian women chanted and wailed, and Indian children added their shrill clamor to the uproar. The Indian braves did not deign to open their mouths, but stood proudly on the bank, decked out in feathers, fringe, and paint.

It was some days after the arrival of the commissioners before De Smet returned with Gall and others to represent the Hunkpapas. The Indians who had come up from Omaha with the commissioners, however, had been given the substance of the treaty the United States desired and met the same evening to discuss among themselves the cause of friction between the two races. The noise of the camps and the beating of tom toms did not subside until a late hour that night or any night thereafter until the conference was ended.

One of the most difficult matters of the conference was the feeding of the multitude. People have to eat, and it is customary on such occasions for the government to take care of the physical wants of the participants in a treaty. When a large crowd is assembled for but a short time no adequate commissariat can be organized. Many of the Indians present had come long distances, and they had to be fed. The steamboat was the only means of bringing in supplies. Among the eatables they brought was a large quantity of hard tack left over from the Civil War, sugar, coffee, rice, beans, and a number of barrels of pickled pork, and barrels of sorghum, tubs of butter, cases of dried fish, and caddies of Climax plug tobacco. The containers were either carried or rolled out and taken up on the bank, where those desiring such food could help themselves. Pickled pork was an article of diet unknown to the Indians. They did not like it, nor would they eat it. When the treaty was over many barrels of this pork with heads knocked in stood around untouched. The Indians poured out the flour issued to them, but carefully saved all the sacks. It was comical to watch them after they had knocked in the head of a barrel of sorghum. They had never seen any before, and were at a loss to know how to handle it. They tried to dip it out with their hands, then with cups, and finally used a stick which they poked to the bottom of the barrel, pulled it out, and passed from mouth to mouth, each of the waiting mob taking a lick of the dripping sweetness. Within a short time molasses was plastered in the hair and over the hands and clothing of the curious throng that crowded around the sorghum barrels. They made no use of the butter and the dried fish. The Indians didn't chew and their efforts at smoking the plug tobacco were unsuccessful.

The time for the conference arrived. Harney, being the eldest member of the commission present, was made chairman. The dozens of shorthand writers, clerks, news reporters, and interpreters took advantageous positions and others took what was left. I will make no attempt to repeat all the speeches or give any one entire.

Harney spoke first, addressing the Indians. He

said, "I am here today to represent the 'Great Father.'
We have been sent here to speak to you as friends and
brethren."

"How, how," came from his auditors.

"The 'Great Father,'" continued Harney, "wants
his Indian children to live in peace, to have homes, to
have churches, to have plowed fields, and schools for
their children so they may learn to read and write and
grow up in the ways of civilization. This country will
soon be filled to overflowing with white people. They
are coming on all sides. There are many white people
all around you. The wild animals you have been de-
pending on for food and clothing will soon be gone.
You are warring among each other on all sides. The
'Great Father' is powerful. He has great armies, but
he also has great mercy. He wants to protect you and
start you in the ways of civilization, to clothe you and
feed you, to build homes for you and schools for your
children. In the past we have fought against each
other. We have long been enemies. This should not
be; it is not good to think upon.

"In our government under the 'Great Father' good
men are selected to make our laws. The laws when
made must be obeyed by everyone. I have talked a
great many times in the past with your great men. I
have respect for their natural intelligence and understanding —"

"How, how."

— "and I think you know as well as I do that there
are good and bad men in every nation; the good are
obedient, the bad are disobedient. The laws of our

country are made to be obeyed; those who do not obey them are punished. You are today living in a country owned by the 'Great Father.' You are his children. He wants you to live on the piece of land reserved for you and live at peace. Today we are to lay before you the plans of the 'Great Father'."

"How, how."

"I want to say that if anything in the past has displeased you or if there is anything you do not understand, bring it forth that we may take the message back to the 'Great Father'."

"How, how."

"I want to say to you that I understand that the Bridger and Bozeman roads will both be abolished and the forts along these trails taken away. Fort Reno on the Powder, Fort Phil Kearney, and Fort C. F. Smith on the Big Horn will be no more."

"How, how," came the approving response from all sides.

"Fort Fetterman on the south side of the Platte will remain. The forts along the Missouri will be kept as a protection to the country, to preserve law. The line of your reservation will be as follows:

"You are to relinquish all lands held by you east of the Missouri. Your land will be between the Missouri on the east, the Yellowstone on the north, the Big Horn mountains on the west, and the Platte River on the south, from Platte Bridge eastward to the forks of the North and South Platte, or until the 100th parallel is reached, thence north to the Niobrara and down it to the Missouri.

"No white man will be allowed to come into this reserve. It is your own. No stock of the white man may graze on this land, and no hunters or immigrants shall pass through it."

General Harney also explained the provisions of the treaty whereby winter clothing and semi-monthly rations were to be issued; also farm implements and household utensils. Stores were to be established, cows given them to milk, oxen to plow with, and later on mares, wagons, and harnesses.

The tract of land set aside as above was for the Sioux, Arapahoes, and Cheyennes only.

Most of the Indians signed the treaty. They had much confidence in Harney and looked upon what he said as law. But in spite of all the protestations that the Indian land would be inviolate, within a few years mobs of people were passing through the choicest hunting grounds of the Indians on their road to the Black Hills. The terms of the treaty, although allowing the whites to hunt outside of the reserve, prohibited them absolutely from entering the reserve. It is little to be wondered that Indian uprisings were frequent later.

Several other speeches were made at the conference, by Running Antelope, Grass, and Red Cloud, but the one that impressed me most was delivered by Gall. As a proper background for an appreciation of Gall's speech it is necessary to know a little personal history leading up to it.

Gall's Indian name was Pizi, although he preferred to be known as the Man-Who-Goes-in-the-Middle.[3]

[3] *Laws and Treaties*, vol. II, p. 1006.

He was not an agency Indian, and for fear that he might be held by the military when he went in to trade, his band always went to a trader's post where there were no soldiers, such as Fort Berthold. A year before the incident narrated, he was, or was supposed to have been a member of a small party of Sioux who made a horse stealing raid at Berthold and ran off some horses belonging to Long Mandan. The military had given out orders to capture Gall at the first opportunity. So the first time Gall's [4] band came in to Fort Berthold,

[4] The narrative here follows the information given in an interview with H. H. Larned, who was present at the Fort Berthold trading post at the time Gall was wounded. Joseph H. Taylor in his *Kaleidoscopic Lives* (143-159) says that Bloody Knife gave to the soldiers the information of Gall's presence. In an interview with Crow Ghost, a son of Hairy Chin, he says that Gall was not shot but that he was bayoneted entirely through his body from both front and back and left for dead; but he walked in severe winter weather to the house of Hairy Chin, twenty miles away. Crow Ghost was then a boy fifteen years old and says that Gall's meager clothing was stiff with blood and that bloody froth was exuding from his mouth, which shows that he had been pierced through the lungs. The old Indians say that he was also bayoneted through the neck, as well as through the body, and was left for dead. This seems to be a correct statement, as it is inconceivable that Gall would have been permitted to escape, wounded as he was, had the soldiers not thought he was dead. In fact, Blue Thunder and others say that he was driven to the ground, and the soldier had to place his foot on the prostrate body before he could withdraw his bayonet. It seems probable that Gall, though left for dead, recovered from the shock of his wounds sufficiently to get away before daylight, when soldiers came for the body and not finding it took up the blood-stained trail. Larned is the only one who says that according to his recollections Gall was shot. It seems more probable that he was wounded only with bayonets since the attack was made at night and a gun shot would be liable to bring on a general engagement, which the soldiers wished to avoid. The Indians whom I have interviewed all say that Gall never had any love for soldiers after his experience with them. It is said that within a year he came in with seven white scalps taken in vengeance for the

Long Mandan slipped down to Fort Stevenson, only
twenty-seven miles away, and secured from De Tro-
briand, the commanding officer, a detachment of one
hundred men to take Gall. This detachment set out at
once and reached Fort Berthold about 2 A.M. Getting
the lay of the camp, they quickly disposed themselves
so as to inclose the whole band of Indians. Larned,
who has already been mentioned, was clerk at the post
at the time, and says that he heard a commotion and
got up to see what it was all about. It was not light
enough to see distinctly, but by using his field glasses
he could see that the Indians were surrounded. He
could hear the interpreter repeating, "We have you
surrounded. No one will be hurt. Come out between
our lines. We want The-Man-Who-Goes-in-the-Middle." When informed of the tepee which Gall occupied some soldiers surrounded it. Gall, aroused from
his slumbers, came out of the door of his tent, whereupon one of the soldiers shot him in the side with a
revolver held not three feet from him. Gall immediately jumped back into his tent, took a knife and slit a
hole in the rear of the tent, thinking to make his escape.
A soldier who stood outside with his bayonet in readi-
ness pierced him. Gall wrenched himself free, and
scantily clad as he was escaped through the darkness
and commotion toward the river bank. As it was too

rough handling the soldiers had given him. Arnold says that on one
occasion he gave a "feast" to some Indians in order to get the privilege
of cutting wood on Indian lands to fill a contract with the steamboats.
Gall came to him and said: "You work hard to get a little property.
If you'll furnish me with ammunition I'll get you all the property
you want without work."

dark to take up his trail, orders were given to wait till daylight. Next day it was easy to follow his trail by blood stains from his freely-flowing wounds. The soldiers who had wounded him felt sure he would be found dead within a short distance. They followed his trail down to the river and across on the ice to the bottom beyond. Luckily for Gall, a snowstorm came up and obliterated his trail. The soldiers returned without him, convinced that his wounds would be fatal and caring little whether they found the body or not as long as he was out of their way. They felt that one so scantily clad as he would soon perish from the cold even aside from the wounds which were known to be severe.

But Gall did not die. Over a month later it was learned at Berthold that he had made his way to friends [5] after much suffering, and was still alive. The revolver ball had struck a rib, breaking it, and glanced around the body cavity on one side, while the bayonet thrust was likewise deflected on the other side. His wounds were severe but his rugged constitution pulled him through, even without white medical help. His wounds were received in the latter part of November, 1867, and his public appearance at the treaty was on July 2, 1868.

When Gall stepped out to speak he wore a long skin robe which draped over his body almost to the ground. His appearance was striking and his attitude one of a

[5] The medicine man Peter, or Padanegricka, treated Gall's wounds according to the Indian practice. His wounds would undoubtedly have proved fatal had they been received in the summer season. As it was, his iron constitution carried him through.

proud and independent spirit. He started out speaking slowly and distinctly. As he warmed up to his subject he became more impassioned; his robe dropped to the ground, leaving him dressed only in a breech clout of embroidered broadcloth and porcupine-decorated and beaded moccasins. He became the impersonation of defiance, of one wronged and dishonored. From one of the wounds in his side the blood trickled down his bare trunk; whether it had been opened for this dramatic occasion or whether it had never healed I do not know.

"I have been driven from one gulch to another, to the mountains and plains far from my home, by your soldiers," he cried. "I have been hunted and hounded and wounded by them. My wounds have not yet healed, and I am not ready to take you by the hand and call you friend. The 'Great Father' has never befriended me. I have never seen his hand extended to me in mercy."

A pause. Then the passionate voice swept on again: "Many of these men before me were at the treaty of Fort Laramie. The promises the 'Great Father' made to us there were utterly false. He told us one thing and did another. He told us that the land set aside for us would not be invaded by white people, that we would be unmolested. Did he keep his compact? Before the treaty was a year old the white people built roads and bridges across our best hunting lands, without our consent and in the face of our protests. Did the 'Great Father' stop his people from trespassing on our land? No!" — and the bitter contempt of the voice was withering, — "he sent soldiers to guard the roads and the people traveling on our trails. They were our enemies; they tried to annihilate us. They attacked us at Killdeer,[6] they destroyed our tents and our winter's food and our women and children starved. Do you call that mercy and kindness?"

He turned fiercely to General Harney. "You say that among all people some are good, some bad. It is so with us. But when one Indian is bad you punish all of us, even our helpless old men and women. If the Santees are bad you punish other tribes too. But if we kill a bad white man who molests us, we are hounded until we have paid with twenty lives for one. You say you do not hurt the good Indians; but with your soldiers no Indians are good, and no white men are bad."

With clenched hands at his breast he continued: "How would you like for some outside nation stronger than you to come into your land and take it for themselves, build forts and station soldiers? How would you like to see your women and children starve, your hunting lands swept clean, while the white man grew rich from your gold? Would you agree to this peaceably? No! But if *we* object," — and all the tragedy of a conquered nation was in his voice, — "your soldiers pierce us with their bayonets, shoot us with their guns, and take our possessions for their own.

"Your hands are red with blood." His arm swept out. "You see the bleeding wounds on my breast. I

[6] The battle at Killdeer Mountain, or Tah-ka-ho-kuty, was fought on July 28, 1864, about twelve miles west of the present village of Killdeer in Dunn county, North Dakota.

cannot shake hands with you until they are healed. Not until this fort is burned down and I can see my footprint in the dead ashes will I believe what you say. Not until the wounds I carry are healed, the lands that belong to us restored, will I sign a treaty with you."

He stood tense for a moment, a bold, defiant figure with head up-flung; then, "You ask, 'Where are your lands,' and I answer you," with a sudden indescribably pathetic gesture, his bare arms swept out, "I answer you, 'Our lands are wherever our dead lie buried'."

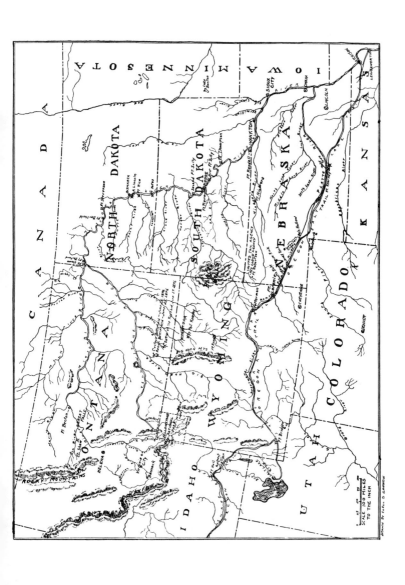

SCALE 100 MILES
TO THE INCH

DRAWN BY CLEM G. GANNON

An Attack on a Train
From an old drawing

OLD FORT RICE

Present site of old Fort Rice, now a State Park under control of the
North Dakota State Historical Society. Photo by Russell Reid

AN ORIGINAL RED RIVER CART

made in 1848. Owned by the North Dakota State Historical Society.
These carts were made without nails or other metal. In the back-
ground is the Roosevelt Cabin on Capitol grounds at Bismarck.
Photo by Russell Reid

INDIAN OUTFITS ASSEMBLED ON RATION DAY
From an old photograph taken at the Standing Rock Agency

INDIAN WOMEN WAITING FOR BEEF ISSUE

From an old photograph taken at the Standing Rock Agency

FOUR OF THE FIRST PARTY TO VISIT THE BLACK HILLS
FROM BISMARCK, NORTH DAKOTA, IN 1875
(1) H. N. Ross, (2) Dick Stone, (3) Harvey Carhoof, (4) Jack
Cale. From an old photograph — the original of which is in the
North Dakota State Historical Society

CHEYENNE FAMILY AND TRAVOIS

From photograph of L. A. Huffman, taken in Tongue River in 1879

INDIAN DELEGATION FROM STANDING ROCK AGENCY IN WASHINGTON, D.C., IN 1888

(1) Louis Primeau, Interpreter, (2) High Eagle, (3) Stephen Two Bears, (4) Big Head, (5) Gall, (6) John Grass, (7) Fire Heart, (8) High Bear, (9) Thunder Hawk, (10) Bear's Rib, (11) Hairy Chin, (12) Black Prairie Dog, (13) Gray Eagle. Mad Bear and Sitting Bull are missing from the group; the former because ill, the latter refused to be photographed

Grave of Interpreter Louis Primeau, Catholic Cemetery, Fort Yates

Graves of some of the Indian Police killed in the Sitting Bull "Uprising," December 15, 1890, on Grand River; Burial in Catholic Cemetery, Fort Yates

SITTING BULL'S GRAVE, FORT YATES

The Sioux Buried in Trees till the Middle 70's, when the
Practice was Discontinued under Pressure

CHAPTER XX

DISTANT PROSPECTS — DISILLUSIONMENT

A NUMBER of other impressive addresses were made, but another that was especially significant was that of Running Antelope. His face is familiar to us as it adorns the old five-dollar Treasury notes. Running Antelope was a more polished orator than Gall but not so masterful in leadership; more ornate and conciliatory but less rugged and fearless. Louis Primeau, interpreter, Jim Gayton, representing the Indians, and Goose all heard Antelope's speech and afterwards vouched for the truth of it.

Said Running Antelope: "The Black Robe [priest] tells us that many winters ago a good man came from Heaven. He was white. But the white people got so bad that this good man had to send his own son among them. But they fell upon him and killed him. White people did this. I don't have faith in white people any more."

While both Gall and Running Antelope talked much against signing the treaty, they were persuaded to sign.[1] The treaty commissioners almost put the chiefs and headmen under duress by the display of presents which were bought to be given to those who signed the treaty.

[1] Gall's name heads the list of the signers to the treaty and appears as Co-kam-i-ya-ya, The-Man-that-Goes-in-the-Middle.

This may serve to explain why Gall signed. Of all the chiefs, Sitting Bull was the most consistent; he never signed anything. He always stayed away and kept himself free from temptation.

After the treaty of 1868 had been signed at Fort Rice, a number of leading Indians who had not signed were called into Washington. Nick Janisse, who went along as an interpreter, told me on his return especially of a speech made by Tall Mandan, a Teton Sioux chief. He was asked by one of the congressmen what he thought of things in the east, and replied:

"My friend, you ask me what I think of your country. You live in good houses. You have large buildings and many railroads. Your men have skill to do many things the Indian does not understand. But as I walk through your streets I see many that are blind standing on the corners of the streets with their uplifted palms begging for help. In the same streets I see women and men in costly carriages, dressed in fine clothes, sparkling with costly ornaments; I see barefooted children in the rain and sleet, all in rags; I see men, some with an arm off, some with a leg off, some blind, all begging. My friends, I do not understand this. These men must have fought for the 'Great Father,' and yet they are begging. Some of these children are orphans, some have no homes. In our lodges the old and helpless are always singing the praises of those who unload the meat of the day's hunt at their door.

"How can you expect me to believe that you would take care of our people when you do not even take care of your own blind and crippled? I have seen the needy

and those who have plenty side by side. I do not believe your people will care for us any better than you
do for your own. That is all I have to say."

When the treaty was consummated at Fort Rice,
General Harney was temporarily assigned to govern
the great reservation including the combined Sioux
tribes, for it was the intention at that time to have a
governor, council, courts, and civil officers over the
Indians. But the patronage of the Indian Bureau was
too strong to permit this type of organization, and poli-
tics did not permit Harney to remain long. Harney,
however, selected a place for his buildings on the east
side of the river fourteen miles below new Fort Sully,
called Peoria Bottoms, where he had wintered in 1855-
56 after his Ash Hollow engagement.

Maj. E. B. Grimes was stationed at this place. I
applied for and received the contract for getting out
the logs and hewing them to build headquarters and
post buildings. We put up a large kitchen and dining
room and suitable barracks for men and officers. The
contract was finished in the fall, but we received no pay
until the following July. Then General Harney paid
workmen for cutting, teamsters for hauling logs, and
myself out of his own personal funds, as the appropriation for the treaty had all been used up. The larger
part was doubtless paid for the boat chartered to bring
the commissioners up the river and to take them back.

Only about six years after the impressive treaty at
Fort Rice, the government by its own orders sent two
separate expeditions to the Black Hills to determine if
gold, of which wild rumors were afloat, was to be

found in paying quantities. In keeping with the provisions of the treaty, however, the forts along the Bozeman and the Bridger trails were destroyed. The government tried to keep the white gold-seekers out of the Hills. In keeping with the terms of the treaty, orders were issued to turn back or drive out all who attempted to enter the Hills region. In one case the military burned up a number of wagons loaded with supplies, because the occupants refused to turn back.[2]

But when the stampede set in, the whole U. S. Army would have been insufficient to keep people out. There were thousands of settlers in the Hills region by 1876, while the treaty modified to recognize existing facts was not confirmed until the spring of 1877.[3] But this is getting ahead of my story.

In 1869 an Indian named Burnt Face came to me and said he wanted to plant some corn on the west side of the river nearly opposite Peoria Bottoms. Major Randall, who was agent at the Cheyenne Agency, told Burnt Face that if he could get some one to do the plowing, he would furnish the oxen and plow to do the work. I agreed to help. James Pearman drove the oxen and I held the plow. A crowd of curious Indians hung around all day to watch the operation. This, I think, was the first furrow ever plowed west of the river in South Dakota.

When I had finished this work I received a letter

[2] The Gordon and Witcher party. Gordon the leader was placed under military surveillance.

[3] The treaty relinquishing the Black Hills was approved by the U. S. Senate and became a law Feb. 28, 1877. — *U. S. Statutes at Large,* xix, 254.

from General Stanley of Fort Sully telling me to come in, as he wanted to see me. I reported to him at once at Fort Sully. He wanted me to act as guide for an escort of soldiers who were to be sent to Lake Benton, Minnesota, to bring back some beef cattle for the post.

"Can you be the guide?" he asked me.

I told him I had never been in that part of the country.

"Well, I'm sure you can do it," he said. "You speak Sioux, and I'll send two Indians with you who know the way. You can take this map of the trail and I think you'll get through well enough."

Under those circumstances I told him I would go.

"Be ready to start in the morning," he said. "Black Tomahawk and Tall Lance will go with you."

I reported as requested the next morning, and we set out on our journey. The escort consisted of two companies of infantry with an ambulance drawn by mules. The two Indians rode their own horses, as I did. We took a southeast direction and celebrated the Fourth of July at a point on James River east of where Wessington Springs, South Dakota, is now located.

The soldiers, unused to traveling on foot, were so tired and footsore that they came straggling into camp at all hours of the night, although we covered only about twenty-four miles a day. The inability of many of them to keep up led to a conference at which it was decided to leave the escort on the James River and to push on to Lake Benton with only Captain Collins, the commander, a lieutenant, the ambulance driver, the two Indians and myself in the company. We continued at an increased speed to the Big Sioux River, where we met those having our cattle in charge. They had become impatient at our delay and had started westward to meet us, so this time we did not get to Lake Benton.

In returning we changed our route somewhat, as the cattle were to be delivered to the Cheyenne Agency. We crossed the James River at a point higher than we did on going. For some distance along the river only sand dunes covered with scrubby cedar were visible.

After we had turned over the beef herd at the agency, I continued on down the river to Fort Sully. Here I was informed that my wife and the Indians left with her had heard that I had been killed by a war party of Indians from Canada who were making trouble about that time, and had returned to their people in western Wyoming. I was grieved to find Itatewin and my baby gone, but these were perilous times and I could not blame my wife for acting on the rumor that had come to her.

A few years later when I was again delivering beef cattle to the Cheyenne Agency, I learned that Itatewin was married to a man there named Charley McCarthy,[4] who at the time was running a trading store. I went as far as his gate and told him that I was Ben Arnold. I asked if I might take back with me my little daughter Marcella, who was then about five years old. Mc-Carthy, however, talked me out of it, saying that he was planning to move to Bismarck where the child

[4] Charles McCarthy is the father of Mrs. Josephine Waggoner, mentioned in the introduction.

could go to school. He had no children of his own at that time, and he knew that Itatewin would hate to give up the girl. McCarthy brought out Marcella and I held her in my arms for a while, then left Grand River Agency not to return for several years. I also saw Itatewin through the window. She saw and recognized me, but to avoid embarrassment I did not go in, nor did she come out.

About this time General Stanley, then stationed at Fort Sully, was ordered up the river to furnish a military reconnoissance for the surveyors of the Northern Pacific Railway in laying out the route westward. This expedition greatly incensed the Indians. The Union Pacific Railway had been completed at that date, much to the chagrin of the Sioux, and now another railway was projected through the heart of the game country still left to them. They were angered almost beyond control. The railroad survey had already reached Bismarck, on the Missouri River.

My first employment after leaving Grand River was with Colonel Denman of Leavenworth and Powers of Salina, who had a contract with the government to furnish beef for some of the Indian agencies. While General Stanley was away on his western trip up into Montana with the Northern Pacific Railway surveyors, I made another trip to Lake Benton after cattle, this time going the full distance. Lake Benton at that time had two settlers, one of them being named Taylor.

During the winter of 1869 and 1870 I worked at the Cheyenne Agency situated on the west side of the Missouri at the mouth of the Cheyenne. We built two block houses of round logs, in the towers of which were to be placed Gatling guns, just beginning to come into use, for the protection of the post. By the time we had finished the desired construction work around the post it was about spring time, and I decided to drive down to Yankton. On this trip I took three discharged soldiers with me, each of them contributing $35 for passage. This was very welcome, as money was scarce and hard to get.

By the terms of the treaty of 1868 a number of cattle herds were sent in to the agency, and it was not hard for one of my experience in taking care of cattle to get a job driving.

In the fall of 1872 Ed Monroe and I were induced to go to Mankato by the report that wages were good for chopping and hewing railroad ties. We left the Missouri River at Fort Thompson, went eastward, and struck the James River at a point known as the "Dirt Lodges." This place received its name from the earth lodges there which Stony Goose and his band had built. They used to go there every summer to raise a little corn and catch and dry fish for winter use. From Dirt Lodges we continued eastward over a long stretch of uninhabited country. The first settlers we encountered were at Lake Benton, Minnesota.

When we reached Mankato, in Blue Earth county, we were shown the spot where the scaffold on which the thirty-eight Sioux were hanged in 1862 had stood, although it was now removed.

Arrived at our destination, we now began to look for work at the princely wages we had been told about.

We finally got to work cutting cord wood from scattering timber on logged-over ground not far out of Mankato for the munificent pay of sixty cents a cord, and we had to pile our own brush too. Try as we might, we could chop only about a cord a day. What we were looking for was work with broad ax, but we couldn't get hewing work.

A rather laughable incident occurred when we were in Mankato. Lewis Hubbell, who was running for some sort of an office, hired us to help him out on election day. He gave us each $5.00, and sent us out with a supply of whiskey to get voters drunk, then bring them in to the polls with ballots marked for him. This, of course, was long before the Australian ballot system came into use. The pay we were getting from him was so much better than we could earn chopping wood that in our zeal to give value received we both voted in each of the two wards in Mankato. We had not been in that vicinity over ten days and of course were not entitled to vote at all. This is merely mentioned to show the laxness permitted in the frontier states in protecting the ballot box.

After we had been in Mankato for a little over a month we set out for Missouri, going through Owatonna, Minnesota, and Ottumwa, Iowa, to Kansas City. We got work at Parkville nearby cutting timber to be sawed and used in making the false bridging for the steel bridge across the Missouri which was to be erected in the following spring, in 1873.

We also worked a while at Cameron, Missouri, for a man named Jesse Reed, cutting cordwood at seventy-five cents a cord. We had· to board ourselves and furnish our own axes. The timber was all hardwood, and we had to go right at it to get a cord and a half each to our credit when night came.

Mr. Reed's home was a social center. He had two grown daughters, and in the neighborhood a play party was almost a nightly affair. The community was quite religious, and dancing was not indulged in; instead these play parties were frequent. We boarded at Reed's, but we had been so long away from the society of women that we were almost too embarrassed to eat what we wanted.

Our language was always very circumspect. One day Mrs. Reed asked, "Are all men out west like you? I haven't heard either of you speak a vulgar or profane word. I always heard that westerners were so rough."

We concealed our amusement until we had got to ourselves, and Ed snorted, "If she heard us some day down on the river when we were whaling away on a water elm, I'm afraid she'd believe that westerners *are* pretty rough."

The Reeds were fine people and our stay there was made pleasant by their kind hospitality.

CHAPTER XXI

Up with a Trail Herd

The Missouri, Kansas & Texas Railway was building toward Texas at this time, and we struck out for the Canadian River in what is now Oklahoma. We hired out to Charles Lefor, the contractor, to cut and peel red cedar logs for telegraph poles. The railroad at that time had reached the Canadian River at a point called Rocky Ford. The melting snows in the Wichita mountains had made this stream high, and we aimed to take advantage of the high water to float our poles down in rafts to the construction camp. We got a number of poles cut in the Creek Nation and started making up a raft by cribbing the poles and fastening them together. We had built it up almost to the desired height when in dropping it down the current to the place where we had more poles ready to put into it we struck a submerged sandbar. The raft broke in pieces, sending the poles in every direction. In some places the Canadian is ten feet deep, in others much shallower. Four of us were on the crib when we struck the sandbar, and we were all thrown sprawling into the water. Fortunately no one was hurt, but Ed Monroe was struck on the head by a log and dazed for a time; if I had not held his head out of the water until he came to, he would surely have drowned.[1] As it was, we all got to shore safely.

We were hired by the month, but the contractor had told us that he could not pay us until the poles had been delivered to the railway company and paid for. It had been our intention to connect eight or ten cribs of some two hundred logs each and float them down like a train of cars. But we were scared out on the rafting business, and, although getting nothing for the work we had done, we decided to give it up. We struck out for Texas but stopped at Boggy Depot on the north side of the Red. Here we met an Iowa outfit owned by three brothers, I think named Simon, who were on the road to Coffeyville, Kansas, where they expected to load and ship to Iowa a herd of cattle they had with them. We helped drive the cattle entirely across what is now Oklahoma to Coffeyville, then set out for Ellsworth, Kansas.

At Ellsworth I met my old friend Bosler whose outfit now had an Indian contract to fill, for which he had just bought two Texas herds from Major George of Abilene, to be delivered on the North Platte just below Scott's Bluffs. Ed Monroe took work with one herd and I with the other, and we set out on our journey north. Each herd had twenty-five hundred head of mixed steers and cows. Steers were worth more than cows in the market but in a case like this when the beef was turned in under contract by the pound, the more cows in a herd the more profitable for the contractor.

[1] Ed Monroe in speaking of this incident said: "Yes, I was knocked senseless into the water, and if it hadn't been for Arnold's help I would have been there yet."

In moving a herd a long distance, the aim is to handle it so that it puts on flesh every day. Cattle graze as they walk and a good herder will keep them grazing towards their destination and make them feel at ease and contented all the time. The herd always goes off the bed ground at daylight, and half their day's journey should be covered by ten o'clock. When possible they are put on water and allowed to rest until three or four when they begin to get hungry again and get up and move off, always northward, until seven or eight o'clock in the evening, when they are bedded.

A crew of ten or twelve men is required to drive a big herd. The trail boss gives all directions about camping places and the manner in which the herd is to be handled, and tells each man what part of the work he must do. The point man directs the course of the leaders and sees that they keep the direction he wants them to go, the others following the leaders. The wing riders keep up along the sides of the herd and see that the herd keeps stretched out and that none stops to block those behind. The drag men push up the tail enders, which are the weak, the crippled, and the footsore. The less experienced men are usually given this work, which is the most disagreeable and the most wearying. The dust is usually bad, often stifling, and the footsore try one's patience by their toilsome and painful plodding and their desire to drop out and lie down at frequent intervals. A drag puncher always welcomes a promotion to some other position on the line.

Then in addition to these, there are the horse wrangler who has charge of the band of saddle horses, usually some seventy-five in number; and the night herder or night hawk who watches the horses at night to keep them from scattering or being driven off by some one who might be in need of them. During the daytime the night herder rides in the bed wagon and gets such sleep as the rocking of the wagon permits.

The cook is an important part of the organization. He always drives a wagon containing provisions, fuel, and such things. When, as is often the case, there are two wagons, one carries the tents, bed rolls, extra rope, bridles, cinches, etc., while the other takes only the provisions. It must be remembered that towns are far apart and repair material and extras must be carried along. Then, of course, camp stoves, candles, lanterns, picket ropes, rope corrals, chaps, and slickers, and change of clothing for the men must be carried also.

In our outfit each of the wagons was drawn by four horses. When the boss directed a certain point for a dinner place, the wagons pulled out ahead. Thus when the herd got in, the riders found a meal ready and the rope corral up to hold the horse herd for a change of horses. Riders always change horses twice a day and want each horse ridden only at wide enough intervals to keep him springy and active. A wornout, logy horse wears on the spirits and temper of a cowboy much more than long hours or poor food.

We always tried to make fourteen or fifteen miles a day and we made and broke camp regardless of the weather. The herders took turns standing guard, each keeping a gentle stake horse picketed close at hand to use in case a thunderstorm or stampede required the whole force to be called out at night time. The days were not so monotonous as one might think. While not always arduous, they were always long, and when a cowboy reached the end of his journey he felt as if he could not get enough sleep. Laughable incidents come up almost daily to break the usual routine, and among the boys is a sort of camaraderie that welcomes one who is whole-souled and unselfish and despises one who is petty and a shirker. On the trail one's short-comings soon find him out, and the boss isn't long in firing the man who doesn't do his share. An inexperienced man of the right spirit could always get help from everybody.

After some thirty days on the road we reached Fort Kearney, guarded by a sergeant and a few privates, and followed the old Oregon Trail on the south side of the Platte up to the forks. Here we crossed and went up North Fork. Fort McPherson was built just below the forks on the south side, but it had no garrison except a few soldiers. We continued up on the south side of the North Platte until we had passed Scott's Bluffs, then crossed over to the north side and continued up the old Mormon Trail to Trout Slough, about fifty miles east of Fort Laramie. Here we held the cattle on good grass until fall.

These cattle were to be used by the Red Cloud Agency on the North Platte and the Spotted Tail Agency on the White River, where the city of Crawford, Nebraska, now stands. Beginning in the fall, we delivered about three hundred and fifty beef cattle every two weeks to the Red Cloud Agency, and four hundred to the Spotted Tail. At times of distribution every chief or subchief was called up and told by the interpreter how many cattle he was to have. He and his followers would then cut them out of the herd and chase and kill them on the open prairies as they would a band of buffaloes. The hides and tongues were usually sold to the trading post, where they were salted down and sold in the east — the tongue of course being sold as buffalo tongue.

There used to be a butcher at Ogallala named Louis Oftengartner, usually called German Louis, who always carried a large amount of dried meat, some cut into large pieces, some into small. The early trains which went through there in 1872 and thereabouts always stopped for some time, and Louie would sell them buffalo, elk, deer, or antelope meat — all off the same piece, and cut from a Texas steer. His business in season was thriving.

Our herd foreman got $150 a month and the men received $50. We established a herder's camp and the work was easy and delightful. We took turns going over to the agencies and visiting around with the agency employees and the Indians. In this manner I became acquainted with Red Cloud, Crazy Horse, American Horse, Man-Afraid-of-His-Horses, Spotted Tail, Crow Dog, and many other famous chiefs. I spoke Sioux and enjoyed hearing them tell of their exploits. I often wrote letters for Crow Dog, who afterwards killed Spotted Tail.

When issue day came round, the agent would come out to our camp and tell us how many head he would need. We would then cut the number desired and drive them in. In those days they had no scales, and sometimes the contractor through some sort of influence was able to turn little Texas cows weighing about six hundred pounds into the agency at a thousand pounds. A few years afterwards when the Indians learned that the government was paying for more beef than they were getting, a howl was set up that led to the weighing of a few average head and estimating the herd at this average. Even then with a dishonest agent a few of the largest cattle could be brought in and averaged and the whole herd, many of them small ones, settled for at the average of the largest. This allowed a steal of about two hundred pounds a head.

Finally the government bought scales and required that all cattle be weighed, regardless of how difficult it was to get these wild animals into a scale pen. But the contractors were equal to the occasion. One time a friend and myself were given $50 to crawl down into the scale pit, take off a few nuts and let some of the scale beams down, thereby disabling the scales. The cattle then had to be estimated, and I presume the contractor made a profit on the transaction. Our part in it was not honorable, but I am giving you a true history and do not feel that I should withhold facts just because they may bear rather harshly on me. It seemed no more wrong to us to help the boss make a big profit on his cattle transactions by such means than it was to sell the Indians beads, blankets, and knives for many times what they cost, or pay them only two dollars for a beaver skin or buffalo robe worth three or four times the amount.

Down at Standing Rock Agency at Fort Yates one time the agent sent a young man, Lieutenant Chance, out to weigh up the issue cattle. After a scale full had been driven onto the platform, the lieutenant started to adjust the weights on the beams so as to get the correct weight. This lieutenant was a sort of dressy fellow and wore white gloves. Shortly he noticed black paint on his gloves. His curiosity and suspicion aroused, he began to look around to see where the paint came from, and wasn't long in finding out. Some industrious fellow had bored out the weights, filled the top of the hole with a cork and painted it over. The weight of the iron removed from the weights naturally made the cattle appear to weigh much more than they actually did. Quite a furor was raised when the discovery was made. But the poor Indian had to have beef. He couldn't wait, and the honest agent couldn't watch all the tricks of the men he had to deal with. Yet the protection of the dishonest man was the fact that all, or nearly all, the white men were making something above a legitimate profit. Most of them were tarred with the same stick, and every one made what he could and kept quiet about the other fellow. The blacksmith and several others at the agency left suddenly after Lieutenant Chance had made his discovery and never returned.

The Bosler Brothers had a strong combination for competing contractors to go against: Jim Bosler stayed in Washington and pulled the wires; Hiram was the middle man and did the buying in the south; and George stayed around the agencies and in the camps to make settlement on issue day.

A rule of the departments at Washington required that substantially all purchases be made by bids. On general principles this is probably the fairest method that can be devised, yet it is the most expensive also, as a rule. In awarding contracts for cattle to be supplied to the Indians, the matter was often handled so as to give a big opportunity for profit. Suppose the number of cattle called for at a given agency was 2,500 head. Only a few companies were prepared to bid on so large a contract or were equipped to handle it. Fifteen or twenty other bids were called for, for possibly equal or lesser amounts. All the bidders in sight might then agree in advance to divide up the business on an agreed basis regardless of who got it. The bids could then be put in at a high figure. Of course the government authorities had the right to reject all bids and call for new ones; but in practice it was rarely done. No one wanted to brook the vengeance of a hungry Indian, and the distance from Texas where the cattle were grown was so great that a contract had to be let at once in order to enable the trail-herds to be delivered to the Indians by the time their beef supply was exhausted. The more stringent the government is in its regulations, the fewer the bidders. We sometimes condemn red tape; but public officers, in order to avoid the appearance of evil, must protect themselves by it. And the people pay the bill, either of too much red tape or too much graft. In business matters governments are not efficient.

The first general contract to supply beef to the Indians that I recall was held by Oldham & Wheeler. Bosler Brothers held the contracts for several years following Oldham & Wheeler, and Jack Morrow and William Paxton attended to the deliveries on the Missouri for them. George Bosler told me that they paid Morrow and Paxton each a thousand a month, and from the way they handled the herds they were worth it.

Morrow, whom I first met at Doby Town in 1863, had a ranch of his own at Cottonwood Canyon on the South Platte. He had a reputation for being a notorious gambler and a sort of all-round bad man. In his earlier days he had been a freighter on the plains, and he had grown up from the ranks through all grades of deviltry. His ranch was the holdout for rough characters. He had likeable qualities, was energetic and forceful, and his word was law. Among those who worked for him any slackness in obeying might bring dire consequences.

In the summer of 1872 when the Boslers had turned in to the Missouri agencies beef believed to be sufficient to carry their contracts through, they had four or five hundred left over and this overplus was started to LeMars, Iowa, the closest shipping point, to be consigned to the Chicago market. After the cattle had been gone almost long enough to reach LeMars, it was found that more beef would be required at the agencies than had at first been estimated by the government authorities. It was too late in the season to get a herd from the south, and there was no other known place near enough at hand where beef could be supplied except from the herd that had started to market.

Paxton came to me and asked me to make the ride to LeMars to head off the herd and have it brought back, and I consented. While he was writing out a general order on all road ranches to supply me with changes of saddle horses as required, I got ready to make the desperate ride. The order was signed by Paxton & Morrow, and as they were well known throughout the northwest, everywhere I asked for a fresh horse I got it. Good riding horses could be had wherever there were people, since a horse was the only method of rapid transportation.

As I swung into the saddle Paxton waved me goodby and said, "Hit only the high places and kill every horse you get on." I don't know whether I killed any horses or not, but I do know that I got the last jump out of several. I rode for thirty-six hours, stopping only long enough to bolt a little food occasionally and make the necessary change of horses. Nor did I reach LeMars any too soon. In another half day the cattle would have been loaded and gone. The distance covered was over three hundred miles, and I consider the speed with which I covered it quite remarkable considering the fact that the roadhouses were not expecting me and there was some delay in the night time waking up the proprietors, explaining my mission, and getting a suitable fresh horse.

CHAPTER XXII

LIFE AS A COWBOY AROUND THE AGENCIES

THE FIRST cattle brought to the northwestern territories from Texas were driven in to fill contracts entered into with the government in supplying beef to
the various Indian agencies. Cattle ranching in the
northern territories had not started at that time.

The old Chisholm Trail was as familiar to the people then as any one of the transcontinental railways is
today. All herds from the South passed over at least a
portion of this trail. The origin of many of the trail
herds was in the vicinity of Austin and Fort Worth,
the trail coming northward through the Indian Territory, now Oklahoma, thence through Caldwell, Fort
Dodge, Abilene, Wichita, or Newton, thence to Ogalalla on the Platte, and then westward into Wyoming or
northward into Dakota Territory. At Ogalalla the
herds were usually divided into small bands and delivered where needed.

One year I helped drive up eighteen hundred head of
cattle in one band and in the following year helped
bring up a drove of three thousand head. In the main
the cattle brought over the trail were steers, but occasionally cows were included also. One time Ed Monroe
and I were on the trail driving a mixed bunch to Wyoming for Jack Morrow, the foreman for Bosler Bros.

It was the spring of the year and we encountered much drizzle and cold rain. The cows were thin, and calves were dropping daily. They gave us a lot of trouble as they always became part of the drags that had to be punched up. I proposed to Ed that we drive along slowly and favor the calves until we reached Nick Janisse's place near Fort Laramie where we could cut them out and give them to Nick, enabling us to travel much faster thereafter. When we got to Janisse's place we had about eighty calves with the herd, but when I told him what we intended to do, he objected for the reason that the calves were not ours to give. All our persuasion could not make him take a single calf, and we were obliged to drive them along with the herd. In one way the calves were not ours to give away, but on the trail they were liabilities rather than assets. Their value was not equal to the loss occasioned by their delaying our progress and wearing out our saddle horses.

Among the calves was one little white one whose pitiful condition especially appealed to me. It was too footsore to keep up, and its mother, being much devoted to it, kept coming back from the herd in response to its bawling. When she went back other cows would usually go with her, which wore out our horses and exasperated us. Consequently I told Ed I was going to kill the calf, and not having any shells handy, cut its throat with my knife. The knife was dull which prevented my doing a good job, and it got up and followed us. Though bleeding profusely and its white coat covered with blood it staggered along until it fell from weakness. This, I think, is the cruelest deed I ever committed and one which I cannot even now think about with approval.

In coming up through western Kansas after some of the dry years, we could see abandoned claims, with shacks for the most part carried away by the wind or by some enterprising neighbor. Small patches of weeds marked the places where the land had been under cultivation. Most of the homesteaders' shacks were built of sod. One of them bore the following significant legend scrawled on a board:

> "250 feet to water
> 50 miles to wood
> 6 inches to hell
> God Bless our Home."

We wore buckskin suits which, when soaked by the rain, stretched until they were all out of shape. As my pant legs lengthened I rolled them up from the bottom and suggested to Ed that he do the same, as his were hanging limp and baggy about his feet. But instead of rolling them up, he pulled out his knife and cut off about a foot at the bottom of each leg. That night after bedding the cattle down, we made a wickie-up, built a fire, and dried our clothes. In the morning Ed's pants were so shrunken that they quit above his knees and in that striking garb he had to ride all the way to the Ogalalla Agency.

Just before we reached the agency we met a band of half-starved Indians who wanted us to turn over some of the beeves to them, which we had no right to do and so told them. We kept on our way, but heedless of our protests they rode into the herd and shot down seventeen head before they quit. They then insolently told us to report them to the agent if we wanted to, as they were only getting the cattle which belonged to them a little ahead of time. We got paid for the cattle, but I don't know whether anything was ever done about their fore-handed way of taking them or not.

One time we were sent to make a delivery of a herd of eighteen hundred head of cattle to the Grand River Agency for Bosler Bros. Capt. William Harmon was then Indian agent there. We swam the cattle across the Missouri River near the mouth of the Niobrara, as was the custom, and took them up on the east side of the Missouri where the going was easier and considered safer. When we were about half-way between Yankton and Mitchell, four hundred head of the best beeves were cut out and sent on down to Sioux City to be sold for Morrow's account, so it was said. When we arrived opposite Grand River, Captain Harmon came over to receive the cattle. He asked, "Are there eighteen hundred cattle here?" "O yes," said Jack, "You and I can count them."

The corral was not large enough to hold all the cattle at once and the herd was cut into several bands; part were driven into the corrals and put through the chutes at a time. When about half the cattle had gone through the chutes, Morrow sent some of his cowboys out to pick up about four hundred head of steers that had already gone through the chutes and tack them on to the rear of the herd yet to be tallied. With insuffi-

cient help and inadequate facilities for handling large
bands of cattle, tricks like this were often worked,
sometimes in collusion with the agent or someone under his employ. As a general rule, however, agents
tried to be honest, and no one ever accused Captain
Harmon of being other than honest in the discharge of
his duties. Morrow was just too slippery for him.

That evening I asked Monroe if he knew we had
counted about four hundred head of the cattle twice
and he said, yes. After the herd was counted and settled for, it was placed in the hands of Ed Donahue to
herd. The next morning when he stretched the cattle
out to graze and got a rough count on them he discovered his shortage. He was much excited over the
loss as he thought the Indians had driven off part of his
cattle during the night. Riders were out all day looking for the lost cattle, but it is needless to say they
found no trace of them.

The question comes up, who profited by the transaction? Morrow's employers who started eighteen
hundred head of cattle to fill this contract thought they
were furnishing all they were expected to furnish;
the government paid for the full number and thought
it was getting them; the herder blamed the Indians for
the theft of four hundred head; the agent blamed the
herder for losing them; and the Indian protested that
the Great Father was deliberately trying to rob him of
his treaty rights. Many of the Indian depredations
were due to the Indians' belief that the Great Father
was making no effort to live up to his treaty obligations; and the Great Father, believing the Indians'

complaints to be unfounded, treated them as malcontents and savages. "Bad" white men did more to originate the Indian question and render its solution difficult than either the parsimony or neglect of Congress or the wickedness of the Indian.

On one occasion a touching incident happened when we were delivering an issue of beef to the Indians, Ed Monroe, Ed Donahue, and I being among the herders. Grand River Agency stood west of the Missouri and between the mouths of Grand River and Oak Creek, which empty into the Missouri from the west side just opposite to the south end of Ashley Island. The beef was always crossed over in the vicinity of Yankton and brought up on the east side of the Missouri River. When we arrived with the herd the water was high, but the Indians had run out of meat and were hungry and ill-tempered; the herd must be got across if possible. The Missouri is always treacherous when high, and at this time the June rise was just about at its crest. The current bore many drifting logs which carried danger to anything which attempted to cross.

It is impossible to make cattle swim even in still water unless they can see the further shore. In swift water, even though they see the shore and take the water well, the current deflects them from their course. So it was in this case. When the leaders struck the current made more angry by the strong north wind, they were swung around and pushed back to the shore they had just left. Only the extreme need of the Indians led us to make this attempt to get the cattle over. We did not even stop with one failure but literally shoved the herd in a second time with no better results.

The Indians congregated at the agency were hungry; many of them had come in many miles from their homes to get their beef issue and had been waiting around several days with scant rations for the herd to arrive. Now, with the beef in sight, the high winds and high waters prevented their getting it. Finally the commanding officer who was Indian agent at the time arranged for a number of Indians to go across on flat boats to kill some of the beeves and bring over the meat to the hungry people lining the west bank. Each boat was in charge of a farmer, usually a white man, sent out by the government to teach the Indians to raise crops and live stock. Both Indian men and women came over in the boats. As is customary, the women did the butchering and dressed the meat, thereby being in position to save the hide, horns, and such other parts of the animals useful for clothing, implements, or adornment.

Some eighteen or twenty beeves were killed and the meat put on the flat boats preparatory to carrying it over to the expectant multitude who had already made camp fires and had pots boiling. The men, women, and beef rather overloaded the boats, and one of the farmers named John Hardy remained ashore to take the last boat after the others had been successfully launched. Hardy had been shooting beeves and wore a large leather belt partly filled with cartridges, and also wore the usual high-topped boots. His boat was so heavily loaded that when it reached the current the load and the wind were too much for it and it capsized, turning passengers and beef into the swirling torrent. Some of the passengers swam out but three or four were drowned, including Hardy himself. He was a good swimmer but the weight of his belt of cartridges and his boots pulled him down almost immediately.

Hardy had a large, well-trained bird dog that was his constant companion, which was on the boat with him when it capsized. The dog saw his master go down and time after time dived his head under the water, as if to see what had become of him. The dog swam around in a circle, barking and seemingly entreating for help. All the calling, whistling, and coaxing from the shore did not avail to bring the dog out. Although at the very moment his dead master lay many rods down stream in the muddy depths of the river, the dog refused to believe he was not where he went down, and continued to swim in circles. He moved slower and slower until his yelps gave way to piteous howls and then to almost inaudible moans. From the shore there was a dismal wailing of the families of those that had drowned, but no sound was more piteous than the feeble whine of the exhausted dog as he gradually sank beneath the water. He had been a constant companion to his master in life, and in death they were not divided.

Charles McCarthy, who had a wood contract lower down the river, and some of his workmen found the body of Hardy on a sandbar, near Ashley Island, to which place they carried it on a blanket, and gave it burial.

CHAPTER XXIII

TROUBLE BREWING IN THE BLACK HILLS

THE cowboys of the early seventies covered a great deal of country. They were on the road most of the time, especially during the summer season.

In the fall of 1872 we had been holding a herd for Bosler Brothers and making deliveries from time to time to the Red Cloud and Spotted Tail agencies. About November 1 word came from the Indian Department at Washington that we should furnish four hundred head of beeves to the Wind River Agency in western Wyoming. As the season for moving cattle had almost passed we lost no time in cutting out four hundred head of the best beeves and heading them westward up the North Platte. Our trail led us over much country familiar to me since 1863. The route led up the North Platte to the place where Fort Fetterman, a garrisoned post, then stood. Our best road from there would have been across the river and up the north side, but the garrison was unable to give us an escort, and without an escort prudence dictated that we keep on the south side. We continued westward or slightly south by west across Laramie Plains and up the Sweetwater (one of the head branches of the North Platte), up to South Pass City where we crossed the Rocky Mountains, and thence north into the Wind River Valley.

South Pass City consisted of only a few buildings, the people all having left. There were several mining camps up the Sweetwater. A few of them, Camp Stambaugh, Camp Brown, and Miners' Delight, which made up, I think, what was known as the Sweetwater group, were located well at the head of the stream. Some gold had been taken out, but the mines didn't amount to much. The high divide which we had to cross between South Pass City and Wind River was covered with deep snow which we wallowed through up to the breasts of our horses. We had to abandon our wagon and carry our provisions on an improvised horse pack-train. But when we finally reached the Wind River Valley we found ourselves in an entirely different world. The climate was summery, and the Snake Indians, who did a good deal of farming, had not yet dug their potatoes.

After we had made the delivery we set out on horseback with a pack-horse outfit on our return journey. We left our wagon stuck in the deep snow and came down the Sweetwater, this time keeping on the north side of the North Platte to Red Cloud Agency. During our absence George Bosler had had the cattle herds moved to the breaks on the Niobrara for winter quarters. A beef issue continued to be made every two weeks until February 1, 1873, when the cattle were all gone.

An Indian out of beef is hungry, and a hungry Indian is an ugly one. An undercurrent of discontent was growing among the Indians. Financial conditions were hard, and Congress was slow to make an appropriation to buy beef. The Indians were entirely without a beef issue at one time for a period of over thirty days until finally Congress passed a measure of relief. Jim Bosler came out from Washington with the word that an emergency appropriation had been passed to buy 3,000,000 pounds of beef on the hoof. Bosler then sent out several of the boys to buy cattle to fill this contract. The first herd, a mixed one numbering 1,600, was bought at Goshen's Hole in Colorado on a tributary to Horse Creek, from a man named Lane. We drove these down to the agency and turned them over to herders on the North Platte, north of Ogalalla. We also bought a herd from Jim Boyd of Omaha, who had a cattle ranch in Nebraska. These odd bands of cattle took care of the Indians' needs until the next regular contract was let.

Ed Monroe and I continued with the outfit until the early spring of 1873 when we quit them on Kiowa Creek. We went down to Cheyenne to take the Union Pacific for Omaha, from which point we expected to go north and get work with the Northern Pacific surveying crew which we had heard was going west of Bismarck the following spring to look up the route for the railroad extension. At Omaha we bought saddle horses and started horseback to Yankton, South Dakato, where we hoped to fall in with Gen. Geo. A. Custer's command, which we understood was to furnish the escort for the railroad surveyors. On our way we got caught in a terrible blizzard and did not reach

Yankton until after Custer had gone, but we followed on up the river after him. We concluded not to try to catch up with Custer but to take work at once. Ed stopped at Fort Sully and I went on up to Grand River and got work with a beef herd. I stayed with this outfit until December when the last of the cattle were killed, frozen, and stored for winter use. During the winter Ed and I cut cord wood on Okoboje Island for Jim Webb of St. Paul, who had the contract that year for supplying Fort Sully with wood. Most of the wood cutters at this place were Bohemians and Norwegians, but Ed Whitney and William Jones did the hauling.

In the spring of 1874, Ed and I went down on the Niobrara horseback and in June joined Walker & Johnson, a cow outfit from the South, who had been making a delivery on the Niobrara. We went with them to the Platte and up that stream to Paxton's ranch on the North Platte opposite Ogalalla. Ed worked for Paxton's and I went over and began work with the Bosler outfit, again delivering contract beef to the Indian agencies.

Shortly afterwards when it looked as if the Black Hills would be opened soon, I went over and started a road ranch on the Running Water, the headwaters of the Niobrara between Sidney and the Hills.

Gen. George A. Custer, who was in command at Fort Abraham Lincoln three miles below Bismarck on the opposite side of the river, was sent on an exploring expedition to the Black Hills in the summer of 1874. Charley Reynolds, better known as Silent Charley, accompanied him as scout and carried the message from

the Hills to the nearest telegraph station at Fort Laramie which gave the sensational "gold in the grass
roots" story to the public. The next day all the daily
papers in the United States gave the news of the discovery of gold and a stampede set in at once, in violation of the treaty with the Sioux. The fabled stories
of gold being found in the grass roots inflamed all with
their golden promise. General Custer was ordered into
Washington, and some knowing ones hinted that he
was to be reprimanded for making the expedition without orders to do so. The treaty with the Indians for-
bade any white man's going into the Hills, and since
the government itself was violating the treaty it dared
not advertise the expedition as having its approval.

Crowds of people from all over the country pushed
up as near as they could get to the Black Hills and
clamored loudly that the treaty be modified to allow
prospective gold seekers and settlers to go in. The
greatest excitement prevailed in the towns nearest the
Black Hills — Sidney, Nebraska; Cheyenne, Wyoming, and Yankton and Bismarck, Dakota, were soon
filled with floaters awaiting an opportunity to get into
the gold region either with or without a modification
of the treaty. The towns were so crowded that in some
of the hotels lodgers even paid two dollars for the
privilege of sleeping on the floor.

The government tried in good faith to keep the people out. But notwithstanding the vigilance of the soldiers, the Collins and Russell party under Witcher and
Gordon, from Sioux City, and consisting of twenty-six
men, one woman, and a boy, entered the Black Hills in

the latter part of December, 1874, with a loss of two of their number, and settled on French Creek. The party was discovered by a detail under Captain Mix in the following March and taken to Fort Laramie by Captain Henry's command. Gordon and Witcher, two of the members of the party, took samples of gold back to Sioux City with them, with which they purchased supplies to take back to the Hills; but they were intercepted on the Niobrara by the military and their loaded wagons burned. This party in coming into the Black Hills had completely eluded the guards, and had not one of Red Cloud's scouts seen the miners living in dugouts and temporary shacks on French Creek and reported the fact to Red Cloud Agency, they might have remained unmolested until spring.

The Indians were growing more restless and even hostile as the whites became more aggressive; so much so, in fact, that it was necessary for General Crook to recall and concentrate troops, now patroling the entrances to the Hills, in a vain effort to maintain the treaty rights of the Indians. As soon as the scattered military detachments were withdrawn, the horde of people anxiously waiting around the border poured in without let or hindrance.

The government had already sent Custer from Fort Lincoln; now it also sent a scientific expedition from Fort Laramie, Professor Jenny being the leading man, to gather such geological and geographical information as was possible. While there he built a structure known afterwards as the Jenny Stockade, which he marked by a suitable monument and used as a base for his scientific observations. I have often camped on this spot.

In the spring of 1875, when all this excitement was rife, I was, as I have mentioned before, running a road ranch at Running Water on the mail route between Cheyenne, Wyoming, and the Red Cloud Agency in Nebraska and Fort Randall on the Missouri River in Dakota. There was a good river crossing at this point and I had an opportunity to see all who passed and get the news. I saw the Collins-Russell party as they were being conducted out of the Hills by Capt. Guy V. Henry's military escort.

As soon as Captain Henry had returned to Fort Laramie he was instrumental in getting a council with the Indians called to meet at Fort Robinson near the Red Cloud Agency. W. B. Allison, a long-time United States Senator from Iowa, was the chairman of the commission. The council was held in the spring of the year and not largely attended by Indians. Many of them were away on their hunt in the western part of Wyoming. Especially is this true of the Cheyennes, as they had departed before the call for the council had been sent out.

The treaty of 1868 contained an agreement that no treaty made with the Indians would be valid and binding until signed by three-fourths of the adult members of the tribe. This provision was doubtless put in by the Indians to prevent their chiefs and headmen loaded with presents from ceding away the tribal lands that belonged to all the members of the tribe and not to the chief and a few leading men alone.

The Secretary of the Interior appointed the treaty commission in June, 1875, and immediately thereafter runners were sent out to all the Sioux tribes asking them to assemble about September 1 at the Red Cloud Agency for a great council. Spotted Tail and Red Cloud were at variance as to where the treaty should be held. A compromise was finally made in which it was agreed that the treaty should be held on the head of White River, about eight miles from Red Cloud Agency. The commission discussed the matters to be brought up at the conference for some days before they could agree on what concessions they wanted from the Indians. As stated above, the treaty of 1868 required three-fourths of the adult males to join in any instrument conveying away their lands. It was easily seen that it would be impossible to get that number of signers. In the first place there were not enough Indians present, even if all signed, to convey title to the Black Hills. It was also felt that the Indians would make no cessions without asking for more money than Congress would be willing to pay.

With these insuperable difficulties in the way it seemed advisable to get the right to mine without asking for title. But the young Indians did not want to part with the Black Hills at any price, and not until the latter part of September did the treaty finally get under way. The treaty was attended by many renowned chiefs and their prominent followers. They were suspicious of the whites and it seemed evident from the first that the conference would not be able to accomplish its purpose — the bloodless acquisition of the Black Hills. Fortunately for me I had brought over the mail from Running Water and had the opportunity of hearing the treaty. I had given out beef issues to every agency represented and interested in the Black Hills. I knew the chiefs and leading men in every Sioux tribe and was able to converse with them without the necessity of an interpreter.

The Indians were not pleased with existing conditions and the commissioners could not promise much, as they were embarrassed by the fact that at the very moment there were over ten thousand white people in the Black Hills with no right to be there. The Indians had the whip hand as a matter of justice, and the commissioners were forced to admit that since the whites had broken the existing treaty they could just as easily break any future treaty that might be entered into.

Tall Mandan, a chief of the Brulés, was the first Indian speaker before the council. The question under consideration was whether the Sioux would be willing either to sell the Black Hills region or lease it for a long term for mining purposes only. He arose and began by saying that most of his tribe were away on a hunt and would not be back before fall. He criticized the government for not sending out the notice sooner and said that he had not had time to confer with his people and get their views. They would have attended the council, he asserted, if the notice had come sooner. It was evident that the Indians could afford to wait and were in no hurry to act. It is probable that the chiefs felt a hesitancy about assuming the responsibility they had assumed at other treaties. The three-

fourths clause was a sort of slap at their former auto-
cratic power, and in order to maintain power with their
people they had to take them into their confidence.

The situation was so tense that soldiers were sent
over from Fort Robinson. Bloodshed seemed eminent.
Had a gun been accidentally discharged, the life of
every white man present would have been snuffed out
instantly. But I must resist the temptation to go into
the details of this conference, much as I would like
to do so.

Several Indians who knew me well asked if the railroad was going to cross the river at Bismarck. Many
of them believed it an impossible feat. Tall Mandan,
Red Cloud, and Spotted Tail had visited Washington,
however, in connection with the treaty of 1868, and
they told the other Indians that on their trip East they
had seen wider streams bridged. Red Cloud said: "The
white people have captured electricity and harnessed
it with wires. In the East the people are as ants, and
they are turning the earth wrong side up! We think
we have this great river between us; but when the
white men get here in numbers, they will cross it.
Nothing can stop them. I have opposed them and have
tried to defend my country, but since I have been East
and with my own eyes seen the wonderful cities and
countless people I know there is no use for us to resist
longer. It is better to live in peace and be friends with
the whites than to oppose them. I have been to see the
Great Father; I know. Sitting Bull and his followers
may refuse to sign treaties. He may resist and fight,
but they will get him in the end."

I heard this speech. True to the opinions he expressed, this doughty old warrior remained with the whites and did not take up arms. A few of the chiefs who signed the treaty of 1868 signed this one proposed by the commission. It accomplished nothing, but it is my belief that if the government had offered a royalty on the ore taken out of the Black Hills, the treaty would have been signed quite generally and future bloodshed avoided.

As it was, all of a sudden the Indians, whether through fear of the soldiers or through protest at their presence, began to pull down their tents, and within a few minutes nothing was left but the dust marking the trail of their departure.

The Indians were much more penetrating and intelligent than we often give them credit for being. Take for instance Spotted Tail's little joke. The commission had proposed to lease the Black Hills for mining purposes for a hundred years, paying only a nominal rental. One day the commissioners had been driven out to the treaty tent in a government ambulance drawn by six mules. Most of the Indians were gone, but just as the ambulance was starting back,[1] Spotted Tail rode up to it on his horse. The driver stopped and Senator Allison put out his head and asked what was wanted. Spotted Tail answered, "I want those mules."

"But you can't have them," protested the senator. "They don't belong to us and we can't sell them."

[1] Wm. V. Wade mentioned herein was a witness to this conversation between Senator Allison and Spotted Tail. He thinks Spotted Tail rather outgeneraled the senator.

"I don't want to buy them," returned Spotted Tail, "I want to borrow them."

"For how long?"

"A hundred years."

"Why, you're crazy. There wouldn't be anything left of them in a hundred years. And besides they belong to the Great Father, to the whole nation. We couldn't let you have them."

"That is what I expected you to say," said Spotted Tail. "The Black Hills don't belong to the chiefs, either. They belong to all of us. We can't loan them or give them away."

Then suddenly he burst out into loud laughter.

"Drive on," commanded Allison, much offended. The driver cracked his whip and the ambulance sped away, leaving Spotted Tail grinning delightedly, sitting on his horse in a cloud of dust.

CHAPTER XXIV

In and Out of the Black Hills

WHEN the treaty council had broken up without accomplishing its purpose, war seemed inevitable. The government could not drive people out of the Black Hills or keep them out with all the military power available. This practical question was set over against our treaty obligations. The Black Hills could not be taken by force except as a result of a war of conquest when the Indians would sign any treaty put before them. The Indians would sign when reduced by necessity to such extremity, but not before.

Gen. George Crook called in all the scattered troops in this region. He was ordered to go out and round up the non-treaty Indians and bring them into reservations. If they refused to come he was to wage a war of extermination upon them. He went to Red Cloud and Spotted Tail and others disposed to be friendly, to hire scouts; but not one would go with him to coerce his recalcitrant brothers to come back. Hitherto the friendlies had always helped the whites in their field operations; but now, smarting under their grievances, they assumed a neutral if not a hostile attitude.

All the fall of 1875 General Crook made saw-buck pack-saddles preparatory to a winter campaign. With the final withdrawal of the troops on guard about February 1, 1876, and their concentration where they would be available for a campaign, white people poured into the Hills without a check.

I carried the mail horseback from my roadhouse to the Red Cloud Agency during the fall. I saw people coming to the Black Hills in every sort of conveyance, and even afoot; ox-teams with mining tools, wagons loaded with provisions and merchandise stocks. One day I ran into two men with four oxen and a large ox-wagon between them. They had owned the outfit in partnership, but after some sort of a disagreement had decided to divide, each taking a pair of oxen and two wheels. They were from Missouri and were bound for the Black Hills in their improvised carts.

About this time General Crook started his drive against the Indians. He soon learned that winter campaigns far removed from a base of supplies were extremely hazardous. Some of the men suffered terribly from frozen feet, and many of the horses were lost. He realized then that a summer campaign would have to be made. The snow had melted before he got back to Laramie; and with mud and high waters and bad crossings he was fortunate to get back, even with nothing accomplished.

The Indian men, women, and children usually settled down for the winter in some well-wooded valley. They carried on no campaigns of their own and were not prepared to withstand attacks from the whites. A winter campaign against Indians was usually disastrous to them and almost inhuman in its cruelty.

General Miles always preferred winter campaigns in which, being unexpected, he could make a night attack, kill a great number, and drive the remainder into the hills. Poorly clad and without tents or blankets, they would perish there in large numbers. The inhumanity and cruelty of such an attack comes from the fact that it is directed not only against men but against women and children and that it destroys their homes and food supply. Among white people to attack non-combatants and burn houses and household goods has always been considered contrary to the laws of war. Only occasionally was a white woman or white child killed or captured by Indians; but in every attack on an Indian village more women and children were killed and wounded than men, and when their tents were destroyed, all their clothing, food supply, and household utensils were destroyed likewise. A winter attack drove them out into the snow without clothing, food, shelter, or fuel, and among women and children the mortality was especially heavy.

I gave up the road house in the winter of 1875-76 and with two companions, John Dewes and George Gafner, set out to trap and poison wolves. We would have to live on antelope meat, as the buffaloes had either been killed or driven from the region in which we operated. Hunting and trapping would give us an opportunity of exploring a good deal of country, and yet leave us unencumbered and ready to make a dash into the Hills at the first opportunity. And we did set out as soon as we learned that General Crook had called in his troops. Our outfit consisted of a wagon loaded with provisions, and a few tools owned in common by the three of us, and three mules and two horses owned by me individually. Two of the mules we used on the wagon while the third was intended to be used as a pack animal when we made prospecting trips. I rode one of the horses and drove the other with the pack mule, my two companions riding in the wagon.

On reaching the road coming up from Platte to Rawhide Creek we found that several gold hunters had gone on ahead of us toward the Hills. One outfit we fell in with consisted of two Chinamen who expected to start a laundry, four or five Mexicans, two yokes of oxen hitched to an old bull wagon loaded with household goods and supplies, and two pack mules with picks and spades dangling on either side.

When we reached the Old Woman's Fork on Rawhide Creek the third day of our journey, we found Scotty Philips [1] in camp with an outfit belonging to Adolph Cuny and his partner. Scotty at that time was a mere lad, but the friendship between us that began then continued during his life. The Indians had made a raid on their outfit while their horses were grazing, and had run off all the horses. There they stood with loaded wagons, waiting for something to turn up! I told them, "When you get to be old timers on the frontier you'll watch your horses better. I'll bet the Indians won't get mine."

[1] James Philips, better known as "Scotty," continued his residence in South Dakota from 1876 till his death a few years ago. He was best known because of a buffalo ranch he operated a few miles north of Fort Pierre, on which at the present time members of his family carry a herd of almost a thousand head. He served South Dakota in the National Congress for a time.

We continued up the rough and devious trail till we reached Jenny's Stockade at the mouth of Camden Creek. Just east of our camp and across the canyon was the high hill on which Professor Jenny had made the mound and placed the stake previously mentioned.

At Willow Springs we struck the trail made by General Custer in July, 1874. The gulches were so steep and the way so difficult that we decided to *cache* part of our provisions and take only what we had immediate use for on our pack horses and hasten on to Grizzly Gulch. It was almost midnight when we finished rigging up pack saddles of the well-known sawbuck pattern. A Colorado outfit was camped about two miles away, which gave us a feeling of security. The moon was full and objects were discernible for some distance around almost as if it were day. Grass was good everywhere and my horses were picketed close by.

Well, when the pack saddles were finally completed, we dug a hole in a sort of cut bank and *cached* about half of our provisions, taking much pains to make the hole deep, and covering it carefully so as to leave no tell-tale evidence of its location. Let me add that we never went back to recover our *cache* and if no one found it the remains are there yet.

One of my horses was a fine runner and I thought much of him, for he had saved my life once. It happened in this way: I was helping make a delivery of cattle to Red Cloud Agency and was returning from a trip on the Niobrara, riding along at a leisurely pace on a divide when I noticed a speck of dust fly up by my side. At first I thought my horse had kicked a pebble loose, but to my surprise another puff of dust flew up and it dawned on me that I was being shot at. I spurred my horse into a gallop. Looking back I could see a party of seven Cheyennes in pursuit. I had confidence in my horse and felt that I could easily keep out of their way. After running for five or six miles I climbed a ridge and could see they were still coming, with two riders considerably in the lead. It seemed to me quite time for me to take a little hand in the fun. By way of arms I carried a Winchester rifle and a revolver. I dismounted, crouched down, and shot, the ball striking in front of the two leaders, who were vigorously plying their whips. They changed their minds about following me in short order, and another shot turned them toward the west, where they disappeared over some hills. The five who were behind stopped and came no further. I kept a sharp lookout, but they were evidently discouraged from any further pursuit.

I had many opportunities to dispose of the horse at a good figure but always refused all offers because of my attachment for him. I awakened before daylight, got up, built a fire and put the coffee pot on. As my horse did not whinney for me as was his usual custom, I decided not to change his picket until after breakfast. When it grew light what was my surprise to find there was not a horse or a mule in sight. I found the picket pin, but the rope was untied and gone. I got my gun and began to look for tracks to determine which way the thief or thieves had gone, but saw only an occasional track. Poor Buckskin! Whoever took him was a master in covering a trail, as he had circled around the camp several times. If the earth had yawned and swallowed the horses up they would have been no more lost to us. I began to regret very sincerely my little joke about the Cuny outfit.

On going over to the camp of the Colorado people, I found them with a broken wheel. Their horses had not met the fate of mine, so we arranged that they should hitch to my wagon and we should all proceed together to Custer City. Snow started falling that day and continued until we reached the town. When we arrived in Custer we found it a place of several stores, all of which sold groceries and whiskey. In several store windows were displayed sacks of flour branded "I. D." in red letters. The Indian Department had bought the flour for the Indians, but in some way it had got out of the agency warehouse into the stores in Custer.

One day a man by the name of Jim Roberts, who was running a store there, came and asked me what I would take to carry mail to Red Cloud Agency. I said, "I'll do it for a dollar a letter, you to furnish me with a saddle horse." He agreed to this, and put a notice in the window on a box-lid, advising people that mail would be sent out the next day for Red Cloud Agency, where it would make connections with the outside world. The package contained, I think, sixty letters. This was the first mail ever sent out of the Black Hills, at least by one whose duty was expressly to carry it. I set out on February 10, 1876.

I knew the direction to the Red Cloud Agency, but had no road to follow or any directions to guide me.

From Custer City I took a southeast course, following down a canyon for about a third of the way. On this trip I discovered the hot springs, and was probably the first white man to see them. Although winter time, the water was warm and the grass was green around the springs. I followed down the stream formed by the hot springs for some distance and found another spring whose waters were cold, and a few miles farther down a waterfall of some four or five feet. Later the county that contains this waterfall was called Fall River county.

My first night out I camped on the Cheyenne River. It had been snowing all day and the night was cold. I built a camp fire in the woods and cut some young cottonwood branches for my horse to browse on and tied him near me. All the bedding I had was my saddle blanket and one blanket carried rolled up behind my saddle. I tried to sleep, but the howling of the wolves reverberating from bluff to bluff made it impossible for me to do so, even if the bedding had been sufficient. As it was, my time was occupied in keeping a fire and turning over, alternately keeping one side warm and getting the other cold. Just before daylight the owls began to hoot, and I recalled what my old friend Chepa had said one time when we were on a hunt. "Don't believe a 'hoot' you hear in the summer time. An owl hoots only in the winter." It is well known that the Sioux often signalled by hooting so like an owl that no distinction could be made.

I carried with me in addition to my bedding a package of coffee, a small piece of bacon, some hard tack, and a cup in one side of the saddle bag, and in the other two feeds of oats for my horse. I had coffee, hard tack, and bacon for breakfast and ate no more until I made camp that night. Days are too short in the winter to bother about making a fire and eating a midday meal.

I reached an Indian camp at the end of the second day, well after dark. In order to get through the camp, I put a blanket around me as the Indians do, when accosted answered in Sioux, and got through unidentified. I afterwards learned that the camp was that of "Man-Afraid-of-His-Horses."[2] I reached Red Cloud Agency about daylight, to the astonishment of the agent. The distance covered in two days and one night on the same horse was over two hundred miles. As before noted, I had carried mail from Running Water to Red Cloud Agency before and was well-known to the people around the agency. I was careful to keep from the Indians the fact that I had come from the Black Hills. Had I been intercepted on the road it is more than likely that my story would have been ended.

I hung around the agency a few days to give my horse a chance to rest up. Then I returned bearing a few letters to some of the business men, one being from the agent to Roberts. On my return I took a different route so as to avoid the camp of Man-Afraid-of-His-Horses; I passed through Buffalo Gap and reached Custer in two days and one night of intensely cold riding. In my absence of ten days from Custer several log houses had gone up and the main thoroughfare began to take on the appearance of a street.

[2] Man-Afraid-Of-His-Horses really means a man who is so brave that his enemies are afraid even of his horses.

A man afoot is no man, so I bought a saddle horse. I talked with a man who had been out prospecting on foot, loaded down with shovels and pans. He told me that if he had a horse he could easily find a good mining claim. I told him to take my horse and find a place, then come back and get me and we would go in together with a supply of bedding, provisions, etc. He had already found gold in scant supply but like most prospectors was looking for a better place. He took my horse and a couple of days' provisions which I supplied him, and set out. And, although I made diligent inquiry, I never saw him again. It is my opinion that the Indians got him, as a lone man's life was worth but little in the Sioux country in the spring of 1876.

Again I hired to Jim Roberts, this time to go down on the Cheyenne trail to meet some freight wagons coming from Laramie, deliver a letter to them, and escort them back to Custer. The wagons contained goods for his store, and as the roads were bad and oxen slow, he was apprehensive that they might encounter a war party. On my way I saw many signs of Indians, but encountered none. I ran into one camp the day before and judged that no women had been with them, as they left an antelope hide and the less desirable portions of the meat. By a careful examination I determined how many horses they had and the direction they were going, which was toward the Hills — a war party certainly. The Indians were thoroughly aroused, and every few days the report that some white prospector had met his death from Indians was brought in.

I did not meet the freighters as I expected, but did

run across a military hay camp on a small branch of
Rawhide Creek some distance away from the main
trail. At this camp was a log house for the men, a log
barn, and a number of hay stacks aggregating about
200 tons. The hay had been cut for Fort Laramie
about twenty miles away and was being hauled from
time to time as needed by teamsters engaged for that
purpose. It was Sunday, I was told, when I arrived at
the camp. At any rate, the men were taking a day off
and lolling about the yard. Just before reaching the
hay camp I saw moccasin tracks made that day, and
knew that Indians were around. I asked, "Boys, where
are your horses?" One of them returned, "They're
turned out to graze on days when we take a lay-off."
I told them, "You'd better get them in; I saw an Indian sign, and not far away, either."

"Oh," one of them said, "We haven't seen an Indian
this winter. There aren't any around here." I then
questioned them about ammunition, and one of them
answered, "We had a lot of it in the early part of the
winter but we shot it away at jack rabbits and sage
hens."

"Well," I said, "I'll stay here tonight."

At my insistence the boys rather reluctantly ran their
horses into a pole corral and gave them hay. It was by
this time about night, and for safety's sake I tied my
horse to the corner of the house and with an army car-
bine in my hand sat in the shadow of the buildings
until daylight. At the breakfast table the boys had a
laugh on me for staying up to watch for Indians that
never came.

They were expecting one of their number back from Fort Laramie where he had gone after a wagon load of corn. It was a bright, still April morning, just the day to invite those cooped up for the long winter out into the open. We sat propped up against the house in the sun, talking over rumors and prospects, especially with reference to the opening of the Black Hills.

The creek ran south with cut bluffs on either side, bordered at their base by box-elder trees. About a mile away along the creek bank I saw a four-horse team coming around a curve in a cut bank with the driver lashing his horses and in full gallop. The report of several shots in quick succession came to us.

"There are the Indians now," said I. "No," said one of the boys, "he's only coming home drunker than a lord." The words were no sooner out of his mouth than we heard another shot and saw the driver crumple up and fall forward.[3] Several Indians came out of the brush, cut the horses loose and made off as fast as they could. I mounted my horse, which stood saddled, and rode down at full speed; but when I got there the driver was dead and scalped.

I came back to the corrals for help. Several of the boys had the old McClellan saddles and could ride. They rigged out as quickly as possible and armed themselves, the shells I had fortunately fitting their guns. Three of them accompanied me and four were left to guard the camp, wagons, and teams. We started out at a swift lope, following the trail to the northeast.

---

[3] The teamster who was killed at the hay camp on the head of the Rawhide was probably Jacob Shroud, although this identification is not absolutely positive.

About ten miles east of the hay camp lived Nick Janisse and several other half-breed families engaged in ranching in a small way. They lived on a small stream which forms one of the head streams of the Cheyenne. They had many horses and a few cattle, and on this fine spring morning all their horses were out grazing except a few saddle horses which they were using at the ranch in branding some late fall colts.

When about half way to Janisse's ranch we noticed a cloud of dust between us and the ranch. I took the leadership of our party as the three with me were without the experience necessary to guide them in the emergency. "Get your guns ready," I told them. All of us were ready, and as we climbed a rather steep hill we came face to face with the horse-herd which the Indians were fogging before them. We spread out so as to bag the herd and hold it. Just then we saw the Indians coming out of the draw, but before we could get time to fire they ducked back into the gulch and fled as fast as their horses could carry them, leaving the herd they had attempted to steal.

We followed the Indians for some miles until they disappeared into a wooded creek gulch which we dared not enter, but never got close enough to shoot at them. Just as we turned to go back we saw another party coming towards us. I could see they were white and conjectured that they were some of the ranchers trying to recover their horses. I held up my hat, which in Chinook is a sign of a white man.

When the group of men came up they turned out to be Nick Janisse and a few half-breeds. We told them about the man at the hay camp having been killed and scalped that morning, and Nick said, "Well, you weren't far from it. It's lucky you lifted your hat when you did, because we were just ready to let go."

Nick and I had known each other since the middle sixties and were glad of the chance to talk over old times. He was one of the most famous Sioux interpreters in the country and had officiated at a number of treaty councils and had made several trips to Washington with treaty delegations. He asked me where I was going, and I told him to escort some freighters into the Hills. He gave me a side look from his little beady eyes and said, "Take my advice, Ben, and stay out of the Hills. The Indians are mad about this stampede of white people into the Hills, and there's trouble brewing. They have the right to the Hills under the treaty and they know it. They won't give it up without bloodshed. If Sitting Bull can get the support of three or four other tribes he will stand pat and repel all invaders. They're gathering all the horses together they can get. Some Cheyennes who were here the other day said that Sitting Bull has called all the Arapahoes and Cheyennes to a council, and he expects them to assist the Sioux."

Nick was in a position to know what he was talking about. He was a half-breed and his wife a full-blood, and thus he had opportunities to get information not available to white men. Nick insisted that we come to his house for dinner and we assented with pleasure. As we rode along toward the ranch we noticed two horses tied in a thick clump of brush. On making an examination we found where the riders had *cached* their saddles, rawhide ropes, and some meat. Several pairs of moccasins were tied on the back of the saddles, and on the front of one was the scalp of the man who had been shot earlier in the day. We surmised that these horses had been left by the Indians where they could rest until they returned with the herd, but that we had pushed them too much to allow them to stop.

We took the horses, saddles, and other plunder down to Nick's place. He said they had just been ready to sit down to dinner when he saw a dust cloud from the horse herd as the Indians put it in motion. They had just finished branding a few yearlings and their horses stood saddled at the gate, so they lost no time in pursuit.

There were some bushes in the door yard of the ranch. One of the men untied the scalp from the Indian's saddle, scooped out a little hole in these bushes, and buried it, since none of us knew any better method of disposing of it.

The soldiers from the hay camp and I washed and sat down at the table with the other men. Mrs. Janisse dished up the food and her daughter Emily waited on the table. The bunch of hungry men certainly enjoyed the good meal set before us. The long, low room was used as a combined dining room and kitchen. Mrs. Janisse stepped outside for a moment when she had caught up in the serving, but only a moment. She came running in screaming, and collapsed on the floor. We sprang from the table, grabbed our guns and while buckling on our cartridge belts piled out of the door, expecting to see the war party of Indians back in force. But there was nothing there except a small brown pup tossing up what looked like an old rag. We went back into the house, and when Mrs. Janisse had revived sufficiently she told us that the pup was playing with a dead man's scalp. We looked more closely at the pup's plaything, and found it to be true. The scalp was of reddish brown curly hair almost the color of the pup's fur. The next time we buried it deep enough that there was no danger of its being dug up.

CHAPTER XXV

Preparing for the Little Big Horn Campaign

As soon after dinner as possible we jogged our way back to the hay camp, much to the relief of those we had left to protect it. They had brought the body of the dead man in and were awaiting our coming before deciding on its disposition. After discussing the matter it was agreed that the body should be taken to Fort Laramie, accompanied by two of the boys and myself. The best conveyance we had was a buckboard with one seat and a bed capacity in the rear of about four feet; so I sat crosswise behind on the floor of the buckboard holding the head of the corpse on my lap while the legs dangled over the rear end. It was four o'clock when we left, but before starting I divided my ammunition with the men who remained at the hay camp, leaving them all I felt I could spare — twenty rounds.

We drove as fast as the fresh team could take us and luckily met with no more adventures that day. It was getting dusk when we arrived at Fort Laramie and I immediately reported to General Crook's headquarters. I told him how unprepared the men at the hay camp were for a possible attack by Indians. He said gruffly, "Those men are in with hay every week, and it's their own fault if they aren't provided with what they need."

General Crook wanted me to take some dispatches to Fort Fetterman and I agreed to do so in a day or two, when the corpse, for which I felt some responsibility, had been decently buried. I was directed to the post chaplain for lumber to make a coffin, but he was unwilling to let me have it as the dead man was a civilian. I argued rather warmly that the man had been working for the military as an extra-duty man and ought to be entitled to lumber enough for a coffin. He said he could not think of letting me have lumber unless it were paid for in advance. So out of my own money I paid him $20, the amount he deemed the lumber to be worth.

Next morning with the help of the two men who came in with me from the hay camp I fashioned a rough coffin. Without too much urging the chaplain unbent enough to perform the burial rites in the presence of the three of us just mentioned and in addition two of the dance hall girls who at our request had come over to sing a hymn. Death was no uncommon thing in Fort Laramie and no one else paid any attention to us. The bugles at the fort were blowing, and the drums beating a tattoo for the soldiers' drill on the parade ground when the chaplain read off the burial ceremony just as quickly as possible in a sort of sing-song intonation with no spontaneity or feeling.

Every now and then the body of a traveler or herder was brought in scalped. The burial ground contained the remains of few who had died from natural causes, and there were all sorts of curious epitaphs carved on the head-boards. Among them were: "Killed by a bear," "Shot in a barroom fight," "Froze," "Killed hisself," "Killed by Indians," "Drug to death."

When through with the burial I reported to General Crook and found him looking for some one to talk to an Indian who was at his headquarters. The Indian proved to be a Crow who had come to enlist in the fight against his hereditary enemy — the Sioux — and of course his services were accepted.

In the course of my conversation with General Crook I asked him what he would do in cases like this murder at the hay camp, and he broke out, "My God, what can I do! I'd look fine taking my men into the badlands to chase two or three Indians. We are outsiders and unacquainted with the country, and the Indians know every nook and corner of it. They've been harassing the garrisons all along the border, stealing stock, killing herders, and running off mules. But what can I do about it? They've changed their methods of attack; they don't come in large bodies but in groups of three and four, do their damage and hide out. It would just be fun for them to have us follow them now, unacquainted with the country and with the creeks all full."

I promised the general that I would set out with his message to Fort Fetterman at once, but when I went to get my horse where I had him picketed, I found that some miscreant had stolen him, rope and all. While I never found out who took the horse, I suspected some Mexicans that I had seen hanging around. It is no pleasant experience to be left afoot when one is used to riding for a living. It is like being left in mid-ocean in a boat without oars. I headed straight for Nick Janisse's ranch where I bought a horse on time, and he came back to Fort Laramie with me. He wished to seek a position as interpreter, and I decided to ask for one as scout or messenger with the military expedition then organizing. We knew a big drive in the Indian country was under way and such positions ought to be open. Two essential qualifications in a scout were a thorough acquaintance with the country and a knowledge of the Sioux language. Long rides had to be made and a man had to be hardy enough to eat what he found and sleep where he had the opportunity and make no complaint about it. He was expected to be a good shot, have sober judgment, and report only what he saw without exaggeration. Janisse urged General Crook strongly to take me on permanently as a messenger, and he agreed to do so.

I met the freighters whom I had come to guide to the Black Hills. They had not even a gun with which to protect themselves, and I gave them mine. I cautioned them to guard their horses well; the Sioux were after horses, and if they had to kill people to get them, they did so.

When I took the message for General Crook he got on his horse and rode with me quite a way in order to get a better opportunity of directing me how to travel and take care of myself and the messages entrusted to me. I promised to use great care. We shook hands, he patted me on the arm and I was off. It was then growing dark, and according to my plans I rode till midnight, let my horse graze till dawn, then resumed my journey. I had all the places where I expected to rest my horse spotted in advance, as the country was well known to me. I had traveled it for the first time in 1863 and had subsequently gone over practically the same trail several times.

Next day as I rode along I saw objects in the distance which seemed to be a rider leading two horses. I loosened the revolver with which General Crook had provided me in the holster and prepared for any emergency that might arise. On coming closer I found that the objects which I saw were three head of stray government horses. I uncoiled my lariat, ran them into a bend in the North Platte where I roped one of them when they attempted to run by me and changed my saddle and outfit onto him. In saddling the fresh horse I forgot and left lying on the ground a small chunk of bacon and some hard tack which I carried to furnish food for the trip. My own saddle horse was snorty, and when I tried to swim him across the river he jerked away from me and I had to leave him. I took the three government horses in with me and reached Fort Fetterman, a distance of ninety-five miles, in two days. When I rode in the post trader, who had known me of old, hailed me and asked, "What have you got there?" I told him I had horses picked up on the way from Laramie and he said, "Well, you're in luck. These are government horses, and there's a good reward out for them."

I reported to Major Randall, delivered the message from General Crook, and told him about the stray horses I had brought in. He paid me a reward of $105 for bringing in the horses, and General Crook paid me $100 for carrying the messages and papers. Major Randall then loaned me a horse to ride in search of mine, which I found not far from where he had jerked loose from me.

On my return Major Randall had me called into his office and told me, "You're just the man I want. I need a guide and scout for our outfit on the next trip. I think I can get you a position with the Associated Press also, as they want a dispatch carrier." I told him I was willing to engage for the messenger service but wanted to be a guide and dispatch carrier only and did not care to enlist as a scout. He agreed to that and I went down to the post trader's store and bought a fine repeating rifle and a stock of ammunition. I still retained the revolver General Crook had let me have. On the 29th of May, 1876, the column which I accompanied left Fort Fetterman for the Tongue and Big Horn rivers.

CHAPTER XXVI

Fort Fetterman to Tongue River

Before going farther with General Crook's journey from Fort Fetterman to "chastize" the non-treaty Sioux, I will give a brief review of the causes of friction between the whites and Indians.

Away back in 1855, by the terms of the treaty of Laramie, all the land between the Missouri, the Yellowstone, the Big Horn, and the Platte was declared Indian land. The Union Pacific Railroad was built through this land and the Oregon Trail laid out against the protest of the Indians, and in 1864 they began to commit depredations in retaliation. In 1865 the Bozeman and Bridger trails were laid out and an order from the military department authorized the construction of three forts on these trails to protect it. These were Fort Reno on the headwaters of the Powder River; Fort Phil Kearney on the headwaters of the Tongue; and Fort C. F. Smith on the Big Horn. This highway and the forts constructed were contrary to the express provisions of the treaty then existing. They cut the best hunting grounds remaining to the Sioux and Cheyenne Indians, occupied at that time chiefly by Red Cloud, Crazy Horse, and The-Man-Afraid-of-His-Horses. These three chiefs were called to a council in 1865 at Laramie and were told that the road and

forts would be built whether they gave their consent
or not; whereupon they withdrew from the council and
prepared to resist. To carry out the written instruc-
tions of General Sherman, then the head of the U. S.
Army, General Carrington was sent to lay out the road
and construct the three forts. The year 1866 was a
bloody one.

In 1867-68, and in other treaties — among which
was the treaty of Fort Rice previously described —
the United States made a complete backdown from its
position, agreed to destroy the three forts in question
and to abandon the Montana road, all of which was
in accordance with the terms of the treaty existing. In
1868 a new treaty of Laramie was entered into which
provided that the Indians might not alienate their
lands except by consent of three-fourths of the adult
male members of the tribe. The years 1870 and 1871
were years of peace.

Then in 1872 the Northern Pacific Railway reached
Bismarck, Dakota, and in each of the following few
years a military reconnoissance was made by surveying
parties across Indian lands to the west. Finally, it was
decided to build the railroad up the Yellowstone on
the south side. The Indians did not want the railroad,
and to build it without their consent was a violation
of the treaty. The Custer expedition into the Black
Hills in 1874 and the Jenny expedition in 1875, both
authorized by the government, were in contravention
of existing treaties.

When gold was discovered in the Black Hills, the
government tried in good faith to keep the prospectors

out, but failed. But when, in 1875, at a treaty council near Red Cloud Agency the Indians refused either to give up title to or lease the Black Hills for mining purposes, the military guard around the Hills was called in and thousands of whites stampeded into the Hills. To force the Indians to relinquish their title General Crook made a winter campaign against them on Rosebud and Powder rivers in February and March, 1876. He destroyed much property, making war on the Indians in a country theirs by right of treaty. By May 1, 1876, there were estimated to be at least 25,000 white people in the Hills; and now they could not be driven out even though the Indians had title.

On December 6, 1875, the Commissioner of Indian Affairs sent instruction to the Indian agents to notify the Indians in the unceded territory to come into the agencies before January 31, 1876, otherwise they would be regarded as hostiles. The letters did not reach the agents until almost the close of the year; winter was severe and the Indians could not have come in within the time limit, even if they could have been notified or had made an attempt to come in. And if they had come in, they knew they would have to leave their winter camps and provisions for an agency which had no means of taking care of and feeding them.

But in spite of these conditions, promptly on February 1 the Secretary of the Interior notified the Secretary of War that the time given the hostiles had expired and he formally turned them over to the military authority. It is very evident that this order for the Indians to come in was given with the realization that it could not be complied with at that season of the year; and with the sole purpose of getting an excuse to make war on the Indians who at that time were taking care of themselves in territory remote from the white man and at peace. But the white man had to have the Black Hills; and the only way to get possession appeared to be by a war of conquest, which would reduce the legal owners to such a state that they would be glad to sign any treaty placed before them. The war was only a pretext for setting aside the existing treaty. I am not talking about destiny or the march of civilization, or anything of the sort, but of a simple matter of obligation.

From February 1 onward war preparations were made by the U. S. Armies, not because the Indians threatened an invasion but simply to give a pretext for holding legally the Black Hills which the whites already occupied illegally. Governments justify themselves in doing things as a result of war which they would not have the face to do without war. The smoke of battle has screened many a high-handed territory seizure. Don't misunderstand me. The United States didn't provoke a war; they merely waged it. What fighting the Indians did was in self-defense. Of all the wars in which the United States has been engaged, the least justification is found in the Sioux War of 1876. The Interior Department can never wash its hands of this crime.

The so-called hostile Sioux were on one or more of the tributaries of the Yellowstone, which they had occupied more or less constantly for some years. The hostiles usually lived on the Big Horn, the Rosebud, the Tongue, and the Powder rivers. The campaign as planned was in three main divisions: General Crook from the southeast, General Gibbon from Fort Ellis on the west, and General Terry, with General Custer second in command, from the northeast. These three divisions were to sweep the country and bag all the Indians in the territory covered. In no other Indian war has there been the equal of these divisions engaged, either in point of numbers, equipment, or fame of leaders.

On such a mission was Crook's army, in which I was engaged as messenger, now leaving Fort Fetterman. It consisted of fifteen companies of cavalry (about 900 men), three hundred infantry, two hundred fifty pack mules, and about seventy-five wagons, to be joined later by nearly three hundred Crow and Shoshone scouts. There were three well-known scouts with the outfit: Frank Grouard, Louis Richaud, and Baptiste Pourier, Grouard received the highest wages. He could speak perfect Sioux and could even pass most places as a full blood. He was dark like an Indian and had lived in Crazy Horse's family for some years. His hair was long and he wore it braided like an Indian's. When our military division reached Powder River the scouts were sent on ahead to bring in the Crow Indians who had signified their willingness to help fight their enemies, the Sioux.

On the march we passed the ruins of old Forts Reno and Phil Kearney, both of which had been torn down in compliance with the terms of the Fort Laramie treaty. At Fort Phil Kearney, Red Cloud and Crazy Horse had killed Captain Fetterman [1] and the whole detachment under him sent out by Colonel Carrington to guard a wood train at the time of the building of the fort. We also saw where Captain Powell had his "wagon-box fight." The scene of both these engagements was between the modern towns of Buffalo and Sheridan, Wyoming.

As I was dispatch carrier I had nothing to do until called on by General Crook, and during the march I rode where I pleased, often with General Crook, sometimes with the scouts or with the officers of the companies. I hunted a little every day and furnished much fresh meat. One day I rode ahead of the procession, selected a place about where I judged camp would be made by evening, killed two fat hollow-horn buffaloes, butchered them and had the meat spread out on the hides when the command got in. It might be well to explain that a hollow-horn is a two-year old, which furnishes the choicest meat, fat and tender. The horns at that time stick nearly straight out, and the inside pith of the horn does not fill the cavity — hence the name hollow-horn. The next day General Crook rode ahead with two men to a place where he thought he might do as well as I did; but when night came he had killed nothing.

After not many days we struck the headwaters of the Tongue River and followed it for some miles. The

[1] Captain Fetterman and eighty-one men under him were killed, all except seven having been killed with arrows. The Sioux had few guns and but a scant supply of ammunition, but they were guided by Red Cloud and Crazy Horse — both daring and resourceful leaders.

first night we camped on this stream a Crow Indian came to the farther bank and tried to talk with us. We could make nothing out of what he said. If it had been daytime I could have talked with him in the Chinook sign language. As it was, we did not get the message he evidently wished to give us. The next day about seventy-five Sioux appeared on a high bluff along our line of march and shot into our ranks, slightly wounding one man. We moved over to Goose Creek, which offered more open ground, and went into camp.

As soon as the command had got safely into camp Captain Davenport sent for me to take some dispatches down to Fort Fetterman. Just about twilight the Sioux made a foray and got off with thirty or forty head of the government beef herd. Before I set out General Crook gave me specific advice, to which I listened attentively, although it added nothing to my knowledge or my caution. But military men are accustomed to giving definite orders to free themselves from blame or responsibility in case things go wrong, and I had to listen.

I exercised much caution on the trip. The messages were important, and besides I wanted to show the officers that I could go through and return. There was much danger, though I felt no fears for my personal safety. About dawn the morning after I had left the camp, I got the odor of camp-fire smoke on the windward side of me. I climbed a high ridge carefully, dismounted, and took a survey of the surrounding country. I found myself within half a mile of a small party of Indians. Just then a horse nickered from the

camp, mine answered, and I knew I was in for it. I
ran to my horse and had scarcely mounted when I saw
three Indians coming toward me whipping like fury. I
ran down across the valley and up the long sloping
ridge opposite. My horse was shod and I knew he
could climb the hill better than my pursuers on unshod
horses. As soon as I had gone over the crest of the hill,
where my horse would be out of sight and out of danger, I dismounted and crept back to the top, unslung
my gun — a repeater with one shell in the chamber
and sixteen in the magazine — and lay flat on the
ground. I took as good aim as possible in the poor light
at the leading one of the oncoming horses. My shot
struck him in the breast, and he coughed and staggered with lowered head. My second shot missed its
moving target, but the third brought down one of the
two horses left. Bullets were whizzing about me but
the Indians had only smooth bores, which are unre-
liable except at close range. I shot several times at the
third horse but failed to hit him. The rider, however,
changed the horse's course and ducked into a bend in
the hill where he was out of my sight, and then went
back to his two companions whom I had set afoot. I
lost no time in moving on, as I feared other Indians
might come up, and three were all I cared to tackle.
Nor did I slacken speed until I had crossed over a level
valley three miles wide and ascended the hills beyond.
On looking back all I could see was a lone horseman
silhouetted against the sky. By this time the sun was
just rising. My horse was getting somewhat winded,
but I dared not try to hide until I had gone on a few

miles further where I would be safe from pursuit. Indians had harassed the army more or less all through
the country I was now in, and I was by no means
secure.

I rode into a brush thicket along one of the branches
of the Powder River, unsaddled and watered my horse,
picketed him where grass was good and lay down to
rest, in the depths of the wilderness, far from any
highway and out of sight.

CHAPTER XXVII

Incidents of the Battle on the Rosebud

The place in which I had made my meager camp was ideal for the purpose — a screen of brush surrounding a garden spot of prairie covered in part by sage. Horses always eat with relish the fine, soft grass that grows among the sage, and there was also some bunch grass which had never been closely grazed over. Before long my horse had eaten his fill and stood on three legs with head lowered, asleep.

I ate of what little I had and lay down to sleep. A soft south breeze wafted the scent of wild plum blossoms and filled the air with their fragrance. I could hear the sage cocks thrumming their tails and crooning in the mating dance. Wild ducks were splashing in the pool nearby. In the distance the buffalo bulls were bellowing, while not fifty feet away a pair of magpies were giving more chatter than labor to a nest under construction. An eagle flying high overhead screamed as he passed. But in spite of the clamor of the early spring morning, I was soon asleep, sleeping as only a tired person can. I awoke in the afternoon, refreshed, changed the picket line and ate again, preparatory to continuing my journey as soon as the sun set and friendly darkness had come.

The horse I was riding was a good traveler but not

well broken. On two different occasions he almost broke away from me. Realizing how dangerous it would be for me to be left afoot, I resolved to get rid of him as soon as I reached the fort. In riding at night one may be guided by the stars in clear weather, provided one studies them closely for several successive nights. But keeping the direction on an almost two hundred mile journey is but a small part of the risks one takes. In the first place the direction you think you want to go is but approximate; in the second place you can see no landmarks to the right or left of your trail, and if you can see the road you can no more locate yourself by this than you could by watching the side-walk in a city.

In the early morning of my third night out I rode into Fort Fetterman, waked the telegrapher, and handed him my press dispatches. Two and a half hours later I turned in the government dispatches. I did not question why I was so instructed; I did as I was told to do, and there my duty ended. New York City, Chicago, Omaha, and other cities had sent out newspaper correspondents to cover this campaign, and each of them sent dispatches and news letters back by me. I received $250 for the trip. Scouts worked by the month, but messenger service was usually paid by the trip. In the case of extremely hazardous trips volunteers were called for, a stated reward being offered to the one who would undertake it.

While I was getting ready for the return trip the captain in charge of the post asked me if I didn't want to carry back some first class mail addressed to members of General Crook's organization, which had been accumulating in his hands. "If you'll take it," he said, "there'll be $100 in it for you, and I'll send a private soldier with you to keep you company." I accepted his offer and bought a pack mule, as the load was too heavy to carry on horseback. My new saddle horse was high spirited and full of life. I paid $80 for him, and he was worth it; he could singlefoot, and to ride him was like sitting in a rocking chair.

My companion sent by the post commander to keep me company, was a sort of a nuisance. He tired easily, would lag behind, then shout to me at a distance if he had anything to say. He could not realize that we were going through a dangerous country where quietness was necessary to safety. Sometimes he would whistle and sing. Finally I told him I didn't want to advertise myself to the Indians, whatever he preferred, and that we would part company if he persisted in his noise making. I was entrusted with important papers and wanted to get them through. After that my companion was more subdued, and we got through without mishap.

The camp on Goose Creek was near where the city of Sheridan, Wyoming, now stands. We arrived there in the morning and I turned over the dispatches and the packet of mail. The letters from home furnished topics of conversation and bits of gossip for many days around the camp.

In the afternoon about eighty Apaches and one hundred Shoshones joined us, and two hundred Crows were due to reach camp that night. They were all enlisted to fight the Sioux and were impatient to move without delay. The next day, June 15, all was in commotion while we prepared for an expedition down the Tongue River. We left the wagons behind. Each man was required to carry six days' rations with him and no pack train was taken. The infantrymen were mounted on mules. Many of the mules were unbroken to ride, and some of the men made a sorry go at trying to ride them. Amid a good deal of confusion and much hilarity our cavalcade of about 1,400 men, including cavalrymen, mounted infantry, scouts, Indians and all, got under way. We were all well loaded with ammunition, and while we took no wheeled ambulances, we did take an ambulance train of two pack mules, somewhat similar to the travois used by Indians.

We made a rapid forced march the first day, but did not see any Sioux. All of us were alert and watchful. I, being a messenger, was not under strict military discipline and was not expected to fight. I was a sort of free lance, but had to hold myself ready to carry dispatches back any time I was asked to do so.

The second day out the Crows, who lived in that part of the country, scouted far out, covering the whole front and flanks of the army and were far more efficient than a like number of white soldiers would have been. They knew the country and the Indian customs, and were good trailers. They returned bearing the news that they had discovered Sioux, who had attacked them and then retreated, but the Crows advised us not to follow, for fear of ambush. The Rosebud had rather high, rough banks on either side and at the "Dead Canyon" there was no bottom land but simply a gorge, in which an army could easily have been ambushed. The Sioux then made a flank movement to cut off the rear company and succeeded in killing thirteen soldiers, five Crows, and seven or eight Shoshones. The Crows were pretty badly scared by the engagement and wished to return home. They feared that the Sioux would drive the soldiers back, and when the army was withdrawn there would be nothing to protect them from the Sioux vengeance. They felt that if they would go home and be good Indians, the Sioux would leave them alone.

General Crook thought he had met the whole Sioux nation, but as a matter of fact it was only a hunting party of Sioux and Cheyennes numbering four or five hundred lodges, under the distinguished chief, Crazy Horse.

When contact was first made and firing began between our Indian scouts and the Sioux, there was one Sioux who seemed to have a charmed life. He skipped back and forth, taking advantage of whatever protection the nature of the ground afforded. When the army had advanced to within firing distance he was still holding his line, and doing effective shooting, too. Naturally he drew the fire of all our skirmishers and fell wounded; even then he sat up and kept pouring in his fire, determined to die selling his life dearly. When the front rank of the advanced line was within easy range, the order rang out, "Halt! Take aim! Fire!" and the wounded Indian crumpled up, riddled with bullets. I learned afterwards that he made this personal sacrifice in order to give time for the Indian women and children to get away.

Another example of personal bravery among the Indians also fell under my observation and is worthy of record. A band of the Crow scouts had attacked a smaller band of about a dozen Sioux warriors in the rough breaks of the Rosebud. While I took no part in the fight I was where I could see and hear everything. The Sioux had withdrawn under the impetuous attack of the superior number of Crows, taking advantage of the rocks that had rolled down from the bluffs above. The Sioux were armed partly with guns, partly with bows and arrows. One of the Sioux warriors named Yellow Ear Rings had fired his gun at the on-coming Crows until it jammed and the breech broke. Thinking his time had come and wishing to inspire his companions he mounted a large stone in plain view of the enemy. With arms extended, dressed only in breech clout and moccasins, he began his death chant in a far-reaching falsetto which could be heard above the crack of the rifles. He expected death, and standing in plain view as he was, I too, expected momentarily to see him drop.

His chant, freely translated, was as follows:

> I love these hills and valleys,
> My friends are in number as the grass.
> But now I am as nothing.
> My friends, I am leaving you.
> You may even now count me dead.

This he repeated, prefacing it with, "I, Yellow Ear Rings," for emphasis.

Such an act of bravery could but inspire his followers, and one of them rebuked him thus: "Yellow Ear Rings, you are too brave to die. We will not let you die. If you are to die, we shall also die with you." At these words his few followers arose as one man and flew at the Crows, who were gradually pushing toward them exultant with apparent victory; put them to flight and saved themselves as well as Yellow Ear Rings. His heroic act of expected self-sacrifice proved to be his salvation; his death chant saved his life and inspired his followers to win the victory.

Knowing many of the participants in after years, I talked with them often of this engagement. One of Yellow Ear Rings' comrades fell shot through the abdominal region in this sally. He asked to be helped to water, and requested his supporter to gather ants from one of the large ant hills so frequently found on the western plains. He then ate of the ants, and although they probably had no curative properties, he got well and lived for many years to tell of his exploits. The family of Yellow Ear Rings is still living at Bull Head, South Dakota.

General Crook decided not to follow the fleeing Sioux any further. He had had about enough, as his forces had received severe treatment from the hands of this hunting party of Sioux and Cheyennes. Our forces camped on the field but early the following morning set out on our return to Goose Creek, carrying the wounded on improvised travois.

Shortly after leaving camp the Crow and Shoshone scouts who worked out in all directions brought in the dismembered fragments of a Sioux they had found, and while the army held up to await the slower movements of the travois with the wounded, the Indian scouts held a scalp dance around the scalps taken from their enemy. The Sioux whom they had killed that morning had been shot the day before across the front of his face, destroying both eyes. They now found him in the breaks of the bluff, weakened from loss of blood, feverish, blind and unable to travel. Hearing riders not far away and thinking them some of his own friends, the wounded Sioux had set up a feeble cry of "Minni, minni, minni," which means water. Hearing the appeal, the Crows went over and took the little life left in him with great glee, savagely tore the body limb from limb and brought the bleeding fragments over to our moving column.

CHAPTER XXVIII

Some Observations on Crook's Inactivity

AFTER the battle of the Rosebud, General Crook retraced his steps to his camp on Goose Creek and settled down to the enjoyment of weeks of fishing and hunting. It was estimated by some of his men that the members of the command took over 15,000 trout out of the streams and the number of deer, mountain sheep, elks, and bears brought in ran into the hundreds.[1] The season was luxurious and the attitude of the soldiers was more that of summer picknickers than of soldiers sent on a serious expedition against hostile Indians.

It is not my purpose to give the history of Crook's campaign but simply to flash a few side lights that will reveal things not mentioned in the official reports, or even in the sober historical narratives. You may or may not be concerned with what I saw and heard, but I am, and this is what I want to tell you.

As I have said, the distance between General Crook's camp on Goose Creek and Fort Fetterman was one hundred and ninety miles. I made the journey between the points every little while, lying over long enough at each terminus to allow my horse to rest and recover

[1] See Bourke's *Campaigning with Crook*, where a rather full account may be found. Also Finnerty's *Camp Fire and Bivouac*.

from the wearing effects of the long journey. Occasionally some one rode with me for his own protection, but for the most part I made the trip in each direction alone. Sometimes I met supply wagons or passed them on the road, and sometimes couriers engaged in work similar to my own, but usually the trail was unoccupied. Most of the hostiles had been withdrawn from our territory and concentrated along the Rosebud and the Big Horn, as we afterwards learned.

On one trip down from Crook's camp I was almost too ill to ride during most of the journey and was compelled to take to my bed for several days on reaching Fort Fetterman. About two o'clock one morning while I was there — I think it was on July 6th — the telegraph agent came to my room with a dispatch conveying the news of Custer's disaster of June 25th on the Little Big Horn. The news had been brought down by the steamboat captain, Grant Marsh, on the *Far West* to Bismarck, Dakota Territory, and from there had been sent out to the world by telegraph. The message had been sent to Fort Fetterman immediately on reaching the War Department.

I knew General Crook would want this information as soon as it could be conveyed to him; so, sick as I was, I got up, saddled my horse, and within half an hour after the telegrapher had waked me was on my way with the sad message.

I passed the supply train freighters at Fort Reno and with but a slackening of pace told them of Custer's death. I then continued to Crook's camp on Goose Creek, reaching it in the early morning of July 10.

General Crook was away on an elk hunt and did not return until the next day, after scouts had been sent to find him.

News of the Custer tragedy threw the camp into the wildest excitement. Many of the members of the 7th Cavalry under Custer were well known to the officers and soldiers under Crook. The messages I carried gave the first news of Custer's death that had reached Crook, although two days later three messengers from General Terry came in with dispatches sewed up in their coat linings which gave more in detail the same intelligence I had brought in.

General Crook sent for me to come to his head-quarters tent. I reported as requested, and he asked me if I would carry a message to open up communication with General Terry on the Yellowstone. I had just made a hard ride from Fort Fetterman and had been ill all the way. I told him that I was in no fit physical condition to undergo the strain of a trip through an unknown country, but he would not take no for an answer and asked, "What will you take to carry a message?" After some hesitation I replied, "$700." He doubtless thought this messenger fee too high, just as I did, because I had made the figure high enough that I would not have to go. When I stated the amount General Crook said, "I'll see you again," and I went my way.

Later a miner by the name of Kelly agreed to carry the message for $300. His plan was to strike for the head of the Big Horn and float down it on a raft as soon as he reached a point where the depth of the water would permit it. He made two unsuccessful attempts to reach the Big Horn and was either driven or frightened back, but the third time was successful.

In the meantime General Sheridan had started reënforcements to General Crook — seven companies of infantry under Colonel Chambers from Fort Fetterman and ten troops of cavalry under General Merritt, from Fort Robinson, Nebraska. Sheridan advised Crook to await the coming of the troops before attempting to join General Terry if he thought best. In this matter Crook was to use his own judgment, and since he did not stir out of his camp it is to be inferred that he thought it unsafe to venture the attempt until Merritt could come from Fort Robinson, a distance of nearly four hundred miles. Merritt's cavalry did not arrive until August 5, and then his command and Crook's started to the Rosebud. Merritt had with him two noted scouts — Buffalo Bill and Captain Jack Crawford, the latter known as the poet scout.

From June 17 to July 10 Crook's command had been inactive so far as hunting Indians or being molested by them was concerned. By the latter date General Terry had withdrawn down the Big Horn and left the victorious hostiles free to turn their attentions to other quarters. A few came to Goose Creek and annoyed Crook's pickets or tried to drive off the horse herd and set fire to the prairie. The grass was too green to burn readily, yet they succeeded in converting miles and miles of grass into a blackened waste. General Crook inside his barricade was perfectly safe, and as long as he preferred to stay there the hostiles did not risk a general engagement. The allied scouts under Chief Washakie had several brushes with the hostiles, but on the whole the presence of the Sioux was only a petty annoyance.

I did not go north with the Crook and Merritt commands but started to Fort Fetterman with my last dispatch after these commands had united. After reaching Fort Fetterman I continued on down to Fort Laramie and from there went to Deadwood.

General Crook did not wish to take his wagon train with him, owing to his doubt of their ability to get through without having too many delays in road-making, and Major Fury took the train back to Fort Laramie. The commands of General Crook and General Terry met on the Rosebud and went on down to the Yellowstone together. Later the commands separated, General Terry going north of the Yellowstone and General Crook coming eastward and across the badlands of the Little Missouri to the head of Heart River and thence southward toward the Black Hills. At Slim Buttes, South Dakota, Captain Anson Mills of Crook's command surprised a small body of Sioux under the young chief American Horse, surrounded them and destroyed them, American Horse being among the killed.

Crook's journey from Heart River to the Black Hills was marked by a shortage of provisions. The soldiers ate horseflesh for several days until word of their plight was taken to Deadwood and provisions sent out to meet them by the citizens. The people of

Deadwood gave them a great ovation, because their title to the Black Hills was expected to come through the army.

Shortly after the battle on the Little Big Horn the hostiles sent runners eastward bearing the news of their great victory. The agency Indians at all the Missouri River agencies knew of Custer's defeat before the *Far West* reached Bismarck with the news. The runners did not have as long a journey to cover, and in bearing messages as important as this they relayed them from one point to another, using fresh horses and riders. The hostiles possibly expected the news of their success to bring recruits to their ranks from among the friendly Indians at the agencies.

There were probably from 2,000 to 2,500 warriors at the Battle of the Little Big Horn, but the country would not support such a large number for any length of time if they stayed together. The Indians had no commissary, and in summer season depended for food upon the wild animals that came in their path from day to day. But the movements of the armies scared the food animals from their accustomed haunts and the hostiles broke up into numerous bands, each under its own chief or sub-chief, and scattered to localities where it was likely buffaloes could be found. Buffaloes were the main dependencies for subsistence among the non-treaty Indians, and at that time there was no herd of these large enough to support a body such as met Custer for any length of time in one place.

I would be going far afield were I to go into a discussion of Custer's last fight. It has been covered by

many writers who condemned or defended Custer. In
fact, so much attention has been given to Custer that it
seems to me General Crook has been overlooked. I
have already spoken of the three columns — Crook's,
Terry's, and Gibbon's, that were beginning to close in
on the hostiles. The plan of the campaign was admir-
able, but there was no way to regulate the speed of the
several columns to enable them to strike at the same
time. General Gibbon joined Terry, but Terry divided
his forces, giving the larger part to Custer, so there are
still three columns to consider, Crook's, Terry's and
Custer's. There was no way to coördinate Crook's and
Custer's movements. The scouts of one had no communication with the scouts of the other. Crook, having
a shorter distance to go, was the first to strike Indians.
His meeting with the hunting band of hostiles under
Crazy Horse at Rosebud on June 17, occurred only
about forty miles from the place where the full hostile
strength struck Custer on June 25.

I have already said that Crook withdrew after this
engagement on the Rosebud to his base on Goose Creek
seventy-five miles to the rear, and remained there fishing and hunting, until August 5. It is probably not
becoming in me to criticize General Crook, but it seems
that his actions deserve criticism. Crook was an experienced Indian fighter — in fact, no other general in
the U. S. Army had the experience or reputation that
he had, and deservedly, at that time.

All Indian fighters know that the first thing one has
to do is to find the Indian. This campaign was organized to find the non-reservation Indians and compel

them to come in to the reservations. Crook struck the Indians first on the Rosebud, and in my opinion he should have remained in contact with them instead of withdrawing to his camp on Goose Creek. He had no need to look for Indians; he knew where they were. His force was far superior to Custer's, and he knew that Custer was somewhere between him and the Yellowstone. He must have realized that the best way for them to support each other would be to approach the common point agreed upon. But Crook, it seems, made little effort to support Custer when he withdrew to a point far removed from the Indian force and to a place where Custer's scouts could not find him. Crook's force was rested; his supplies were adequate, and the topography of the country was such that he had easy access to his supply train.

Custer, on the other hand, was looking for Indians. When he struck a fresh trail he followed it. If Crook had done the same thing, the hostile force could not have combined against either — their attention would have been divided.

I have no word of criticism for Crook's scouts, Grouard, Pourier, and Richaud: there were no better anywhere; or of the Crow, Shoshone, or Ute allies, who gave us their service without owing us anything. In the battle of the Rosebud the percentage of loss among the Indian allies was far greater than among the white soldiers.

After June 17 Crook, to all practical purposes, was out of the campaign. He remained at his base inactive in a military way until Terry's scouts, after scouring the country, found him seventeen days after Custer's death. Had Crook been where he ought to have been the scouts could have found him in time to use his forces in conjunction with Custer's.

Terry's scouts reached Crook's camp on July 12. How much longer he would have remained in camp had Terry not hunted him up is vain to conjecture. Crook had a right to anticipate that Custer would need his assistance, and his assistance surely could not be given while in his camp on Goose Creek. Of course, it may be contended that after his battle of the 17th Crook felt that the hostile forces were too powerful for him to meet alone; but in such case, he must also have realized that Custer, whose man-power was much less than that of Crook's, would be even less safe.

The whole plan of the campaign contemplated the use of the combined columns against the hostiles, and the failure of the campaign was due not so much to alleged rashness on the part of Custer as to an almost criminal inertia on the part of Crook with his superior force.

CHAPTER XXIX

AFTER the Battle of the Little Big Horn the hostile bands scattered to their various homes. The Cheyennes went south along the Big Horn Mountains, Crazy Horse and his followers came over on Powder and around the Black Hills, while Sitting Bull, Gall, and Rain-in-the-Face and their followers went north of the Yellowstone, and when pursued by General Miles, took refuge in Canada in the following year.

The whites poured into the Black Hills during the whole of 1876, and the Indians became more incensed at their encroachments. Indians and miners alike went armed for each other, and murders were of almost daily occurrence. Most of the murders were doubtless committed by hostiles from the Little Big Horn who were working back toward the agencies where they could be counted in for supplies. Military campaigns were carried on in the late fall and winter against the tribes who refused to come in. By military orders the horses and guns were taken away from the friendly Indians at the agency, as it was believed that the hostiles were trading buffalo robes for ammunition and other war material.

During the winter campaign of 1876 I served as packer under Dave Mears, a brother-in-law to General

Crook, who had been brought from Oregon to take the job. The pack train was large, cumbersome, and only a useless bill of expense, as it proved. Mears's previous experience had not fitted him for such work.

While on this campaign a few of our rear guard were having a little brush with the Indians — when one of the soldiers fell from his horse. An Indian not far off rode over to him and the soldier handed up his gun to the Indian who was still on his horse. Whereupon the Indian threw open the breech block, saw the gun was loaded, closed it and shot the soldier through the head, jumped off, cut the cartridge belt from his victim, mounted, and was away almost before we could realize what was taking place. The whole scene was enacted in full view of our train. The Indian was armed only with a bow and arrows and we could not account for the soldier's action in handing up his gun in token of surrender on any other ground than extreme fright, as neither whites nor Indians took men prisoners.

In the treaty of September 26 to October 27, 1876, the Indians unwillingly relinquished the Black Hills and all the unceded Indian country between the Yellowstone and the Platte. The buffaloes had been killed off except in favored localities and the winter campaigns had destroyed the Indians' tents, household goods, and clothing until there was nothing for them to do but submit to the demands of the treaty commissions, place their marks on the dotted line, and accept the subsistence dole offered. Congress ratified the treaty on February 28, 1877, and on this date the Black Hills ceased to belong to the Indians. At that time it was estimated that the white population of the Hills exceeded fifty thousand. Instead of Indian depredations the citizens were henceforth afflicted by white outlaws who held up mail coaches, freighting outfits, and treasure coaches with alarming frequency until the better element took the law into their own hands and killed many of the desperadoes. The bandits sometimes dressed as Indians to protect their own identity and to direct the blame to the Indians who were then in bad odor.

On one occasion when I was running a road ranch a man came to stay over-night with us. According to custom strangers were taken in and no questions asked. The weather was cold, and of evenings the guests sat around a large stove in the sitting room. Later the same evening another man came for lodging who proved to be a peace officer on the lookout for some of the bandits who had been making travel unsafe for some months.

After supper as we all sat around the stove, the peace officer made known the fact that he was out looking for some of these robbers, and especially for Doc Middleton, known to be one of the most dreaded of these law breakers. He didn't mince matters in the least but told us in emphatic English what he would do to Middleton if he ever ran across him. When he had about talked himself out, my other guest, who had sat silent and unperturbed throughout the peace officer's monologue, spoke up and asked:

"You say you have a warrant for Doc Middleton?"

"You bet I have," was the prompt reply.

"Well, I'm Doc Middleton," said the stranger composedly.

The peace officer gasped, and it became immediately evident that he had decided that he was not looking for Middleton.

"Well, why don't you serve your warrant? I'm here."

With trembling fingers the deputy sheriff pulled out the warrant and began to unfold it in the uncertain light of the kerosene lamp, whereupon Middleton reached over in an unconcerned sort of way, took the paper and threw it into the stove.

The deputy had taken off his revolvers before eating supper, but Middleton still carried his buckled around him. The deputy hadn't a chance, and he knew it. Middleton was not only a desperate character but fearless and unbeatable in a gun play. I have never seen any one whose face revealed less of what was going on in his mind. He permitted the deputy to go his way without his guns, but never joked or said a word about the affair. As soon as it was over it was as if it had never happened.[1]

One time while I was holding a beef herd opposite the mouth of the Grand River the government brought up flour and issued it to the Indians to fulfil the terms of the treaty. The Indians had never used flour before, so they poured it out on the ground. They made good use of the sacks for leggins and breech clouts.

[1] After a career of crime almost without parallel, Middleton was led into an ambush by some of his confederates and captured. After serving a term in the penitentiary, he lived the life of a decent citizen.

About the same time several hundred barrels of ground coffee were turned over to the agency for distribution among the Indians. It was found to be so adulterated with ground pine bark that it tasted like pitch. There may have been a little coffee in the mixture but it couldn't be separated, so the whole issue was thrown away. The government was trying to live up to its obligations, but there were so many opportunities for such accidents that those with evil designs could not pass them by. The Indian could not get a hearing and those committing the frauds usually went unpunished, largely because the Indian had no standing in court and had no means of compelling justice. The juries were always packed against him.

In the spring of 1870 or '71 I worked in a wood camp on Medicine Knoll Creek, on the west side of the Missouri. Our outfit consisted of Charles Clark, riding boss or camp tender, a Mexican named Pedro, a half-breed named Sidwell Consula, Ed Whitney, Ed Monroe, and a few others besides myself.

In the summer of the same year Consula, Whitney, and I made a trip over to James River. As we expected to find game on the road we carried no provisions; but most of the road lay across an open prairie, and on the whole trip we found no animals larger than meadowlarks. When we reached Crow Creek Reservation on our return we were getting desperately hungry, and as we entered an Indian village Whitney cried out, "Five dollars to the first man who calls me to a feast." Almost immediately an old man stepped to the door of his lodge and called a feast, which consisted of sections of beef intestines and green corn boiled together. We were hungry enough, however, to eat anything with relish. The Indians prepare beef intestines by removing the inside lining, blowing them up and drying them. After that they are cut into sections and cooked with corn or tipsin.[2] Hunger is a good sauce; the Indian got his $5.00 and we enjoyed the meal.

I have spoken of the hard winter of 1865-66 at Fort Union. On coming down the river I learned that around Grand River the Indians had suffered terribly from hunger. The government at that time gave them no rations. Being on the point of starvation, they would sell anything they had for a pocket full of corn. They ate all their dogs and horses, and it was believed that over five hundred died from starvation in the immediate territory before the winter was over.

Very few of the Indians had guns, and such as they had were Hudson's Bay smooth bores that carried an ounce ball — very inaccurate except at close quarters. These Indians were too poor to buy powder and balls, and too weak and famished to go on long hunts even when provided with ammunition.

The Hudson's Bay Company used to buy up flintlocks that had been thrown into the discard in the Old World, ship them over and trade them to the Indians for furs. An old trapper on the Missouri River named Marcelle, who formerly worked for the Hudson's Bay Company, said in selling an old flintlock he would

[2] The scientific name of tipsin or tipsila is *Psoralea Esculenta.* It has been called Indian turnip by white people. Among all the prairie tribes the perennial storage root of the tipsin was an important article of food, eaten either fresh or dried.

stand it on the floor and the Indians would pile up beaver hides as high as the gun to pay for it. Any sort of a gun was superior to a bow and arrow, and the Indian, living as he did by the chase, had to have weapons of some sort. White traders took advantage of his necessity and drove hard bargains.

The white man's business was also hazardous. At one time in the later 60's there were 20,000 buffalo skins, the property of Durfee & Peck, stacked in long ricks at Fort Union with tarpaulins thrown over them. These hides had been bought from the Crows among whom the smallpox had been raging, and the government would not allow them to be shipped. I do not know what final disposition was made of these robes, but I presume they found their way to market sooner or later.

Whiskey has always been a demoralizing factor, wherever used. Its sale has never been legal among the Indians, but they got it just the same.

On one occasion two men rode up to my camp to stay over-night. One of them asked, "Ben, ain't you got something to drink?" "Yes," I replied, motioning to a nearby tent, "but we can't pass it around, the inspector is over there."

"What do I care for the inspector," said he, "Show me the drinks."

So I uncovered a keg, and before morning my visitors had the inspector drunk and got his signature to some papers they desired signed.

On another occasion I went into partnership with a man and we bought eight gallons of whiskey and engaged in the Indian trade on our own account. An Indian came along and we traded a gallon of it for a pony. We made similar trades with others as fast as we could show our wares. As soon as our stock ran out the Indians to whom we had first sold began to sell one-half of what they had for a pony to other Indians who had not come in time to get a supply from us. Thus the Indians who had bought from us ended up with a pony and a few drinks left, which they considered profitable dealing.

As soon as our supply was exhausted we started out with our horses and ran plump into the Indian inspector. He knew what we had been doing, but made no fuss as he knew we had something on him. Ordinarily I was not a law breaker, but I sometimes liked to "put something over" on a fellow whose own evil ways made him afraid to open his mouth against others.

Canada has had many Indians to deal with. England is the mother of many colonies and knows how to handle native subjects better than we do.

During the years from 1860 to 1880 we spent many times as much in fighting Indians as we did in annuities. On the other hand Canada has been at peace with the Indians and her per capita cost of taking care of them has been far less than ours.

The reason for this is not far to seek. The Indian service in Canada has been better paid and in consequence has attracted a higher class of men. In the United States in the early day the agents received for the most part around a thousand to twelve hundred dollars per annum each and out of this meager allowance they had to find subsistence for themselves and their families. It looks as if Congress expected them to make up the deficiency either in private business on the side or in getting "contributions" from Indian traders.

While we have had many able, honest, and well-meaning Indian agents, yet they were so in spite of the system rather than because of it.

In the early '70's Secretary of War Belknap was impeached for graft in the Indian service. One agent who was receiving a salary of $1,000 testified that he had contributed $15,000 to get the position. The positions of trader or agent were sought chiefly because they gave opportunity to make a profit at the expense of the Indian. Harpies always hovered around the Indian camps dogging their footsteps, debauching them with whiskey, and cheating them out of their scanty supplies, in spite of the vigilance of the authorities. Want and starvation often urged the Indians, even when friendly, to deeds of violence. The Indian held the white man responsible for his woes, as the usurper of his country. The white man had killed the buffaloes, used his wood, and confined him to a reservation with insufficient annuity and nothing to do. The Indian had to give up the chase in which he was skilled and take up tillage in which he was unskilled. He had no civil ambition to take the place of a war-like one. He had no reserves to sustain him when crops were blasted and no means to make up deficiencies which his honest labor usually failed to provide.

I must say a word about a well-known character in

the early days of the Black Hills, known now as Calamity Jane.[3] While Calamity Jane was not in a sense an outlaw, yet she was a picturesque character of the Old West. Her real name was Jane Somers, although she appeared at different places under many different assumed names. Much has been written and told about this remarkable woman, but the greater part of it is untrue. The stories of her being a scout or a guide are inventions of people who never knew her. Jane Somers was born in Princeton, Missouri, in 1852, and came to Virginia City, Montana, in 1864, making the journey overland with her parents, to the Alder Gulch gold camp.

Jane was then but a girl of thirteen and her mother being poor she took in washing from the miners. Jane gathered and delivered laundry for her mother, and many knew her as an attractive, vivacious girl. Shortly afterwards she was led astray, it was claimed, by a man whose name one of the gold gulches still bears. Her mother died at Blackfoot, Idaho, in 1866, and her father at Piedmont, Wyoming, in 1867. Thus left an orphan, she soon became a follower of the freighting teams, and learned to be a good driver. She visited many places, and when the Union Pacific reached Corinne, Utah, she went thither and traveled up and down the line till 1875 when she went to Cheyenne and to Fort Laramie, and from there, dressed in male attire, she accompanied the mule teams that hauled the supplies for the army escort under Colonel Bradley from

[3] Calamity Jane's real name is often given as Martha Cannary. Some of the other names she bore are, Hunt, Blake, White, and Dalton. See Freeman's *Boating down the Yellowstone.*

Fort Laramie. This is the same escort that took over Professor Jenny who went to make geological explorations of the Hills. From that time on she made her home at Deadwood, although she visited from time to time all the outlying cities.

The career she followed required a constitution of iron. While she never was a government scout, Calamity had many stirring adventures and many true stories could be told of her, but most of them would not look well in print.

The last time I saw her she was in the town of Evarts, South Dakota, then the end of the Milwaukee Railroad. At first I could hardly believe it was Calamity, as she was old and haggard beyond her years. To make myself sure, I asked her if she knew Bill Bivens at Virginia City in 1864, and she said: "I can go to his grave as straight as an Indian goes to dog soup." Her answers to other questions satisfied me as to her identity.

In her prime she was known as a good teamster, a skillful roper, and a crack rifle shot; all qualities admired by western men. She told me that she was fifty years old. She had traveled extensively and knew many people, especially among the old timers, and carried photographs of herself dressed in buckskin costume, which she sold. Many made small purchases and refused to take change, as they considered her a fit object of charity.

This woman was a strange mixture of the wild and wayward, the generous and unselfish. While she lived a life of shame, yet she was as good as her associates. She never posed; her personality was her own.

In 1878 a smallpox epidemic broke out in Deadwood, hundreds were bedfast from the scourge, and many died. It was here that this outcast woman, true to the better instincts of her sex, ministered day and night among the sick and dying, with no thought of reward or of what the consequences might be to herself. Her unselfish labors during this great calamity all but blotted out the past in the eyes of many, and the people gave her the name, "Calamity Jane," as a mark of recognition if not affection; and by this name she has been since known throughout the West.

On August 1, 1903, at the age of fifty-one, she entered her last sleep, and was buried in Mount Moriah Cemetery in Deadwood by the side of her one time pal, Wild Bill Hickok, mourned by a few, pitied by all.

CHAPTER XXX

The Homesteader Vanguard

As the Indian war was now over the Black Hills began to take on a more peaceful and substantial aspect. The fear of trouble with the Indians kept many of the more timid Easterners at home. Now that this danger was removed, many flocked not only to the Black Hills but to all the surrounding territory open to homestead entry.

In the spring of 1877 my friends, Ed Whitney and Ed Monroe, the former then freighting into the Black Hills and the latter cattle inspector at the Red Cloud Agency, and myself arranged to go down on the Niobrara in the vicinity of the fort by the same name, with a view to locating. Our prospects didn't pan out and Whitney went up to the Medicine Knoll creek in South Dakota, Monroe returned to his inspecting work at the Red Cloud Agency, and I went down on the Elkhorn.

The winter of 1876 was a hard one. The grasshoppers had destroyed much of the vegetation the summer before and the people were so hard up that there was no local market for anything. Not far from the town of Neligh I ran into an old Scotchman named John McKinnon who had plenty of corn. I was looking for a place where I could feed my horse during the winter, so I stayed over with him. In return for my keep I furnished much of the provisions for the table and enjoyed the life of a settled community for a season. I am sure the people of the neighborhood thought I was an outlaw seeking an asylum.

During the winter the neighborhood had a literary society which was attended by nearly every one for miles around. The greater part of each evening's program was given over to a debate, often with eight or ten on a side selected by the two chief disputants. The debaters had no sources of material at hand and their arguments were mainly unsupported assertions, made often with much vehemence. Like all pioneer farming communities, the people always attended court for the gossip and the entertainment it afforded, even going miles to do so, and their style of speaking in debate was patterned largely on the noisy harangues of the pettyfoggers who made up the small town bar of that day. The people who attended the literary society may not have received much information, but they did get the ability to stand on the floor, and they developed a certain ready, rough wit in rejoinder that was enjoyed by the listeners. While staying with McKinnon I first met the girl I married January 5, 1878.

The following spring Ed Whitney and I went north to the Niobrara to take up homesteads but I shortly afterwards relinquished mine to him, as down on the Elkhorn I could see in the doorway of a log cabin the slender silhouette of a sweet rosy-checked girl waiting for me. She clung to me through the years until she was taken from me but a few years ago. I remained on the Elkhorn for a few years, where our first baby daughter died and another was born to us.

My next move was to the Niobrara near where Alliance, Nebraska, now stands. Fort Niobrara had been established and I took a hay contract and for a time lived on the Sharp ranch.

We got a fair start in farming. After my years of adventure and frequent moving from place to place the life of a farmer seemed rather prosaic and tame. Yet I might have remained there permanently had not a catastrophe overtaken me. Some Texas infected cattle were brought in and all my cattle took the Texas fever and died, not a hoof remaining. At that time the nature of the infection was not known, but it was later learned that it is traceable to the Texas tick. The southern cattle had become immune to the disease, but when they were brought north they carried the ticks whose bite infected the northern cattle, which died with alarming rapidity. To show how rapidly the disease worked I give one instance. One of my neighbors was teaming to an Indian agency with two pair of oxen, and while he was on the way all four head died, leaving him on the road with his loaded wagon and nothing to draw it.

Being discouraged by the loss of my cattle, I sold my corn for eight cents a bushel, disposed of all my other possessions except what I could haul in a covered wagon, and set out for Fort Fetterman, Wyoming. Our family now consisted of two children, a boy and a girl, and shortly after arriving at Fort Fetterman another son was born to us.

A railroad was under construction through the Fort Fetterman country, and one of the engineers told me of a place where there would be a town; if I desired I could file on land within the proposed town-site. But I did not file. The town is now Douglas, Wyoming.

When the railroad work suspended for the winter of 1885-6 I returned to the head of White River in Nebraska for the winter. In the fall of '86 I moved to Chadron where an old friend, Don Pape, and I joined forces in pulling young cottonwoods to sell to the incoming settlers who were taking up tree claims. The federal lands laws allowed one to take up a homestead of 160 acres, a like amount as a preëmption, and an additional 160 acres as a tree claim. The law was intended to encourage the planting of groves and shelter belts over the treeless west. Millions of acres were taken up as tree claims; but few people have ever seen a single grove as a result. In proving up, the claimant made affidavit that he had planted to trees the number of acres required by law. Most of the planting was done in such manner that the trees had no chance of growing, and those who had the claims knew it. For the most part they were stuck in the sod and left uncultivated. Even if the seedlings grew a few years under good care a chance prairie fire that occasionally swept the country always burned everything before it. The trees always held the combustile drift carried by the wind and thus prepared the way for their own destruction.

At any rate, the demand for cottonwood seedlings was very great. We sold over a million in 1886-7 and made a good thing on the venture. Those who bought from us were actuated for the most part only by the motive of getting an additional 160 acres of public domain.

Most of the homesteaders were single men without the means to handle even their homesteads successfully, much less the 480 that each filed on, and a good many took preëmption claims for an additional 160 acres — at least those who had the $1.25 an acre that the government required for payment on this sort of claim.

While we were at Chadron another daughter was born to us in 1888. In the spring of 1889 I moved into South Dakota and located on Bad River, twenty-two miles west of Fort Pierre. This land had previously been on an Indian reservation and had recently been thrown open for settlement. The region round about was fertile but wholly unsettled at that time, though crowds were elbowing their way in, in a frenzied endeavor to file on these free lands before the supply was exhausted.

I started a little store and asked that a postoffice be established. My request was granted and the name Bovine [1] given to the postoffice. That was a great cattle country, but those who took homesteads were poor, and the distance to haul grain, its low price, and lack of roads retarded farming operations. In my little store I had much call for credit. Being an old time westerner I took promises at their face value, but for some reason or another pay day never came, for them I mean. After the birth of my youngest daughter at Bovine in 1891, I moved to Pierre to get the advantages of a school for my children, several of whom were old enough to attend. For nine years I lived there, but even then the

[1] The postoffice of Bovine has given place to Capa of the present day.

call of the frontier was always strong. When the Milwaukee railroad was under construction and the survey had been staked to the Missouri and the town of Evarts platted, I moved there to take employment congenial to my restless spirit.

For a time Evarts was one of the largest primary cattle shipping points in the United States. Large cattle outfits that held Indian lands under lease drove their cattle to the Missouri and at first swam them across. Later the Milwaukee constructed a pontoon bridge on which the cattle were crossed. While this was less than a quarter of a century ago, the cattle were wild and many of the cowboys were wilder still. Knowing the country as I did, I made trips into the cattle country under the employ of the railway and laid out trails with reference to the water supply. When there was no natural water supply, an engineering crew was sent out with workmen to construct reservoirs along the main trails.

For two years I ran a ferry across the Missouri at the mouth of Oak Creek, near the postoffice called Grass. In 1896-7 the Milwaukee crossed the river and in pushing its extension passed through much virgin country, in South Dakota, North Dakota, and Montana, and incidentally killed the ferry business. Homesteaders came in by the train-load. Tent and tar-paper shack towns sprang up every few miles, as a rule ahead of the track laying. My knowledge of the country served me in good stead in locating some of these settlers on good homesteads. The old time cow man and prince of good fellows, Ed Lemmon, laid out the trail which the Milwaukee engineers followed in making the survey. It was his intimate knowledge of the topography of the country that led the Milwaukee to tear up the tracks and abandon the roadbed into Evarts and make its river crossing some miles higher up at Mobridge, from which point an easy grade up Oak Creek was obtained.

The town of Lemmon, South Dakota, situated on the boundary line between the two Dakotas, was named after Ed Lemmon. For years he was the manager and heavily interested financially in the Lake, Tomb & Lemmon Cattle Company, that ran thousands of cattle on the ranges of South Dakota. Only a few men of the old West such as he is are left.

From the building of the Milwaukee to the present time my experiences have not been unusual, and for this reason are too common to be interesting. To give a narrative covering this period would be of too personal a nature. I have tried in the foregoing pages to give my experiences only when they connected the reader with something of greater importance than any one individual, and this plan will not be abandoned now.

CHAPTER XXXI

Indian Characteristics

THE INDIAN is a human being and in most ways is not unlike the whites, although his training and environment have been different. Economic forces rendered his skill with the bow and arrow and in the chase nugatory. Farming is too tame and prossaic, and too uncertain in unskilled hands, to appeal to one who had spent his life on horseback.

In traits of character the Indian was steadfast in his friendships. Personally, I have been as well treated by Indians as by white people. Among Indians, as among white people, there are some good, some bad. The love of money among the whites has made the good ones grasping and ready to take advantage of the necessities of the weaker, and has made the bad ones into thieves and robbers. The chief property of the Indian — that which gave him his living — consisted of wild animals, property common to all. When one killed a buffalo, the meat was distributed among those in need. The sense of individual proprietorship was not strongly felt. What belonged to one belonged to all. Consequently the Indian felt no shame in asking for what he wanted (begging) from his white neighbor or of taking it (stealing) if it were not freely given. No one ever visited an Indian camp who did not have set before him the best the village afforded — food and bed — with no pay expected for it. The Indian felt that when he went to a white man's village he was entitled to a return of courtesies. If such courtesies were not extended voluntarily, he felt free to ask for them. Begging was not considered an offense. It was simply calling to the attention of the one who had possessions his short-comings in not making a voluntary offering, as the Indian would have done under similar circumstances. The idea of common property weakened the sense of individual ownership among the Indians, and while it tended to make them generous, it tended at the same time to make them improvident.

To steal horses from an enemy was considered a *coup* worthy of the highest praise — next to taking an enemy's scalp. Horses were in great demand. A man's social and military standing were determined largely by the number of horses he had. A warrior had to furnish himself, and each strove to get as good an outfit as possible. Stealing horses from an enemy was the easiest way to cripple him and build oneself up, and was just as praiseworthy among Indians as a fair degree of thrift is among white men. In their dances and social functions, certain marks of recognition were given to those who had stolen horses that were not given to those who had not. To steal required bravery and cunning, which were both desired virtues. It is easily seen, then, that with a weak sense of individual ownership, the strong need for horses, and the high standing accorded one who could steal them without getting caught, the moral sense covering the sacredness of private property would not be in accord with our own. We must judge the Indian by his standards, not by ours.

The Indian in his line is bright. He has been called a savage, but he is not dumb and stupid; he is superior intellectually to many of the white peasant population of Europe. There were no better trailers, scouts, or skirmishers than the red race produced on the frontier. They were adapted to the life they led, and their efficiency must be measured by the way in which they responded to their environment.

The Indian man is called lazy. His chief duties were to catch game and defend himself from his enemies, and in these attributes he showed skill and industry. Like white people, he was not too anxious to work; unless stimulated, encouraged, and made to see that it meant his immediate benefit and advancement. It was always hard for an Indian to comprehend why his reservation was taken from him and given to the whites as soon as it gave evidence of being worth anything. In some way he was slow to see the justice of taking away his home lands and sending him away to another home less hospitable. We probably would have felt just as he did had we been in his place.

In 1875, when the order was sent out that all non-treaty Indians among the Sioux must come in and be enrolled, Crazy Horse and Sitting Bull refused to comply. They did not see why anyone should assume to control their movements so long as they lived within the territory assigned them by treaty. Louis Richaud, the interpreter who was sent to confer with them, brought back this message from Sitting Bull: "The Big Chief of the white men must come to see me. I will not go to the reservation. I have no land to sell. Game is plentiful and we have enough ammunition. We don't want any white men here."

Most of the trouble between the Indians and whites was caused by young Indian men and bad white men. The bad white men took advantage of the Indian and sent in false reports to Washington and to the agencies. The Indian had no one to present his side of the case and the evil inclined whites knew it.

As I have already said the Indian was generous, and as a rule any favor shown him was reciprocated. He was honorable in his dealings, especially with those whose conduct had been above suspicion. I am not using honorable in the modern restricted sense that ascribes this quality exclusively to one who pays his bills promptly at the first of each month.

The lurid writers have always portrayed in vivid coloring the "tomahawk and the scalping knife of the savage." The Indian was not more inhuman in warfare than the whites he fought against. Neither side as a rule took prisoners. The Indian fought men; the white men attacked a village and killed more women and children than warriors. The Indian wars were fought on the Indian's land, where the white man had no right to be. The Indian's tents, his household goods and provisions, were destroyed, and many died in consequence from starvation and freezing. With few exceptions the white men's houses were free from attack.

One of the clauses of the treaty of Laramie, in speaking of the lands assigned to the Indians, reads thus: "And the same is set apart for the absolute and undisturbed use and occupation of the Indians herein named," yet all the Indian wars of the Northwest from 1864 to 1877, were fought in the territory set aside for their "undisturbed use and occupation."

In 1870 when Red Cloud and Spotted Tail headed a delegation of Indians to Washington, the former said in a speech he delivered: "When I come to the white man's land [Washington] I leave no trail of blood. When the white man comes to my land he leaves a trail of blood behind him. When you send goods to me they are stolen all along the road; so when they reach me there is only a handful. They held out a paper for me to sign and that is all I got for my land. You might grant my people the powder they ask. All I ask is for enough to kill game. The Great Spirit has made all things I have in my country wild. I have to hunt them up. With us it is not like it is with you, who go out and find what you want."

After 1876 not only the guns but the horses were taken from the agency Indians, and in this respect they were placed on a plane with the hostiles. The Indians knew the use of fire arms, but even in their last war, 1876-7, many were still armed with bows and arrows and most of the guns in use were antiquated flintlocks and smooth bores. They had no chance to wage a successful war, and men like Red Cloud knew it. While they did not want to give up their hunting grounds they knew they must either do so or be driven from the face of the earth. Bishop Whipple, a member of the treaty commission of 1876 in speaking of the treaty of 1868 and its violation by the United States, said :"I know of no instance in history where a great nation has so shamefully violated its oath."

The treaties with the Indians were made because of the pressure from the whites for the white man's benefit. Indian forays almost without exception were reprisals for injuries they had sustained. The non-treaty Sioux always claimed they wished to get to a place where the white soldiers wouldn't follow them. Consequently they took up residence in the remote regions of the Powder, the Tongue, and the Rosebud, where the buffalo could still be found.

The buffalo was the Indian's main dependence for food, clothing, and shelter. The white man slaughtered the last buffalo for its hide, although this slaughter was contrary to law and in contravention of treaties with the Indians. The magazine gun, the white robe hunter, and the railroad doomed the buffalo, and with its passing the Indian had to settle down to farming and stock raising or be supported by government issues at the agencies.

The annuities offered the non-treaty Indians amounted to less than the value of one robe per capita. From a business standpoint it was to their interest to remain away from the reservation, hunt buffaloes, and sell their robes to traders and buy what they needed for subsistence, and not depend upon the agency issues which were never sufficient to keep them from feeling the pinch of hunger. This fact alone sent many friendlies to the hostile band, where they could be better clothed and fed. The wild bands without agency assistance were in better physical condition than were the agency Indians. Barring the molestation of the military, life in the hostile camps was more desired than inactive life on an agency. The complaints of the hostiles against the soldiers were well founded, as at no time did they live outside their treaty rights.

The Congress of the United States shortly after the Battle of the Big Horn passed a law that provided,[1] "No subsistence to be furnished them [the Sioux] until they relinquish all claims" to certain described lands, including the Black Hills. The law applied as well to the friendlies as to the hostiles; those who had stayed at home were deprived of subsistence. If caught away from the agency they were treated as hostile; and if they stayed at the agencies, no subsistence would be given till they signed a treaty alienating the lands desired by the treaty making power of the United States. But the whites must have the Black Hills and it would be ungracious to quarrel with the means they used in accomplishing that desirable result. Land grabbing was made necessary by the force of circumstances and was approved by all the whites, although a few looked upon it in a way as disagreeable, and piously to be regretted. We have been trying ever since to figure out justifying arguments to prevent our acts from being classed as a vulgar crime. In theory, a treaty is an agreement between two or more parties, but this one was prepared in Washington, and not a dot of an "i" or the cross of a "t" was permitted to be changed.

[1] Act of Congress, Aug. 15, 1876, *U. S. Statutes at Large*, xix, 192.

CHAPTER XXXII

Some Famous Sioux Chiefs

From time to time in these reminiscences I have had occasion to touch on some of the famous Indians of the old days, now long since gathered to their fathers. My work on the frontier brought me into intimate contact with the great leaders of the Dakota Nation. Having married a member of that family, my knowledge of the language enabled me to get into their life, habits, and thoughts as few men could. Therefore I have an excuse, if not a justification, for stating some opinions relative to a few of the leaders of the most populous and powerful Indian family of their day, the Dakota or Sioux Nation.

I shall speak briefly of Red Cloud, Spotted Tail, Crow Dog, Crazy Horse, Gall, and Sitting Bull. Red Cloud, long time chief of the Ogalalla Teton Sioux, was born on the forks of the Platte in 1822. While not a hereditary chief, yet by force of character he made himself a leader of his people. He set himself firmly against the encroachments of the whites and it was through his leadership, as I have already stated, that the forts on the Bozeman road were destroyed. Red Cloud agreed to cease hostilities as soon as these forts were torn down, and true to his promise he came in, signed the treaty, and remained at peace with the whites during the last forty years of his life.

It is said that Red Cloud earned eighty *coups* for bravery and daring exploits against his enemies, red and white. Undoubtedly he was one of the greatest warriors of his day, Crazy Horse alone equalling him.

As soon as Red Cloud had made his peace with the whites he showed ability in peace equally as great as he had shown in war. His counsel and advice were always sought by his people and usually followed. He took a prominent part in all treaty councils where his people were interested, and on several occasions was a delegate to Washington. I knew him well and always found him a gentleman in every sense of the word.

At one time when a member of a delegation of Indians in Washington he made a pitiful plea for what he considered his rights. Weak and defenseless, resigned to his fate, yet with an appeal for justice that is touching in its simplicity he said: "I am not hard to swindle, because I do not know how to read and write. The Great Spirit will not make me suffer because I am ignorant. I know I have been wronged. The words of my Great Father never reach me and mine never reach him. There are too many streams between us. The Great Spirit raised me on wild game. I do not ask my Great Father to give me anything. I came naked and I will go away naked."

All his appeals availed him little. He was talking of a past that few knew, and of which no one cared enough to listen. The last time I saw Red Cloud, he was over eighty years old, emaciated and blind, who a generation before had been the most distinguished Indian of his day, a pathetic figure but now feeble and fretting under the alleged neglect of the Great Father.

Another noted chief associated with Red Cloud is Spotted Tail, always a firm friend of the whites, but it is not of him so much as of Crow Dog, his murderer, that I would speak.

In his earlier life Spotted Tail had killed Big Mouth, his rival for the hand of Appearing Day. According to Indian custom and belief it was considered the duty of some one to avenge the death of Big Mouth. It is probable that Crow Dog also had some aspirations to become head of the Brulé tribe in Spotted Tail's place, if the latter were put out of the way. Consequently Crow Dog, who was at this time head of the Indian police at the Rosebud Agency, murdered Spotted Tail without provocation. Crow Dog was arrested and tried according to the Brulé custom and was found guilty. As a penalty for his crime he was required to deliver several ponies and robes to the relatives of the murdered chief. According to the Sioux law, Crow Dog had paid in full the penalty for his crime. But owing to the high standing of both men connected with the tragedy the United States could not pass the crime over in silence. Consequently Crow Dog was arrested, taken to Deadwood, and tried in the March term of the United States court in 1882. His friends engaged Attorney A. J. Plowman to defend him; but in spite of Plowman's best efforts Crow Dog was convicted and sentenced to be hanged. In his defense Plowman maintained that Crow Dog had already been tried and had paid the penalty according to the customs of the Sioux, and furthermore that the United States had no jurisdiction over the case. In some ways the United States treated the Indians as if they belonged to a foreign nation; for instance, they made treaties with them, just as they would with a foreign power, and it was on this ground that Attorney Plowman claimed lack of jurisdiction.

The case dragged out for some time, and while an appeal for a stay of execution had been granted, the sentence of death still stood against him. Crow Dog was given the liberty of the court yard, a privilege not granted to a white man under a similar sentence. The day of the execution had been set.

One evening the prisoner did not report to be locked in the jail, as was his custom. Thinking that he had gone to his home on the Rosebud Reservation, a United States deputy by the name of Wilson was sent to bring him back. When he got there Crow Dog told him he had wanted to see his family, especially a baby that had been born after his arrest, hence the reason for his leaving Deadwood. After considerable storming around Wilson was obliged to return to Deadwood without his prisoner. Crow Dog told the officer, however, that he intended to go back to Deadwood, and that it was unnecessary for any one to come after him, and furthermore he would start back after two more "sleeps." The deputy got drunk on the way back and when he reached Deadwood, Crow Dog was already there ready and expecting to pay the penalty of murder on the following day.

Court was called and Crow Dog's presence was required. He dressed himself in his best costume and decorated himself with all the medals in his possession, which he cherished with pardonable pride. In the meantime a telegram had been sent from Washington granting a pardon, but Crow Dog did not know it.

He walked into the court-room with great dignity to meet death as only a brave man can, and was much surprised when informed by the interpreter that he was a free man and at liberty to return home.

I was much gratified when I learned that Crow Dog had been pardoned. I knew him well and wrote several letters in his behalf. He had made a journey of nearly four hundred miles on foot to see his family and friends and bid them good-bye. I have never heard of another case where a man condemned to die was suffered his freedom and permitted to come unattended on his own honor to be at the appointed place at the set time to meet his own execution.

Crow Dog was a sincere friend of the white man. On one occasion after his pardon for the crime of killing Spotted Tail he was sent into the Sand Hills of Nebraska to capture an Indian who had killed a cowboy. Not being able to arrest the murderer Crow Dog shot and killed him, although a member of his own race.

On another occasion white men had stolen some Indian ponies. A detachment of United States soldiers was sent out to capture them. They took Crow Dog along as trailer and scout. While scouting, Crow Dog ran into the thieves asleep in a secluded spot, whereupon he gathered up the stolen Indian ponies and also the horses of the thieves and brought them back unaided. The soldiers remonstrated with him for not killing the thieves as they slumbered. He replied that he could not do so, as in all his life he had never taken the life of a white man. He had held positions of trust among the whites and always lived up to the confidence reposed in him.

Crazy Horse was probably the most daring and brilliant leader among the Sioux Nation. Crazy Horse through the intervention of his uncle, Spotted Tail, came in and voluntarily surrendered in the late fall of 1876. While at the agency the whites always feared that he would leave the agency and become hostile again, although the guns and horses had been taken away from all the Indians. He made his home at the Red Cloud Agency.

On one occasion he was taking his sick wife to Spotted Tail Agency, when he was stopped. He retorted haughtily: "I am Crazy Horse! Don't touch me! I am not running away!" The authorities at Washington had issued an order that Crazy Horse should stay on the Red Cloud Agency, and he felt that he should be privileged to go and come as he pleased, so long as he behaved himself. The authorities took him back to Red Cloud Agency, but to the military post instead of to the agency itself.

Owing to an unfortunate error made by one of the

interpreters there was an unjustified fear that Crazy Horse would leave the agency and become a hostile again. When they took him to the post it was ordered that he be placed in the guard house. When Crazy Horse saw the bars he realized that he had been deceived and tricked and his proud spirit rebelled at being placed in a prison cell. He jumped back and drew a knife that he had secreted on his person and made a dash to get outside where his Indian friends were, when one of the soldiers pierced him with his bayonet, giving him a fatal wound.

Some call it dastardly murder. The whites feared him, although his conduct was exemplary. There was suspicion on both sides, and it was doubtless planned by the agency and the military to get him out of the way, but not necessarily to kill him.

Thus passed Crazy Horse, one of the most gallant and resistless military leaders of his generation. His steadfast friend, Touch the Clouds, folded the dead chief's hands on his breast, and tenderly said: "It is good. He has looked for death and it has come." [1]

The aged father and mother came sorrowing to beg the body of their distinguished son that they might give it Indian burial. Out from the white man's forts to the hills on foot, alone and with tottering steps they followed the travois to which was bound with rawhide thongs the broken staff of their declining years.

The Hunkpapa chief, known in history as Gall, was called in early life the Man-That-Goes-in-the-Middle. He acquired the name because of his bravery, i.e., he

[1] Homer W. Wheeler, *From Cowboy to Colonel*, Los Angeles, 1923.

advanced in the attacking line where there was the most danger — in the middle or center.

We have already had occasion to speak of some of Gall's exploits. To him and Crazy Horse belong the credit for the skillful leadership that won the victory on the Little Big Horn. Gall is one of the big three military leaders in the Sioux nation, the other two being Crazy Horse and Red Cloud. Red Cloud and Gall were orators of ability as well as warriors of distinction.

After the battle of the Little Big Horn, Gall went to Canada where he lived for a few years, when a difference arose between him and Sitting Bull, and Gall left for the United States, taking his followers with him.

He signed the treaty at Fort Rice in 1868 under the name The-Man-That-Goes-in-the-Middle, not as Pizi or Gall, as I have previously stated. In his later years his face lost much of its earlier sternness; and with features softened he looked not unlike Henry Ward Beecher. More liberal and less puritanic than Sitting Bull, he was able to make compromises when his own best interests were at stake; consequently he adjusted himself to the white mans' ways with less friction and was permitted to die a natural death in 1894 at the age of fifty-four years. His remains rest in the Saint Francis burying ground near Wakpala, South Dakota, under his baptismal name John Gall.

Sitting Bull [2] has received more notoriety than any

[2] For a succinct account of Sitting Bull see *Sitting Bull and Custer*, by A. Mc G. Beede. The estimate he gives of Sitting Bull is quite the best in print. It is based on hearsay reports obtained from Indians who associated with him and knew him well. In talking with

other Sioux chief. He has been condemned unmercifully by white men, all the low epithets being used for the purpose. He has been called a man of low propensities, a disturber, an agitator, a malcontent and a bulldozer, a coward and a liar. He may have been some of these, but after all I can't help but admire his consistency.

From the Indian's standpoint he was a straight-laced patriot. He stood consistently against the encroachments of the whites at all times. He strove to make a great confederacy which would stand as a barrier against the aggressions of the whites. In all the Indian wars the whites used Indians to help them against their own race. He maintained that all the Indians should compose their own differences and join hands against the common enemy — the whites. The Indian, however, was more bitter towards his hereditary red enemy than he was against his white enemy, and Sitting Bull's efforts to form a federated alliance among the Indians met with only partial success. Yet it was through his influence that the Cheyennes attached their fortunes to the Sioux. He tried to unite the Assiniboines and the Utes and the Crees with the Sioux. He fought the Crows because they would not unite with the Sioux and tried to drive them over the Rocky Mountains, to get them where they could not help the whites.

He wanted to maintain the Black Hills. He knew the buffalo and the antelope were being killed and that

the old Indians I find Sitting Bull is held in high regard. The opinions expressed by writers as a rule are neither based on an acquaintance with the man or any first-hand evidence concerning him.

the fur-bearing animals were becoming scarcer and that in a short time they could not make a living out of game and furs. He knew that the Black Hills held gold that the white man wanted, and he promised that all Indians who united with him in keeping the whites out, would be entitled to share in it.

As an orator Sitting Bull had few equals among Indian public speakers. He was always serious; never joked, which added to the reverence his people had for him. He was kind to old people and required young hunters to supply meat to the tents of the old and helpless. It pained him to see any one in want. He always tried to prevent the holding of white captives; instead of putting them to death as most tribes did he strove to have them returned to their people. To hold captives, he asserted, invited reprisals and brought trouble, which he tried to avoid.

Sitting Bull never sold out his people's interests for a mess of pottage.

In 1882 when Sitting Bull was one of a distinguished Indian delegation in Washington he refused to sit with them for a group photograph. He was not a poser and personal ambition never influenced him, as it did a number of chiefs who now stand in higher regard among the whites. He never signed a treaty, because to do so would compromise some of his people's rights. He was not lured by the offers of presents, by position or power, to deviate one jot or tittle from the strict adherence to what he considered the best interests of his people. He stood so straight that he leaned backwards. All he wanted was to be let alone. He wanted peace and fought that he might have it. His own welfare he subordinated for that of his people, and among them he was the unselfish, dominant leader.

On one occasion when a treaty commission went to Canada to induce Sitting Bull and his followers to come back to the United States, give up their horses and guns to be sold and the money invested in cows, he said:

"They ask me to give them my horses. I bought my horses and they are mine. They do not belong to the government nor do the rifles. The rifles are mine also. I bought them; I paid for them and I will not give them up."

And furthermore he said: "I never treated with the Americans to surrender my people's rights. Why should I? The land belongs to my people. I traded with them [the whites] but I always gave full value. I never asked the government to make me presents of blankets or cloth, or anything of that kind. The most that I did was to ask them to send me an honest trader that I could trade with, and I proposed to give him buffalo robes and elk skins, and other hides in exchange for what I wanted. I told every trader that came to our camps that I did not want any favors from him, that I wanted to trade with him fairly and equally, giving him full value for what I got, but the traders wanted me to trade with them on no such terms. They wanted to give little and get much."

In the summer of 1879 Finnerty, an American newspaper correspondent, visited Sitting Bull in Canada and the latter said:

"I want nothing to do with Americans. They do not treat me well. They cheat me when I trade. They have my country now. Let them keep it. I never seek anybody; least of all do I seek Americans."

Notwithstanding his independence, some two years later, 1881, he came into the United States and gave himself up. The Americans seemed to be worried when he was in Canada and still more worried when he came to the United States. This fear is what finally led to Sitting Bull's undoing.

Few think that Sitting Bull in the Ghost dances had any designs on the peace of the United States. There is little in his conduct that points to war-like preparations. Everything he did was under suspicion, and those in authority were looking for a pretext to put an end to their own uneasiness. Sitting Bull had passed the prime of life, was heavy and slow, and those who knew him best considered him harmless. He was aggrieved at the menial treatment accorded him, a chief, since his surrender; but his was the petulance of a child.

Sitting Bull was consistent to the last; a leader of his people in the ways of his fathers. On December 15, 1890, on Grand River, but a short distance from the place of his birth, and near where most of his active life had been spent, he met his death at the hands of the Indian police acting under the pay and direction of the military. His body was hauled to Fort Yates, placed in a rough pine box and covered with quick lime, as a mark of contempt, and lowered into his six feet of earth in one corner of the post cemetery among his bitterest enemies, the soldiers. The remains of the soldiers that then had sepulture here were removed years ago to the national cemetery on the Little Big Horn to be with their comrades of the old Seventh Cavalry on the field where Sitting Bull and his followers had touched them with glory.

In life Sitting Bull wished isolation from the whites; in death he lies isolated in the unfenced commons — not only isolated from the whites but from those of his own race. With a pile of rough boulders at the head and a slender marble slab at the foot he rests in his narrow bed, overgrown with choking weeds, an evidence both of neglect and the disesteem born of racial conflict.

CHAPTER XXXIII

Reflections

I have already spoken of some of the well-known white men with whom I had a close acquaintance in the early days of the Dakotas. I would gladly speak of a number of others if space permitted; of a few who are still living I shall speak.

Ed Monroe, now of Springview, Nebraska, and I were intimately associated for some years. During our cow punching days we were together most of the time. He is now living in the comfort his age and industry entitle him to, on the Niobrara, near the scenes of some of our earlier exploits, a worthy asset to his community.

Horatio H. Larned has been spoken of several times. He is living in retirement in Lansing, Michigan. We ate and slept around the same camp for some months over a half century ago. By recent correspondence he shows that he still has a vivid recollection of the old days on the Missouri.

Another man whom I casually knew in my early wood-chopping days is Wm. V. Wade, of Shields, North Dakota, who still lives on his Cannonball ranch, which he has occupied for over thirty-five years.

Only a few of the old fellows are now living. These three men are typical of the early West, surrounded by temptations yet yielding to few; of rugged strength, resourceful, and above all endowed with good horse sense.

Among those for whom I had a high regard who have already passed on I would pay a tribute to the following: Capt. William Harmon, Maj. Chas. E. Galpin and wife, Basil Clement, Ed Whitney, James B. Gayton, A. M. Willard, Seth Bullock, Scotty Philips, George Bosler, and Maj. James McLaughlin. All these did a worthy work and a grateful people should not let their memory die.

I knew all of the interpreters and most of the army scouts and so-called "characters" of the Missouri and Platte River countries from 1863 onward, a few of whom are: James Bridger, Buffalo Bill, Frank Grouard, Louis Richaud, Big Bat Pourier and Little Bat Garnier, Charles Primeau and his son Louis, Geo. Florey, Nick Janisse and brother Antoine, Louis Agard, Frank La Frambois, Basil Clement or Claymore, Louis Bordeaux, Charles Tackett, Father de Smet, California Joe, Charley Reynolds, Joe Merivale, Capt. Jack Crawford, Wild Bill Hickok, and many others of deserved prominence, less widely known.

My life has been much the same as any pioneer of the West. Having been a soldier, a gold seeker, a messenger, a cowboy, a bull-whacker, a hunter, a trapper, and a river man, I have faced the hazards of the West but have never had the courage to face the people back in Ohio who knew me as a boy and who, I felt, might brand me for my desertion from the army.

I am seventy-seven years old and have lived fifty-eight years among the wildest, most lawless people of America, including Indians, Mexicans, road agents, horse thieves, gamblers, and "bad men" generally. I have lived and worked and eaten and slept with them, moreover have never had serious trouble with any of them.

My aim has been to play the game fair. I may have killed a few Indians, never caught a horse-thief, and helped to hang but one murderer. Throughout life I have tried to be on the side of the right-thinking and right-acting class. I have not always lived up to my best; sometimes through a spirit of bravado, sometimes to hold my own with other wrong-doers, sometimes through force of circumstances I have gone wrong. Many times I have erred; when my error was made plain to me I have tried to be frank in acknowledging it; if in the right, I never gave up. A disagreeable person I let alone; an agreeable one I did not let tire with my company. My efforts to play the game fair have been rewarded not in money but in friends. I have been an adventurer, a rover; a money-maker settles down and waits for his properties to mature. I have got so much out of life that money can not buy that I would not exchange places with the money grubber. With all classes of rough people I have been accorded substantial justice without having to fight for it; from the genteel, who love gain too much to be fair, I have suffered most. A frontiersman, such as I, is untrained in holding his own against the approved trickery of civilization. But in all walks of life I have found most people fair. The few who are unfair we can usually leave alone; and this I have studiously tried to do.

The modern days are too near at hand to stand out conspicuously. Civilization casts a drab uniformity over places and peoples, hence I shall say nothing of the later days.

In bringing these reminiscences to a close I want to emphasize the fact that I have tried to give a few sketchy pictures of the old trail-blazers; those who lived and labored in subduing the wilderness — the frenzied miner, the obscure scout, the patient bull-whacker, the picturesque cowboy riding the plains, and the old time rancher, sometimes harassed or brought to poverty by blizzards, Texas fever, grasshoppers, and drought, yet through it all cheerful and heroic; and last of all to give credit to individuals of the Red race who with honesty and courage resisted the white men by whom they were despoiled.

I have tried to give the truth without animus or ill-will. Whether I have succeeded well or ill is left to the judgment of the reader.

CHAPTER XXXIV

THE WRITER has picked out of Ben Arnold's experiences those things that give a picture of the past and that have a historic interest. His wanderings naturally gave him a wide acquaintance with men and affairs in the states where he spent sixty years of his life. In many cases the facts stated in the narrative are confirmed by men still living or by written or printed records. In instances where no confirmation is at hand the statements made are believed to be substantially true.

Arnold had enough Irish blood in his veins to give him a good sense of humor, and he was welcomed in any company because of his ability to tell with fidelity and wit stories of the frontier. His memory of men and events was remarkably good up to the time of his death, October 28, 1922. He had a restless spirit that would not let him settle down or stay in one place for long. Adventure he loved; such a spirit as his was the very essence of the pioneer.

When three days old his mother died and he was left to the care of a grandmother until he was fourteen, when she, too, passed away. During his early years he had such schooling as was common to the youth of his age in the country schools of Ohio. Notwithstanding his scant school opportunities in youth and the lack of books and libraries on the frontier, yet his mind was well stored with the information that can only come with travel and intimate contact with people of vigorous mould.

Being thrown on his own resources at the age of fourteen, he obtained work as a mule driver on a canal boat for a short while, and later got a job as a sort of "flunky" on a steamer that plied between Cincinnati and St. Louis. His duties consisted mainly in polishing silverware and running errands for the boat's officers. This work continued until his enlistment in the Civil War at the age of seventeen, in 1861, as has been stated in the narrative.

His father, Patrick Dougherty Connor, and two brothers also enlisted in the Union army. One brother, Fernando, became a noted spy and was twice captured by the enemy and once condemned to die, but managed to escape, and the other, Lieutenant Winters, went with Sherman to the sea, and was killed in the siege of Atlanta.

Ben Arnold served during three enlistments in the Civil War. He craved excitement and was not content with service unless it were active.

Those who knew Arnold best say that he was an expert marksman, a good packer, and could trail like an Indian; and that his sense of direction and consequent ability to find his way in the night-time was perfectly uncanny.

With him money had little value. He would part with anything he had for a comrade in straits. His training was of the old generous frontier type. In this world's goods he was poor, but his happiness in life was never disturbed by what he lacked. A happy unselfish disposition made him a favorite around the camp fire. Among all the old time Indians at the various agencies he is well known, not as Arnold, but as Wa-si-cu Tam-a-he-ca — Lean Whiteman. Physically he was slender but muscular, and weighed about one hundred and fifty-five pounds.

In some places in the narrative the Indian proper names have been used, as it is impossible to translate the proper names into their exact equivalent in English. Many of the younger Indians can read English and some of the older will relish some stories in the foregoing pages, as characters well known to them are the chief participants. For this reason it was thought best to give in some instances names in Dakota. Arnold was always a friend to the Indian, and they speak of him as being a man who had no forked tongue — a high tribute indeed, when given by people who were so often deceived by those who would take advantage of them.

Arnold lived at a time when he could see the whole procession of the Old West — the fur trader, the soldier, the prospector, the miner, the big rancher, the squatter, the homesteader, and the farmer — come; and most of them go.

Civilization, or destiny, or right, or might, or whatever it is that determines national progress, doomed the Indian. His ways and the white man's were different, and a clash, followed by a readjustment, was inevitable. In this clash both the Indian and the frontiersman lost step; the new-comer took the front rank.

Arnold always liked the live stock business, and he said that the years spent as a cowboy were the happiest of his life. Around the round-up wagon and the camp-fire were formed friendships in which there was no shadow of turning. He wrote a poem of some merit which has suggested the name for this volume, and I can do no better than to quote it:

> Through progress of the railroads,
>   Our occupation's gone;
> We'll get our ideas into words,
>   Our words into a song.
> First comes the cowboy —
>   He's the spirit of the West;
> Of all the pioneers I claim
>   The cowboys are the best;
> We'll miss him in the round-up,
>   It's gone, his merry shout,
> The cowboy has left the country,
>   His camp fire has gone out.
>
> You freighters, our companions,
>   You've got to leave this land;
> Can't drag your loads for nothing
>   Through the gumbo, and the sand;
> The railroads are bound to beat you —
>   So do your level best,
> Give it up to the granger
>   And strike out farther west.
> Bid them all adieu
>   And give the merry shout, —
> "The cowboy has left the country
>   And his camp fire has gone out."

When I think of those good old days
  My eyes with tears will fill;
When I think of the tin can by the fire
  And the coyote on the hill.
I'll tell you, boys, in those days
  Old-timers stood a show, —
Our pockets full of money,
  Not a sorrow did we know;
But, how times have changed since then,
  We're poorly clothed and fed;
Our wagons are all broken down
  And horses most all dead.
Soon we'll leave this country,
  Then you'll hear the angels shout,
Oh, here they come to Heaven,
  Their camp fire has gone out.

May the reminiscences herein recorded serve to re-kindle the camp fires, and bring back to memory the days that were.

THE END

APPENDIX

BIBLIOGRAPHY

This brief bibliography suggests a few of the titles that any one desiring to make a more comprehensive study of matters touched on in *The Exploits of Ben Arnold* will do well to read or consult.

BEEDE, A. McG. Sitting Bull-Custer, Bismarck, 1913.

BELKNAP, WILLIAM W. Proceedings of the Senate sitting for the Trial of William W. Belknap, Secretary of War, on articles of impeachment exhibited by House, 1876. 1166 pages.

BRADY, CYRUS TOWNSEND. Indian Fights and Fighters, 1866-1876.

BRIDGER, JAMES. Life of, by J. C. Alter. Salt Lake, 1925.

BROWN, JESSE, and A. M. WILLARD. The Black Hills Trails — The History of the Struggles of the Pioneers in the Winning of the Black Hills. Rapid City, S. Dak., 1924.

CHITTENDEN, CAPT. HIRAM M. History of the American Fur Trade of the Far West. 3 vols. N. Y., 1902.

CHITTENDEN, H. M. History of Early Steamboat Navigation on the Missouri River — Life and Adventures of Jos. La Barge. 2 vols. N. Y., 1903.

COLLINS, J. S. Across the Plains in '64. Omaha, 1904.

CONNELLEY, WM. E. Quantrill and the Border Wars. Cedar Rapids, Iowa, 1910.

COOK, JAMES H. Fifty Years on the Old Frontier. New Haven, 1923.

COUTANT, C. G. History of Wyoming. Laramie, 1899.

DODGE, COL. RICHARD I.   Our Wild Indians. Hartford, 1883.

DUNN, J. P.   Massacres of the Mountains.   N. Y., 1886.

FISKE, FRANK B.   The Taming of the Sioux. Bismarck, 1917.

FLETCHER, ALICE C.   Indian Education and Civilization. 48th
Cong., Sen. Ex. Doc. No. 95.   Washington, 1888, 2d Sess.

FREEMAN, LEWIS R.   Boating Down the Yellowstone.   New
York, 1922.

GRINNELL, GEORGE BIRD.   The Fighting Cheyennes.   N. Y.,
1915.

HANS, F. M.   The Great Sioux Nation, 1907.   Chicago.

HANSON, JOSEPH MILLS.   The Conquest of the Missouri, Being the Story of the Life and Exploits of Captain Grant
Marsh.   3rd ed.   1916, Chicago.

HEBARD, GRACE RAYMOND, and E. A. BRININSTOOL.   The
Bozeman Trail.   2 vols.   Cleveland, 1922.

HOLLEY, FRANCES C.   Once Their Home, or Our Legacy from
the Dakotahs.   Chicago, 1891.

INMAN, COL. HENRY, and COL. WM. F. CODY.   The Great
Salt Lake Trail.   Topeka, 1910.

JOHNSON, WM. PRESTON.   Life of Gen. Albert Sidney Johnson.   N. Y., 1878.

KELLY, FANNY.   Narrative of My Captivity among the Sioux.
Hartford, 1871.

LANGFORD, N. P.   Vigilante Days and Ways.   Chicago, 1912.

LARPENTEUR, CHAS.   Forty Years a Fur Trader on the
Upper Missouri, by Elliott Coues.   2 vols.   N. Y., 1898.

LOUNSBERRY, COL. CLEMENT A.   Early History of North Dakota.   Chicago, 1919.

McLAUGHLIN, MAJ. JAMES.   My Friend the Indian.   Boston,
1910.

MILES, NELSON A.   Personal Recollections and Observations.
Chicago, 1897.

MONTANA.   Contribution to the Hist. Soc. of Montana.   9
vols.   1876-1923.

NEBRASKA.   Nebraska State Hist. Col.   20 vols.   1885-1922.

NORTH DAKOTA HIST. COLL.   7 vols.   1906 to 1925.

THWAITES, R. G. Early Western Travels. 32 vols. Cleveland, 1904-7.

TOPONCE, ALEX. Life and Adventures of, written by himself. Ogden, Utah, 1923.

U. S. INTERIOR DEPARTMENT. Annual Reports, Commissioner of Indian Affairs.

U. S. WAR DEPARTMENT. Annual Reports and Files. 1855-1891.

VICTOR, F. F. Eleven Years in the Rocky Mountains, and life on the Frontier. Also a history of the Sioux War and Life of Gen. Custer.

WHEELER, HOMER W. From Cowboy to Colonel. Los Angeles, 1923.

YOUNG, C. E. Dangers of The Trail.

Three volumes now in preparation that I am sure will be of value on the period are: Granville Stuart: Forty Years on the Frontier, edited by Paul C. Phillips, published by The Arthur H. Clark Company; Ed Lemmon's Reminiscences (publisher not determined), and Luther S. or "Yellowstone" Kelly's Reminiscences, to be published by the Yale Press.

INDEX